This is the One

Daniel Taylor has covered Manchester United for the *Guardian* since 1998, and lives in south Manchester with his wife Zoe. This is his second football book, following on from the critically acclaimed *Deep into the Forest*.

This is the One

Sir Alex Ferguson: The uncut story of a football genius

Daniel Taylor

The author would like to thank his colleagues on the *Guardian*, in particular Ben Clissitt, and everyone at Aurum Press for their support and advice, especially Natasha Martin.

First published in Great Britain 2007 by Aurum Press Limited
7 Greenland Street
London NW1 0ND

www.aurumpress.co.uk

This paperback edition first published 2008 by Aurum Press

A catalogue record for this book is available from the British Library.

ISBN 978 1 84513 354 2

Typeset in Palatino by Saxon Graphics, Derby
Printed and bound in the UK by
CPI Mackays, Chatham ME5 8TD

CONTENTS

INTRODUCTION

TAKING ON THE WORLD (PART I)

He's an amazing man. Let's establish that straight away. Sir Alex Ferguson is a manager of uncommon ability. He has brought football of butterfly beauty to Manchester United. He bought Eric Cantona, the rebel with a cause. He nurtured the Golden Generation. He discovered Ole Gunnar Solskjaer, the baby-faced assassin. He signed Wayne Rooney, the assassin-faced baby. He has brought trophies, glory, prestige and the kind of happiness, over twenty years, that United supporters once only dreamed of. No one has managed at the highest level for so long. Or with such competitive courage. Nobody has beaten the system like he has and accumulated so many trophies.

When Ferguson swept into Old Trafford in 1986 Boris Becker was the teenage Wimbledon champion, Nick Berry was at number one with *Every Loser Wins* and Steaua Bucharest were in possession of the European Cup. It was the year of Chernobyl and *Top Gun*, Charlene marrying Scott, Andrew marrying Sarah, Diego Maradona's 'Hand of God' and Wayne Rooney's first birthday. Ferguson posed in the centre-circle for his first photo-shoot and, behind him, the Stretford End was a concrete terrace with steel fences topped with spikes.

Two decades on, Old Trafford is a gleaming all-seater stadium, the capacity has risen from 55,000 to 76,000 and the 'Keep Off The Grass' signs are in five different languages. It has been an epic journey of 6 a.m. starts, nerve-shredding football and relentless drama. He has outlasted eleven different Manchester City managers. He has seen off Thatcher, Major and Blair, and could easily add Brown to that list as well. He has been knighted and immortalised and he has turned United into one of the most prolific trophy-grabbing machines in the modern game. In his own words, he has 'knocked Liverpool off their fucking perch'. Nine league titles, one European Cup, five FA Cups, one European Cup Winners' Cup, two League Cups. Plus enough individual awards to fill a museum. Those of us who are football writers in Manchester should never forget how lucky we are to have witnessed it. Even in those moments when it feels like the hardest club in the world to cover.

We journalists regale our friends with anecdotes and enjoy the certain social cachet that comes from dealing with him. We have boxed away stories for our grandchildren and our office walls are lined with signed books and photographs. But we know, deep down, that he doesn't like what we do.

Trying to establish a relationship with him is a continuous, Forth Road Bridge process. We'd love to swap numbers, to high-five after important victories, to bear-hug and clink wine glasses. But, deep down, we have all had to accept there is never going to be a day when he invites us back to his for scones and tea and some Scottish hospitality. Or a press conference when he finishes with the words 'Drink, anyone?' Ferguson, you quickly learn, has erected a brick wall around himself to keep out the national newspaper journalists who work on his patch. Even in the good times he likes to keep his distance. We see him once, twice, sometimes three times a week, and we travel around the world hanging on his coat-tails, season after season. Yet we are still not sure if we know him properly. He is always that little bit out of reach – which, on reflection, is probably just how he likes it.

The caricature is of a flint-faced authority figure, steam shooting out of his ears as he stands in the dugout, menacingly chewing gum, ranting at the fourth official and pointing to his stopwatch. Yet that's exactly what it is: a caricature. The real Ferguson is far more complex than the tabloid portrayal. He isn't always 'fuming' or 'exploding'. He doesn't always 'slam' and 'blast'. We have lost count of the number of times we have arrived for press conferences to find him waltzing with an imaginary partner through the reception area at Carrington, the club's training ground. Or breaking into song as Kath, the receptionist, hoots with laughter and tells him to shush. On his worst days, he can be dictatorial, hostile and standoffish. But he can also be warm, charming and convivial, with kind edges and an infectious laugh. He would be on any guest-list for a fantasy-football dinner-party XI. Ferguson is a natural storyteller. He has an outstanding memory for the tiniest snippets of information and varied interests beyond the four white lines that have contained much of his life. He has taught himself French using audiocassettes. He has learned how to play the piano. He 'gets' jazz. He has a global knowledge when it comes to food and is a connoisseur of fine wines.

He is past retirement age, yet he seems to have an immunity to exhaustion. Complete strangers are often astonished about how friendly and charismatic he is. They are struck by how different he seems in real life from how he appears on television or in the press. They talk about a sexagenarian of fierce intellect and a student of human nature with an impressively high IQ and an astute appreciation of what makes other men tick.

But then there are times when it is difficult to square his more appealing characteristics with his darker sides – the Ferguson who can be cold and ruthless and, in the vernacular of football, a bit of a bastard. His family probably wouldn't recognise the grumpy journophobe who could argue a point without even the shadow of a leg to stand on. Or resort to the infamous 'Hairdryer' treatment, leaning into your face and shouting with such force it feels like you are in a wind tunnel.

His press conferences can be tense, joyless affairs, crackling with friction. He can be impregnable, leaning back, hands behind his head, bored and fidgety, abrasive to the point of being monosyllabic and so downright exasperating you could drop a flowerpot on his head.

His one-liners are legendary. One World Cup year we – 'we' meaning the Manchester press corps throughout this book – annoyed him, by having the temerity to ask if he planned to go to the tournament. 'None of your business,' came the answer. 'Do I ask if you're still going to those fucking gay clubs?'

Then there was the time, at the end of a trophy-less season, when a *Daily Telegraph* reporter innocently asked what had gone wrong. 'That's a good question,' Ferguson replied, with a vast grin. 'But it would take a whole interview to get it and that's an interview you're never going to fucking get.'

Alternatively, his press conferences can be entertaining and revealing, full of laughter and off-the-record anecdotes and bristling comments about what is wrong with the game and what should be done about it. He does not open up easily, but when the mood takes him he can disarm his audience with long, impassioned homilies about football, politics and the world in general. And in those moments you absorb every word and remind yourself that time in his company, with the shackles off, is both rewarding and fascinating.

When Ferguson is on good form put aside the caricature of the empurpled curmudgeon with little red puffs of smoke coming out of his ears and think instead of a gregarious raconteur with an unstoppable enthusiasm for life. A man's man, good for a drink and a game of golf and determined to grab life by the balls. A man so intensely competitive he would stop to watch two children playing a game of Pooh sticks.

He is also a man of great humour. 'What has happened to diving headers these days?' he will ask, eyes twinkling. 'You know, the kind of goals Denis Law, Tommy Lawton, Nat Lofthouse, Dixie Dean and Alex Ferguson used to score.'

He will pick out a reporter who hasn't shaved, or whose hair is a little unkempt, and ask whether he has walked into an Oasis concert. He will complain about someone's match report and gently chide the journalist for thinking he writes for 'the *Dandy* comic strip'. Ferguson takes pride in his repartee and in his ability to make people laugh, and he will often send himself up too. He knows how others see him. We tried to guess his team on one occasion and he interrupted with a smile: 'Never try to read the mind of a madman!'

Beneath that brusque exterior and ferocious partisanship there is a different Ferguson, one that is not seen often enough. The soft-focus Ferguson has been known to ring newspaper offices, demanding to be put straight through to the editor after hearing that a reporter who works on his patch might be in danger of being made redundant.

When John Bean, the former *Daily Express* man, had a heart attack, the first contact he had from the outside world was a nurse bringing him a bouquet of flowers, with Ferguson's spidery handwriting asking: 'What have you been doing to yourself, you silly old tap dancer?'

He has grown to dislike the newspaper industry but he does not regard the whole of the species with disdain. Some of his oldest friends are football writers and he has never forgotten the journalists who backed him when it looked like he could be sacked early in his United career. When Steve Curry lost his job at the *Express* Ferguson was one of the first people on the phone to commiserate. When Bean was forced to retire on medical advice Ferguson called him to say: 'Any time you want to come to Old Trafford give me a ring and there will be a seat for you in the directors' box.'

In 2003, David Meek, the former *Manchester Evening News* correspondent, was diagnosed with cancer. 'I had to break the news to Alex that I would be unable to ghost-write his programme notes for the first time in sixteen years,' Meek recalls. 'He wanted to know why and when I told him I was going into hospital for an operation he looked me in the eye and said exactly what I wanted to hear: "You can handle it." There was a huge bouquet waiting for me at the hospital. Then I was convalescing at home a week later and, out of the blue, the phone rang. There was no introduction. He didn't even say who it was. A voice just growled down the line: "The Scottish beast is on its way!" He was at my front door twenty minutes later and the point is he didn't have to do that. He's an extremely busy man and it was the middle of the season and David Beckham's will-he-go, will-he-stay saga with Real Madrid. "You'll never guess what that Beckham wore to training today," Alex said to me. "He had this bloody spingly-spangly tracksuit on – he looked like Gary Glitter!" We had a pleasant afternoon, chatting about football and families. I'll never forget how kind and supportive he was.'

No doubt there are some who prefer to see a different side but those who know Ferguson best say he has a heart the size of the Old Trafford trophy room. He can be overwhelmingly generous, a devoted worker for charities. He goes out of his way to attend the funeral of a loyal supporter, an unsung member of staff or one of his many old acquaintances. Often when his mobile is clamped to his ear he is offering advice and encouragement to a struggling manager. There are invitations for a sacked manager or coach to help him out with training for a few days. Cards are sent to injured players. Visits are made to schools or businesses run by friends of friends. Letters are sent to Elizabeth Thomson, his first teacher at Broomloan Road Primary in Govan, the unloved district of Glasgow where he grew up.

When George Best died nobody spoke more passionately than Ferguson. Or with greater warmth. And of who? Yes, a brilliant footballer and Old Trafford legend, but also someone who was never slow to criticise Ferguson. Best once recommended that Terry Venables should be brought in and told the newspapers he 'wouldn't walk round the corner to watch United play'. Yet Ferguson, usually such a grudge-bearer, came into his own after Best's death. Nobody could have done more to represent United with greater dignity. Nobody could have been more eloquent in his tributes. 'George burst on to the scene at a liberated time, with an explosion of music, the Beatles, style, fashion and a freer way of life,' he said. 'He carried the dreams of everyone in the Sixties. As well as his talent as a fantastic player, what remains in my mind is his courage. I can see him, even now, flying down the wing, riding tackles. He has left us with a million memories and all of them good. The best talent our football has ever produced.'

This is the side of Ferguson his friends and colleagues cite. A man who often displays unusual consideration and warmth. There is the story of him visiting Anfield after the Hillsborough disaster, arriving quietly, making it clear he didn't want any publicity, that it must be kept under wraps. He was the first public figure from outside Liverpool to travel to the stadium to show his grief and support and, without the media ever getting wind of it, he presented a substantial cheque for the disaster fund.

Then there was the time, a couple of weeks before Paul Hunter's death, when Ferguson sent the former world snooker champion a video message telling him he should be proud of everything he had achieved and praising him for his bravery and dignity in fighting his cancer. 'He had never met Paul before but his message was so genuine and heartfelt,' says Lindsey, Hunter's widow. 'He came across as sincere and kind. He said Paul was very special, a proud Yorkshireman, and that he could see similarities with Alan Smith. He said he was praying for Paul to get better and that he knew what a lovely lad he was. All we knew of Ferguson was this hothead football manager we saw on television. Yet he went out of his way to be so caring and that really touched us.'

Geoff Thomas, the former Crystal Palace player who has successfully battled leukaemia, was equally astonished when he organised a re-match of the 1990 FA Cup final and Ferguson threw himself into the project, offering to manage the United team and going out of his way to help with the arrangements. Likewise, we journalists were surprised the morning after United had gone out of the 2007 Champions League semi-finals to Milan to see him on television arriving for Alan Ball's funeral at Winchester Cathedral. The previous night, we had sat with Ferguson in Malpensa airport waiting for a delayed flight home and he was clearly devastated. When the plane finally arrived the baggage went missing and we were kept on the runway for another hour. We didn't get into Manchester until 5 a.m. and Ferguson must have been physically and emotionally drained. Yet he somehow made it to Winchester by midday, paying his respects to one of England's World Cup heroes.

As for us, the football writers, you certainly never forget the first time you meet him. His eyes squint, his brow creases. He leans forward. 'Who are you?' he might demand. You aren't sure where to look or what to call him. You try not to show weakness but it isn't easy.

His favourites tend to be older journalists such as Hugh McIlvanney of the *Sunday Times*, Glenn Gibbons of the *Scotsman* and Bob Cass of the *Mail on Sunday* although, even then, it is always on Ferguson's terms.

It is when reporters below the age of forty turn up that he sometimes gets edgy. One London-based reporter from the *Daily Star* – in his mid-thirties and married with kids – came on a European trip and politely held out his hand to introduce himself, only for a look of astonishment to cross Ferguson's face. 'Jesus Christ,' he said. 'Do they get them straight from school these days?'

He drives us mad sometimes, but he is wrong when he says the press hate him. You hate the man who has stolen your wife. Or keyed your car. Or burgled your house. But Ferguson? Not a bit. Some journalists have grievances. Legitimate ones too. But how can anyone not have a soft spot or, at the very least, a sneaking regard for someone who has filled one of the most demanding jobs in sport for twenty years?

The problem is that it is unfathomably difficult to predict whether we are going to get him on a good or a bad day. One minute, he will be singing at the top of his voice, as if he didn't have a care in the world. The next, his mood changes and he will be staring at you with hard, penetrative eyes.

We want to like him, of course, and we want him to like us. We want to get on, to have an understanding. Nonetheless, there have been times under his management when it is not just respect when we go to see him. It is genuine anxiety.

Generally, the stronger the manager the less reticent he is when speaking to the press and the less sensitive he is to what we write. But Ferguson is different. He has been known to ban reporters for criticising his players. He will convince himself we are trying to lay traps and complain that we do not ask enough about the actual football. Then we will try to engage him in conversation about tactics and he will sarcastically shake his head and say, sorry, he forgot we were the 'experts'.

Alistair Campbell, his close friend and former government spin-doctor, sums up the Ferguson media relations strategy: 'I'm just doing this because of contractual obligations but you are all . . .'

And yet we would sit outside Ferguson's door for hours if it meant getting a few minutes on tape.

On good form Ferguson is gold dust – trenchant, droll, controversial, forthright, never boring – and when he wants to get something off his chest our sports editors will gratefully clear the pages. This is an era when most football managers see nothing and say even less. Yet Ferguson has never been one for surrounding himself with an entourage of puffed-up advisors. He resists any temptation to descend into deliberate blandness. He doesn't talk about his players giving it 110 per cent. Or of taking each game as it comes. He would rather speak in plain English.

What we have is a basis of understanding. Yet Ferguson is the only manager in England who refuses to speak to the press after Premiership games or the early rounds of the FA Cup and Carling Cup. His policy is generally one of avoidance. He will speak to us after Champions League ties (UEFA will fine him otherwise), but the Football Association and the Premier League turn a blind eye in the domestic competitions and he has decided he just doesn't need the hassle. 'I don't get the press coverage I think I'm entitled to,' he says, 'and I no longer see it as part of my job to fulfil their interests.'

It is sad that it has gone this way. In the old days he would accept we had a legitimate role to play and hold separate post-match briefings for the Sunday and daily newspaper reporters. He respected the fact we were the medium between the club and the supporters and that, in our number, there were journalists who understood the game, who could be trusted and could be useful allies.

Everything has changed now. 'There are some excellent journalists, honest journalists, and respected journalists,' he says. 'But the media has become a monster. They know all the answers, right and wrong. They want exclusive stories and confidential background. They want their cards marked. They want gossip. And believe me, if they don't get it, you're in trouble.'

What we are left with is a process in which MUTV, the club's subscription channel, is the only media organisation he indulges. He stops for them for five minutes after every match, answers a dozen questions and then he is gone. Occasionally, a press officer at an away ground will innocently offer to show him to the pressroom, but he will quickly make it clear it is not necessary.

We improvise. At away games we give a tape to his press officer Diana Law (one of the nicest people at Old Trafford). She records his MUTV interview in the tunnel and brings the tape to the pressroom so we can recycle the best bits. For home games we gather round the pressroom television until MUTV announce he is about to come on air. Then we jostle for position and hold our tape players to the television to record whatever he says. It is an undignified process: taping another man's interview to reprocess the more usable quotes.

There are old-timers in the pressbox who can remember the days when journalists were encouraged to travel and socialise with the team and Sir Matt Busby told his players to 'treat the press the same way you would treat a policeman'. You could argue that any objectivity was compromised by such close association but at least it gave the readers (i.e. the supporters) detailed knowledge about what made the club tick. No journalist has such insight now and, for us, that's a source of permanent disappointment. Not unhappiness, exactly, but a kind of deep regret because we are deeply conscious we must be missing out. We try to get into Ferguson's mind, to second-guess him and work out his body language, but sometimes we might as well be writing about what is at the bottom of the ocean. We don't really know what he thinks about the crucial goal, the opposition's tactics, whether such and such a player ought to have been marked closer, and so on.

At most clubs, reporters will be allowed into the tunnel, or a special interview area, at the end of every match to speak to the players. At United, it is considered trespassing. The last person to make that mistake was Arsenal's press officer Amanda Docherty, who had offered to escort Matt Dickinson, the chief football correspondent of *The Times*, to the changing rooms so he could speak to Arsène Wenger's players. They were waiting in the corridor when Fergie emerged and allegedly shouted: 'Get that cunt out of my tunnel!'

In recent times, the club have started to allow one newspaper reporter into the tunnel after league matches to speak to the opposition players. Otherwise, the only media personnel allowed tunnel passes are from television (usually MUTV, BBC's *Match of the Day* and Sky Sports) and a local radio reporter who records an interview on a disc that is shared between all the different radio stations apart from the BBC (whom Ferguson despises). The radio reporters call it the 'Disc of Doom'.

As for the rest of us, there is nothing we can do. Ferguson is hard and in control. 'Your days are numbered,' he told us once. 'Television gets everything now. All you lot can hope for are the crumbs that remain when television has had its fill.'

There are rules in place. Rules about where we can go and what we can ask, and if anyone rocks the boat Ferguson hoards grudges like other people collect stamps. The Press Association were excluded from his conferences for three years after he told their correspondent Dave Anderson (now of the *Daily Mirror*) he asked 'too many questions'. *The Times* and the *Guardian* have been frozen out at various intervals. The same goes for the *Daily Star* and the *Daily Express*. The *Sun* and the *Daily Mirror* are banished, on average, two or three times a season. The BBC is regarded as a sworn enemy *sine die*, and the *Daily Mail* was denied access for several years until a change of sports editor and a major peace-making exercise in 2002. Ferguson had been convinced the *Mail* was 'running a campaign against myself and the club' and that it was a 'disgrace' and a 'vendetta'. He then got it in his head that Peter Keeling, a freelance reporter who has covered United for forty years, was sneakily tipping off the newspaper.

As Keeling took his seat at Carrington one day, Ferguson ordered him into the reception area, frogmarched him out of the pressroom and pointed towards the toilet.

'In there!'

'He'd been misinformed,' Keeling recalls, 'but I was too astonished to be coherent and I apologised for whatever it was I hadn't done.'

The truth is that ninety to ninety-five per cent of the stories that are written about Ferguson and Manchester United are hugely complimentary, and rightly so. On other occasions, though, he is entitled to feel like the newspapers are ganging up on him. He lives his life in a blaze of headlines and it has become fashionable in some parts of the media to knock him. This book is not an attempt to portray our profession as perfect (it's not). Reporters are under pressure every day to come up with big stories and there is so much competition, particularly between the tabloids, that there will always be some who cut corners and take chances. Trivial incidents will be blown up and exaggerated. Transfer gossip will be written as fact. Quotes will be subtly spun to take on new meaning. The culprits even have their own name for it – 'twirling'.

Back in 1986, newspapers were thinner and had none of the glossy football supplements that weigh them down now. There was a London-based chief football correspondent, known as the Number One, and maybe half-a-dozen regional operators, including a United specialist. Two decades later and there are Number Ones, Number Twos, regional staff, feature writers, colour writers, website correspondents, stringers, bloggers, podcasters, diarists, agency staff, foreign reporters and wires correspondents, all ravenous for news. It is an era of 24/7 breaking news. Ferguson's idea of hell.

'The press conference of today is a total waste of time,' he says. 'There are young guys sitting there . . . I don't know who they are, what they are or how they got there. They don't want to know about the football side any more. They want the reasons why you didn't pick such and such a player. Or they want to find disarray in the dressing room. I don't think they are interested in football at all. There was a time when sports journalism was about what happened in the twentieth minute, how the goal was scored, how good was the final pass. We've nothing like that now.'

Ironically, we too would prefer to go back to the old days. Journalists can be world-class moaners and we have a few of our own gripes as well. But, essentially, we should never lose sight of the fact that this is a fascinating job and that Ferguson has enriched all our lives. Some reporters support United. Others don't. We are all seduced by the club and that is Ferguson's doing. He is a propagandist of genius, obsessed with excellence and, in many ways, truly unique. Working out his idiosyncrasies is just part of the journalistic adventure.

2005–06
Annus Horribilis

THE BEGINNING
8.8.05

Press conferences are usually held at Carrington every Friday at 12 noon sharp – Ferguson, you discover, is never late and regards it as extreme bad manners if we are – but he also sees us on the day before mid-week matches. If it is a Champions League week his briefings are switched to the Europa Suite, in the South Stand at Old Trafford.

Today is the first time we have seen him this season. United play Debrecen of Hungary in a Champions League qualifier tomorrow and, traditionally, this will be one of the more enjoyable sessions. Everyone is happy to be back. Ferguson will be light-hearted, his batteries recharged, raring to go. He will tell us we get uglier every season, asking in an incredulous voice how we manage to make him look so young. The questions will start and, if he is feeling generous, he might have some information deliberately stored up. 'Make something with that,' he will say, as we gratefully scribble it down knowing that the next day's back-page splash has just been organised. Then he will shoo us out with a wave of the hand and his favourite payoff line. 'Now get out my sight. Go on. Away and write your shite ...'

However, nothing can be taken for granted. Getting to grips with Ferguson is like riding a bucking bronco. One minute you feel you are in control, your senses tuned in to every bump and jerk, convinced that you can ride the beast on your terms and that you have it mastered. But you're kidding yourself. Suddenly, one violent twist later, you are on your backside, dazed and confused and dusting yourself down, covered in bumps and bruises.

He loves to keep us on our toes. It is part of what makes him so fascinating in this conformist age when so many Premiership managers are as colourless as tap water. Yet it can be maddening too. Ferguson comes into the Europa Suite through a side door, and the speed at which he bustles in takes everyone by surprise. He looks tanned and healthy, damn good for a man of his age. But there isn't a flicker of a smile. His face is hard and uncompromising. His eyes are scanning the room, burning holes in everyone, sending coded signals that he would rather be anywhere than in this room at this time. There are no pleasantries, no comparing suntans, none of the football banter that you normally get from him at this time of the year. When someone says hello, he barely responds and it signals, to anyone who has not guessed already, that it is going to be a difficult press conference.

We know what he is doing, and why. A few weeks ago, Ferguson took the squad on a trip to Vale Do Lobo, a five-star resort for sun-seekers and golfers-with-money in an exclusive part of the Algarve. It was a chance to get some sun, introduce the new signings and start plotting how to win the title back from Chelsea. The press were not invited. But, three days in, a story was leaked to the *Sunday Times*, a newspaper with a reputation for accuracy, about an argument between Ferguson and the team's captain, Roy Keane. Keane was unhappy with the training arrangements and had complained to Carlos Queiroz, the assistant manager. Ferguson told him he was out of order and to snap out of it. Keane went berserk and suddenly they were yelling at each other in front of all the other players. Pointing fingers and shouting abuse. Two potentially lethal chemical agents, both capable of spontaneous combustion.

Manchester is the City of Gossip. There have been rumours ever since that the rift has become unbridge-able, that Ferguson and Keane, once as close a manager–player partnership as any in football, have come to resemble an old married couple, still sharing the same oxygen but none of the old joys. The fans have been getting jittery and Ferguson blames the press for stirring things up. 'It was blown up out of all proportion,' he says. 'Roy and I had a few words but an argument is nothing. Did he walk out? Did we come to blows? Of course not. We are both combusti-ble characters and we are always having arguments. I wish I had a pound, in fact, for every row I have ever had with Roy. He cares and I care, and every so often we clash. That doesn't affect the respect I have for him and I don't think it lessens my standing as man-ager in Roy's eyes.'

He is angry because he thinks we have sensational-ised what happened. Today, in this room, is the first opportunity he has had to exact his revenge. There is a bad vibe, from the moment he arrives, and our worst fears are confirmed when Diana Law, United's press officer, gives a little welcome speech and invites the first questions. There are twenty or so journalists lined up in several rows of seats. A television reporter asks Ferguson what he makes of the coming season and, specifically, whether he thinks United are equipped to win the title back from Chelsea.

'That's some question, that is,' Ferguson shoots back. 'Do you seriously think I'm going to answer that?'

A *Daily Mirror* reporter, doing his best to pretend

that everything is all right, holds up his hand to ask about possible transfer business, particularly speculation that United want to sign Michael Owen from Real Madrid. That hits a nerve too and Ferguson says he is not going to answer. 'I've seen what you've been writing over the summer,' he says. 'I'm not helping you one bit.'

It carries on for a few more minutes but it is fizzling out already. Ferguson is sour and impenetrable and the barriers are not going to be broken down. Not today. At the first appropriate pause he says 'Right' and he is off his chair and out the door and the one Hungarian journalist in the room is looking bewildered. She asks us if he is always like this and, oddly, we find ourselves apologising on his behalf, telling her there is stuff going on behind the scenes and, please, don't be too put off. For some reason, we don't want to shatter her illusions.

The truth is that it is a lousy way to start a new season, with grim portents for the next nine months. Ferguson is under extreme pressure going into this season, United's first under Malcolm Glazer's ownership, and history tells us that when he comes under a lot of strain the leg-pulling and mickey-taking stop and he starts to think of the press with something approaching revulsion.

Glazer is seventy-six – too old, he says, to visit Old Trafford in person – and completed his £570 million takeover of the club in the summer. He lives in Florida, where he built his empire buying and selling trailer parks. A quick internet search shows that when he bought the NFL side Tampa Bay Buccaneers, in 1995, he fired the popular, long-serving manager. There has been no suggestion that he has contemplated doing

6

the same at Old Trafford but, even so, his reputation makes it a potentially treacherous season for Ferguson. Glazer is no Jack Walker at Blackburn Rovers, Jack Hayward at Wolverhampton Wanderers or Steve Gibson at Middlesbrough, proud football men who poured tens of millions of pounds into their clubs out of sheer love. Neither is he another Roman Abramovich. He is an opportunist, a profit-seeker, and it is Ferguson's job to provide him with some till-ringing trophies – and fast.

The fans have waged a hate campaign against Glazer, convinced that this strange, whiskery American will take the club into financial ruin. There are protests planned before tomorrow's game. But he's here to stay, and that must be unnerving for Ferguson at a time when Abramovich has a third of the Russian oil industry to spend at Chelsea and a manager, Jose Mourinho, who is intelligent enough to make sure it is spent well. Stamford Bridge has become a giant fruit machine, a club for the haves and the have-yachts, and these are worrying times for Ferguson. Pre-Abramovich, his achievements were as solid as the Old Trafford stadium and it seemed as though nothing could end United's hegemony. He won the league eight times, the FA Cup five times, the League Cup, the European Cup Winners' Cup and, in 1999, the most dramatic European Cup in history, a 2–1 defeat of Bayern Munich sealed by a pair of goals from Teddy Sheringham and Ole Gunnar Solskjaer in stoppage time. At his peak, the Premiership trophy found its way to Manchester like a homing pigeon. United inspired envy and admiration. They were brilliant and successful and there was no club in the country that could live with them.

You think some things will remain for ever. But last season Arsenal beat them in the FA Cup final, Liverpool won the European Cup and, in the league, Chelsea cruised to their first championship for fifty years. In the previous decade, the title was a straight battle between United and Arsenal but the duopoly has been well and truly smashed now. Chelsea finished eighteen points clear of United with a record number of points (ninety-five), wins (twenty-nine) and clean sheets (twenty-five). Mourinho was named as Manager of the Year and when he accepted the award he described himself as the 'Special One'. Modesty is not one of the qualities at Stamford Bridge and Mourinho has predicted Chelsea will finish as champions again, possibly by an even greater margin.

Ferguson still has reasons to be optimistic when he looks round the Old Trafford dressing room. He has an inspirational captain in Keane, plus new signings such as Edwin van der Sar and Park Ji-Sung and seasoned campaigners such as Paul Scholes, Ryan Giggs and Gary Neville. He has two of the world's most exciting young stars in Wayne Rooney and Cristiano Ronaldo as well as a goalscorer, Ruud van Nistelrooy, who is the kind of striker every fan dreams about having in their team. And yet it is difficult not to be swept away by Mourinho's self-aggrandisement. Mourinho was recruited from Porto, where he won the European Cup in his final match, having knocked out United in the last sixteen. His overcoat is long and very, very expensive. His shirts are cut in Savile Row. His cufflinks are solid silver and he holds your attention like Michael Corleone in the *Godfather* movies. He talks about Chelsea dominating English football as if nothing could be more natural. Between him, Abramovich and Glazer, it is a season fraught with danger for Alexander Chapman Ferguson.

PEACE, OF SORTS
9.8.05

Manchester United	3
Debrecen	0

Champions League qualifier, first leg

We aren't sure what to expect tonight. But it is an important victory and an audience with Ferguson is a far more cordial experience. No drama, no fuss. The team all but book their place in the Champions League with goals from Ronaldo, Rooney and Van Nistelrooy, and Ferguson lifts that hard mask, Darth Vader-style, when he comes into his press conference.

The room is full of South Korean journalists, one of whom asks him what he made of Park Ji-Sung's first appearance for the club. Ferguson comes out with a couple of run-of-the-mill compliments but his Glaswegian accent is too much for the Koreans to understand. Clearly embarrassed and very, very nervous, they have to ask him to repeat himself.

'Do you know that the most perfect English in the world is spoken in Scotland?' he says good-naturedly. 'That's absolutely correct by the way. If you go up to Inverness for a day you will learn how to speak English perfectly.'

The poor Koreans don't have a clue what he is talking about. Yet they smile politely and bow their heads, as if in the presence of some higher authority. 'Thank you,' they say. 'Thank you so much, Mr Ferguson.'

The press conference is a peacekeeping operation and it goes well. We nod in agreement at every observation and ask questions that make it clear we like what we have seen. Ferguson seems a lot happier, maybe even a little relieved. Glazer's sons, Joel, Bryan and Avi – now United directors – were at their first match and the players have put on a convincing performance.

'The Glazer brothers have been in the dressing room and spent twenty minutes congratulating the players,' Ferguson says. He seems keen to do a spot of PR on their behalf. 'I think they're reasonably acquainted with the game and they have great enthusiasm for it.'

Not everyone is happy, however. Before the game, more than 3,000 fans march in protest outside the stadium. There are scuffles with the police and chants of 'We can do this every week.' Emotions have been running dangerously high ever since the Glazers took control and it needs a major security operation to smuggle them into the stadium. There are riot vans on Sir Matt Busby Way, dog-handlers on the forecourt and a police helicopter hovering above. The Glazers arrive in a car with blacked-out windows, a posse of bodyguards and an escort of police motorcycles, sirens wailing. They arrive early to get there before the crowds, and they leave deliberately late for an unspecified out-of-town hotel. United say it is not deemed safe for their whereabouts to be known.

AIRPLANE
23.8.05

We fly to Budapest today for the return leg of the

Debrecen tie. As we are coming into Ferihegy airport the plane hits awful turbulence. There are some nervous flyers among Ferguson's players and, apart from the odd expletive, everyone falls silent. It is much worse than the usual light vibrations. It is a stomach-churning sequence of lunges and lurches and even the aircrew look slightly panicky as the plane starts to judder violently. Drinks are flying everywhere, bags are banging about in the overhead lockers. Everyone is feeling queasily apprehensive.

It stops as suddenly as it starts and – ding! – the pilot comes on to apologise. The air hostesses flit around, straightening their hair and checking everyone is OK. The players hold their stomachs, full of bravado and trying to laugh it off, but are obviously shaken.

Then the lavatory door bursts open at the front of the plane and out staggers a bright-red Ferguson, looking as if he has gone through a tumble-dryer.

'Jesus Christ!'

As a comedy moment it is up there with David Brent's dance in *The Office* and Del Boy falling through the bar in *Only Fools and Horses*.

Ferguson is trying to smooth down his side parting, reaching unsteadily for his seat, when he suddenly realises the entire plane is watching. People are standing up and pointing, craning their necks to get a better view. The players start cheering and it makes him go redder and redder. The sponsors and corporate guests start cheering. Then the journalists join in. He is going the colour of a ripe tomato. You wouldn't believe a man could go such a shade of red.

'Who the hell locked me in?' he calls down the plane, playing up to his audience as an air hostess totters down the aisle to help him to his seat.

'I hope you haven't splashed, Sir Alex,' she says, and there are more loud cheers.

At least he sees the funny side. One of Ferguson's more endearing traits is his ability to laugh at himself and, half an hour later, he is still chuckling about it in the arrivals hall, holding up his trouser leg to show his shoes are urine free: 'Quite clean, I think you'll find'. He has agreed to do an interview by the carousel, so we find a quiet corner where we won't be disturbed. The incident with Keane seems to have been forgotten and his mood is light and jovial.

But then all the bonhomie and levity is shattered.

Three supporters, in their thirties, have landed on a separate flight. When they see the squad waiting for their luggage they head straight for David Gill, the chief executive, and start tearing into him, shouting and swearing and accusing him of 'selling out' because of the way he has rolled out the red carpet for the Glazers.

Everything happens so quickly that Gill is caught off guard. He is a big man, well over six feet, but he visibly seems to shrink as the men crowd round, accusing him of betraying the club and collaborating with the enemy.

'You've fucked us over big-time. How could you sell us out to Glazer? How could you betray the fans like that?'

Gill is speechless. He doesn't know where to look or what to say. For a split second a look of annoyance crosses his face but he doesn't want to take on these guys. He knows there is nothing he can say to calm them down so he just stands there with a thin and nervous smile, looking unhappy.

When the Glazers set about buying the club Gill did everything he could to delay and block the take-over. He described their plans as 'unworkable' and 'aggressive', and he was championed by the support-ers because of the way he was trying to protect the club's traditions and save them from a family with no interest in football.

His was a courageous stance for as long as it lasted. The problem was it didn't last very long. When it became obvious that the Glazers had the financial muscle to get what they wanted, Gill unexpectedly made a U-turn. Suddenly he was welcoming the Glazers with open arms, gushing about how excited he was to work alongside such interesting people … and Long Live America!

The supporters fought long and hard against Glazer, at great cost and emotional sacrifice. They feel let down. These guys are giving Gill a really hard time. A circle has formed, like a playground scrap, and he looks utterly miserable, totally out of his depth. The blood is draining from his face.

'You turned your back on us. How can you work for the Glazers?'

Suddenly Ferguson is in the middle of the circle. He gets on well with Gill and it seems to us that he thinks he can calm the situation just because of who he is. The reaction takes him by surprise.

'You've fucked us over too, Fergie. You could have spoken out about it. Why didn't you say anything?'

'The fans want some answers, Fergie.'

Ferguson was opposed to the Glazers' takeover of the club but the sum total of his resistance was a few paragraphs in his programme notes. After that, he kept well out of it. It wasn't easy for him. He was in an invidious position. Anyone who criticises him should ask themselves whether they would dare to speak out against the people who might be their future bosses. Yet Ferguson has always prided himself on standing up for what he believes. Rightly or wrongly, the supporters expected something that he wasn't willing to give them – his backing.

He is temporarily stunned, barely able to take it in. Most fans tend to treat the manager of their club with a certain reverence and Ferguson is used to a level of veneration usually reserved for high-ranking priests. Fans wave to him in his car or wind the window down to shout something supportive. Children will rush towards him in the street and then fall silent when they reach his side. Grown men will blink in disbelief, then nudge each other in wide-eyed excitement, unsure whether or not they should speak to him.

Not here. These guys are hardcore anti-Glazer militants. They are eyeballing him, accusing him of letting them down, making it clear that, in their eyes, there is a big difference between being a great football manager and a great football man. It is shocking, unprecedented.

It takes Ferguson a few seconds to digest what is happening and then he returns fire. 'I've got a job to do here,' he snaps. 'Let me get on with my job.' He says the criticism is unwarranted and makes it clear he has no intention of resigning. 'I've got fifteen staff to think of. They come first for me. So let me get on with my job.'

By now, Gill has melted into the background, relieved to be out of the firing line. Gill is the kind of guy you would find swapping anecdotes at a Round

Table dinner or swinging his racket at a lawn-tennis club in some leafy Cheshire village. Airport rows are not his speciality.

Ferguson is different. He has been embarrassed in front of a large audience and he is not going to take that from anyone.

'How long before the Glazers put up the prices?' one of the fans asks him accusingly.

'If you don't like it, go and watch Chelsea,' Ferguson snaps. 'Go and see how much it costs for a ticket there.'

He phrases it terribly. He is trying to point out that it is far more expensive somewhere like Stamford Bridge and that the supporters shouldn't jump to conclusions about the Glazers hiking prices. But he puts it so clumsily that it comes out as if he is saying: 'Well, if you don't want to support Manchester United you can always sod off to Chelsea.'

The fans hold their ground for a few more minutes before shaking their heads and turning to go. 'You're out of order,' they tell him. Ferguson stares back then turns to the twenty or so journalists who have made the trip. We are making notes and he realises we have seen and heard everything.

BUDAPEST
24.8.05

Debrecen	0
Manchester United	3

Champions League qualifier, second leg

On foreign trips the press are allowed to fly with the team. The club are happy to have a 'united front', although we are aware it is a source of irritation to Ferguson and a privilege he occasionally threatens to take away from us. At least once he has raised it with the board of directors, presenting a case for us to be left to fend for ourselves. The directors are reluctant to take him on but they don't understand why he has such a problem. We sit at the back of the plane, the players sit at the front, and the curtains are pulled across. It might as well be a steel shutter.

His grievance is that we delay them before flights home. After matches the team travel straight to the airport, with a police escort, as soon as they have showered and dressed. Before we leave the stadium we have to write our final-edition match reports and quotes pieces and there are no flashing blue lights in front of our coach. The players are tired, they have training the next day and they just want to get home and into bed. We are keeping them waiting.

We are even later than usual tonight and there isn't a great deal of friendly interaction as we make our way apologetically down the plane. Some of the directors nod hellos but behind them, in the players' seats, there are at least two comments along the lines of 'about bloody time'. Ferguson is midway through the *Daily Express* crossword and we shuffle past, trying not to bang him with our laptop bags.

We can see the newspapers in front of him:

Ferguson hit by four-letter volley
Ferguson clashes with fans over Glazer
Fergie tells fans: go support Chelsea
Fergie's row

We move further down the plane. Past Ryan Giggs, Edwin van der Sar, Rio Ferdinand, Paul

Scholes. But Gary Neville is out of his seat, holding up a copy of the *Daily Mirror*. The closer we get to him the more obvious it becomes that he is waiting for us. There is an apprehensive hush. Then David McDonnell, the *Mirror*'s Manchester correspondent, tries to get past and suddenly Neville is shouting. United have won, qualifying for the Champions League, but Neville looks as if he has lost the biggest match of his life.

'What was that shit you wrote about me this morning?'

McDonnell is knocked back on his heels. 'I beg your pardon?'

'You've misquoted me. When have I spoken to the papers for you to be quoting me?'

He is pointing to an article, on the inside back page, that quotes him saying United should not think about winning the European Cup until they have shown they can win the Premiership.

'I'm sorry, Gary, but I haven't misquoted you about anything,' McDonnell says. 'There's been a misunderstanding. Those quotes were sent directly to my office by Press Association. It's nothing to do with me.'

Press Association, or PA, is a national news agency that provides a 24-hour service for every arm of the media at press conferences, matches and other newsworthy events. Most newspapers have only one correspondent in the main football regions (i.e. Manchester, Merseyside, Yorkshire, the north-east and the Midlands) and maybe three or four in London. PA provides extra manpower. As part of the service, it monitors MUTV and distributes the players' quotes to the newspapers.

Neville shouts: 'Don't give me that. You've misquoted me. Do you hear me? Don't ever fucking misquote me again.'

McDonnell tries to deny it again but Neville shouts him down. 'You're lying to me ...'

Everyone on the plane is watching. The sponsors. The air hostesses. The directors. The players. The manager. Diana Law tries to intervene but Neville isn't listening.

McDonnell starts to move off. 'I think you should calm down, Gary. Nobody's lying. Those quotes came from PA and I can prove it to you.'

'FUCK OFF!'

Diana Law: 'Gary! No!'

Alan Smith is in the next row, laughing. 'Whooh! Whoooooh!'

But Neville has a face like murder. 'Don't ever make up quotes from me again.'

We move to the back of the plane and sit there in stunned silence, collectively digesting what has just happened.

SIX OUT OF TEN
29.8.05

Newcastle United	0
Manchester United	2

The team have made a good start to the season, maintained today by goals from Rooney and Van Nistelrooy, but things ended so badly on the way back from Budapest that, for once, we are quite happy not to have any contact with Ferguson after the game. Kath, the tea-lady in Newcastle's pressroom, has a freshly brewed pot and a plate of chocolate digestives waiting for him but we know she is wasting her time. She waits and waits then, huffing loudly, clears up her crockery. She has been serving tea at St James's Park since 1968 and it is obvious she feels put out. 'What's he like when they lose?' she asks.

We saw him for ten minutes at Carrington yesterday and the events in Hungary were never brought up. Sometimes, though, it's enough just knowing that he's in a flaky mood. It was a classroom atmosphere, like detention. Ferguson sat behind a wooden table, brusque and intimidating. We were lined up in two rows of seats, being as polite as we could, our questions designed not to antagonise him, much as you wouldn't ruffle the fur of a sleeping bear. Our survival instincts have kicked in since Budapest and if that means buttering him up for a week or two then so be it.

The Neville business is different. We haven't seen a player throw a tantrum like that since a very wound-up David Beckham had a go at a reporter from the *Manchester Evening News* for giving him six out of ten after a game against Leeds United a few years ago. It is amazing how seriously the players take those marks. A few years earlier the team bus overtook the same reporter on the motorway and Neville and Beckham came to the window, holding out both hands to indicate that they deserved a ten. On this occasion, Beckham had scored lower than Nicky Butt, who was given a seven, and he never spoke to the *Evening News* again.

Neville is generally media-friendly. None of us reported his rant from the other night and we are hoping it won't turn into a long-term grudge. He is usually one of the players who is OK about talking to the press and his dad often has a drink with us on European trips.

THE HAIRDRYER
9.9.05

So far this season Ferguson has restricted himself to a few mild tremors. But when the pressroom door bangs shut today we get the full volcanic eruption. It has been building up and we aren't particularly surprised. He lets off some steam and hopefully we will be able to start again with a clean slate.

His complaint is that quotes have appeared in the *Daily Express* and the *Daily Mirror* from an old interview in UEFA's Champions League magazine and he thinks he has been stitched up. He is evidently angry as he takes his seat, and addresses Richard Tanner of the *Express* and David McDonnell of the *Mirror*.

'Right, Richard and David, I'll call you by your first names on this one occasion but, hear this, it's the only reference I will ever, ever give you.'

McDonnell, who has been on holiday, is beginning to think he would get the blame for the half-time oranges being sour. He tries to cut in but Ferguson shouts him down.

'DON'T GIVE ME THAT! That shite in your paper, absolute crap ...'

He is remarkable when he gets going: half out of his seat, neck muscles straining, eyes protruding, more swear words than you might hear in an entire afternoon at Old Trafford.

'I don't give any of you credibility, do you know that?' he shouts. 'You talk about wanting to have an association with people here and you wonder why I don't get on with you? But you're a fucking embarrassment, a real embarrassment. One of these days the door is going to be shut on you permanently.'

He is fine for the remainder of the press conference, good-humoured even. His responses are calm and measured and the flares behind his eyes burn themselves out. But he has turned us into a bran-tub of nerves. We are on edge, aware that one question might trigger that outrage reflex again. We have seen it too many times before. All will be well and then someone will ask something slightly too daring, or phrase a sentence badly. He will take it as an affront to his authority and react.

The mother of all eruptions came in December 2004, a week after television cameras had caught Wayne Rooney pushing his hand into the face of Taib Ben Haim, the Bolton Wanderers defender, during a match at Old Trafford. Haim had gone in for some pretend agony, as if he had been bludgeoned with a sledgehammer, but Rooney had screwed up. He was facing a misconduct charge from the Football Association and a three-match ban. There was a very uneasy atmosphere as we filed into Ferguson's press conference.

'Alex, we have to ask you about the Wayne Rooney incident, him slapping the Bolton player.'

He started off calmly. 'Well, because it's Wayne Rooney, because it's Manchester United, yes, I can understand there is going to be a focus on it. But my bigger concern, and you are not even addressing it, is the Bolton player, what he did. He laid down on that ground pretending he was injured for two whole minutes.'

'I think we accepted that he did that …'

'You accepted it …?'

Bang!

' … WELL YOU'VE NOT FUCKING WRITTEN ENOUGH ABOUT IT! You're fucking on about Rooney, because he has a wee slap in the face and no matter whatever fucking else matters in the fucking game? You see fucking behaviour like that! He should fucking be up before the FA, not fucking Rooney. You are allowing that fucking cunt to cheat.'

What do you say to a man who is this angry?

'You're on about Rooney all the time, why not go and fucking blast him, that fucking Ben Haim? Why Rooney?'

'He's probably the most famous …'

'FUCK OFF! It doesn't matter. He's a human being like everybody else. He's nineteen years of age. Jesus Christ, what do you fucking want? Blood out of the boy? You fucking crucify him every fucking time. He's a fucking nineteen-year-old boy. Right?'

'He wasn't crucified …'

'A joke it is. Their fucking boy should be up before the FA for that. It's a fucking disgrace. And I'm not fucking saying anything more about it now. It's up to you to fucking do it. It's not for me to do it. Fucking joke he is, lying about, rolling about in fucking agony. Any other player than Rooney you wouldn't have bothered your arse.'

He was so angry at this point that he swung his arm at the tape recorders on his table and sent them flying into a wall ten feet away. One smashed open. The batteries flew out and scattered across the floor.

'It's over, right? You can get out. Press conference finished. You've got me to lose my temper. Wonderful!'

The remarkable thing about Ferguson is that he can switch from fury to good humour in the space of sixty seconds. The most innocuous remark can have him laying into a journalist, releasing everything two or three inches from his victim's face. It goes on for a few minutes and then he will be done. His face will return to its normal shade and he will be asking whether we have any more questions, as if it had never happened. He will finish with a cheery 'All right boys?' and clap his hands together to wrap it up, joking that he would rather have a 'week in jail' than another five minutes in our company. It is an unnerving process. If you are not the victim, he might even give you a crafty wink or a knowing smile as he ushers everyone out. Then the next time you see him he will act as if it was a trick of our collective imaginations. He never refers back to the same incident. But he never forgets either. It makes reporters think twice before asking something that he might not like.

THE DERBY
10.9.05

Manchester United	1
Manchester City	1

Appearance is important to Ferguson. He usually wears a blazer to games, dark blue with the United crest, sometimes beneath a black overcoat, plus a club tie, pressed trousers and polished black shoes. He likes to be smart and well turned-out. But today, inexplicably, he goes for a cotton tracksuit that seems a size or two too small. It clings to him unflatteringly as he appears on the touchline and the Manchester City fans are on their feet, pointing and cackling.

Tracksuit from Matalan!
Tracksuit from Matalan!
Tracksuit from Matalan!

It is usually the other way round: Ferguson taking the piss out of City. He calls the City of Manchester stadium the 'Temple of Doom' and he loves it when Paul Hince, chief sportswriter for the *Evening News*, turns up to his press conferences. Hince is an old-school Mancunian and devoted City fan who, in the 1960s, was briefly on the club's books as a pro. He calls Ferguson 'Sir Taggart'.

Ferguson, in return, uses City's failures to beat Hince around the head. His favourite line is to tell Hince, who is close to retirement, that he should still get a game. Or, if City have had a run of bad results, he will ask him whether he has remembered his anti-depressants and offer to put him in touch with a 'good counsellor'.

When Hince asked a question on one European trip, Ferguson just burst out laughing. 'What are you doing here?' he wheezed. 'Can't get into Europe with your own team so you have to latch on to us. Is that it? Well, I'm telling you nowt, you little Blue spy.'

Hince tried again. Ferguson playfully shook his head, telling him not to confuse him with Kevin Keegan (City's manager at the time). 'You think you are talking to Kevin, don't you? And Kevin would give you an answer, wouldn't he? But you're not talking to Kevin – and you ain't getting my team. That's it, press conference over.'

There is no joking today, though. Ferguson is under a lot of pressure right now, more than he probably cares to let on, and there are the signs of a man who has just gone through a wedding set's worth of crockery in the dressing room. City are not even a good side. They will be marooned in the bottom half of the table by the end of the season. Yet the rivalry seems to inspire them when they play United. Van Nistelrooy scores first but Joey Barton equalises and Stuart Pearce, Keegan's successor, is pumping his fists in front of the United fans. There are enough chances for United to win handsomely, but it is City who finish the stronger. In the final few minutes Andy Cole, the former United striker, nearly wins it for the visitors. 'Blue Moon', City's adopted anthem, is echoing around Old Trafford when the final whistle goes.

It is a bad result for United, not just in terms of points but for the morale of their supporters. There are boos at the final whistle and Ferguson looks really down. Chelsea have won their opening five games without conceding a goal and if it is to be United's year they cannot afford to drop points against middle-of-the-table sides. Manchester City at home is the kind of game they have to win and worryingly, there are signs that the supporters are beginning to doubt the team. Some of the fans behind Ferguson's dugout let him know exactly what they think of it. As he walks down the tunnel, he is shaking his head. The worry lines on his face stand out like contours on a map.

VILLARREAL
13.9.05

We're on an early-morning flight to Spain today for United's opening Champions League group game, against Villarreal at the Estadio El Madrigal. Everyone is excited about the start of a new Champions League campaign and Ferguson is in a jovial mood when we check in at Manchester airport. The players are in their club suits but Gerard Piqué, an eighteen-year-old defender signed from Barcelona's youth team, doesn't know how to knot his tie. Blushing, he has to ask if there is anyone who can do it for him. The check-in girls are teasing him and Ferguson is quietly chuckling.

He doesn't even fake a smile, however, when a Liverpool fan swaggers over at passport control and starts to have some fun at the players' expense.

'Eh, lads, how's your summer been?' he crows. 'Mine's been absolutely mint. Been to Istanbul. Won the European Cup. You wanna hear about it?'

This guy is a moron. He has a sunburnt nose, a pot belly, peroxide hair and a long-suffering wife. He is wearing a white shellsuit, unzipped to show a red T-shirt bearing the words: 'Liverpool – five European Cups'.

When Wayne Rooney walks past, the loudmouth can't believe his luck. 'Wazza lad, do you wanna buy a T-shirt? Might be a bit tight but it's yours if you want it.'

Ferguson walks off briskly. He signs a few autographs, ruffles a young boy's hair, poses for photographs. One girl takes an age getting the camera working on her mobile phone but he sticks around, smiling sympathetically when one or two of his players (Keane, for example) might have made their excuses and left. Ferguson is really good when it comes to meeting the supporters in public.

It is when we arrive at Valencia airport that he drops his bombshell.

His itinerary on European trips has traditionally included a ten-minute briefing, exclusively for the daily newspaper journalists, once we have landed and are waiting for our luggage. But today Ferguson sends a message via Diana Law that the arrangement has been cancelled. He cites what happened with the supporters in Budapest, saying we broke his trust by reporting it and that we have nobody to blame but ourselves.

It is another sign that media relations with Ferguson are going the same way as red telephone boxes. There is still the official Champions League press conference, organised by UEFA, but those airport briefings were precious to us in terms of beating early-evening deadlines. By speaking to him in a private huddle we could also get some exclusive news away from our television or radio rivals. In happier times, he has even been known to turn on broadcast journalists he has caught trying to eavesdrop. He would be quite protective, clearing them off with a flea in their ear. But no more.

RED CARDS AND RED MISTS
14.9.05

Villarreal	0
Manchester United	0

Champions League, Group D

Wayne Rooney gets himself sent off tonight. He is booked for tripping a Spanish player and turns on the referee, breaking into exaggerated, sarcastic applause. It is childish and unnecessary. A second yellow card appears, followed by a red. Even then he wants to prolong the argument. The other players have to usher him away before he makes it even worse. He completely loses the plot.

It is usually very hard for Ferguson to see his players in a bad light. Unless someone has thrown a killer punch and knocked an opponent clean out he nearly always says the referee got it wrong or that he needs to see it on video. He defends them out of loyalty because, in the long term, he thinks they will repay that loyalty.

Tonight, though, we can tell from his body language that Rooney will be in for it in the dressing room. Albert Morgan, the kit man, is despatched from the dugout to shepherd Rooney down the tunnel and Ferguson deliberately blanks him as they pass on the touchline. United have been on top for most of the game but, a man down, they have a desperate battle to hold on for a draw. Rooney's petulance has cost them any chance of winning.

The press conference afterwards is in a whitewashed room in the bowels of the stadium. It is sweaty and airless and buzzing with mosquitoes, and Ferguson's face is red enough for us to suspect he has been shouting in the dressing room.

'In the circumstances, Alex, you must be pleased to have hung on for a draw, but can we ask you first for your thoughts on Wayne's sending-off?'

He chooses his words carefully. 'I think Wayne reacts to injustices. He felt it was a wrongful booking and he reacted. The fact is, however, you can't applaud

a referee like that. He's given himself no chance whatsoever, especially with that referee. We've had
problems with him before, y'know?'

'Do you think Wayne invited the red card then?'

His reply is loaded with exasperation. 'What have
I just said to you?'

'We've seen this behaviour quite a lot from Wayne.
Is it time for him to cut this sort of thing out of his
game? He's been playing long enough to know what's
right and what's wrong.'

'Oh yeah, he's been playing a really long time –
two years, is it? Really long … really long …'

'Well, long enough, surely?'

'Listen, he's a young lad. He's nineteen. We hope,
through maturity, that these things evaporate. The
important thing is to retain his good points and eradi-
cate the bad ones …'

Someone's mobile goes off – *Cock-a-doodle-doo!*
Incredibly, a Spanish journalist answers it.

'*Hola.*'

This guy is jabbering away at a hundred words per
minute, apparently oblivious to the fact that there is a
press conference going on. Other reporters are trying
to shush him but he isn't paying attention. And
Ferguson is gaping, scarcely believing what he sees,
blood pressure 170 and counting. The next question
could easily tip him over the edge.

'Has Wayne apologised, Alex?'

'Right, I've said enough about that,' he says. 'I'd
like to talk about something else, if you don't mind.'

Subject closed.

YOU WOULDN'T PUNCH A MAN IN
RED-TINTED GLASSES?
16.9.05

Ferguson has fallen out with MUTV. He has been tipped off that while we were in Spain one of the presenters, Paul Anthony, broke ranks and apparently indicated on air that United should change their tactics to 4-4-2. Ferguson has developed a fondness for 4-5-1 this season, with Rooney shunted out to the left wing, and Anthony suggested it was too negative. He was merely repeating what every journalist in Manchester has been writing but Ferguson has taken it badly, as if he has suddenly found out his best friends have been bad-mouthing him behind his back. He is refusing to speak to anyone at MUTV until he gets an apology and a promise it won't happen again.

Even by Ferguson's standards this is extraordinary. MUTV is known in media circles as 'Pravda TV'. A station where interviews are about as demanding as *Hello!* magazine. The general rule for MUTV presenters is to agree with everything Ferguson says and explode with laughter every time he makes a joke. If he were caught stealing flowers from Southern Cemetery, they would find some way of defending him. If he landed a right hook on Arsène Wenger's chin, they would argue he was provoked. For Ferguson to refuse to speak to MUTV is not like Tony Blair turning down a one-on-one with Jeremy Paxman on *Newsnight*. It is Blair refusing to be interviewed by Ant and Dec because one of them looked at him in a funny way.

The issue is a familiar one for anyone in the media who has covered United for any length of time – that

Ferguson weighs each ton of praise as nothing beside a hundredweight of criticism.

After the Manchester City game Paul Parker, a former United player now working as one of MUTV's pundits, criticised the decision to leave out Ryan Giggs. Lou Macari, another pundit and ex-player, has made it clear he would rather United go back to 4-4-2. Paddy Crerand, who won a European Cup medal with United in 1968 and has the reddest-tinted glasses of them all, says the same. And now Anthony, a man with no football background, has questioned whether playing with only one striker goes against the club's attacking traditions. Ferguson has been working it over in his mind, getting increasingly wound up, and he has decided that MUTV, and Anthony in particular, need to be taught a sharp lesson.

It is ludicrous, of course. Anthony might have touched a nerve but surely Ferguson could have pulled him up about it in private. An apology would have been forthcoming, presumably. Anthony could have explained that he was a fan and that he cared deeply about the club. And that could have been the end of it, without anyone else knowing.

Instead, we have the crazy situation where Ferguson is boycotting a television station operated by the club and watched exclusively by its own supporters. It's the first time anything like this has happened with MUTV. The station is used to getting privileged access and Anthony, we're reliably informed, is having a terrible time.

POLITICS
18.9.05

Liverpool	0
Manchester United	0

There is talk in the pressbox today that David Gill is going to have to involve himself in sorting out Ferguson's differences with MUTV. Gill is a good negotiator. In theory, he should be in a position to stand up to Ferguson and tell him to snap out of it. It is not a conversation he will necessarily look forward to, but it is one that needs to take place. Because, as it stands, Ferguson has made it very clear that he is not in the mood for making up.

The interesting thing is that most of the supporters seem to be on Anthony's side. United won the European Cup, scattering all before them, by playing in a 4-4-2 formation and it has been baffling that Ferguson should change to a more conservative approach. Ferguson is an admirer of the top Spanish and Italian teams and his Portuguese assistant, Carlos Queiroz, has had spells at Sporting Lisbon and Real Madrid. Together, they have decided that the team should adopt a more continental style, with Keane operating as a holding player in a five-man midfield and Van Nistelrooy operating as a lone striker. This is a different United – more methodical, less gung-ho – and they have managed only five shots on target in their last three games. They have not scored in 225 minutes of football and, to be brutally honest, they have not looked like scoring. They are seven points behind Chelsea already and the fans are starting to question Ferguson in a way they have not done for years. On the internet messageboards some of them have even been campaigning for him to go. They are in the minority, but it is still shocking to see Ferguson, the master manager, getting so much flak, and sometimes abuse, from his own supporters.

A draw at Anfield is a satisfactory result but it is another drab and defensive performance. And, with five minutes to go, things get even worse. Keane goes into a 50-50 and feels a sharp pain in his left foot. He carries on for a few minutes but eventually he gives in to the pain. The X-rays confirm his fears: his third metatarsal is broken.

He will be out for two months, which is a terrible blow. Gabriel Heinze, the club's player of the year, ruptured his cruciate knee ligaments against Villarreal and suddenly Ferguson is without his best midfielder and his best defender. The season is still is in its infancy but, already, it's beginning to look as if everything is conspiring against him.

MUTINY
24.9.05

Manchester United	1
Blackburn Rovers	2

All the frustration comes to a head today. The crowd turn. Effing this. Effing that. Thousands of them, in every part of the ground, but particularly around the dugout. Ferguson is a 'disgrace'. He is 'fucking clueless'. He does not know what tactics are. He is a 'shambles'. It is time he 'fucked off' and took Queiroz with him.

Towards the end, a big fat guy in a leather jacket to the right of the dugout is jabbing his finger at Ferguson, all pent-up anger. Nearby, on another row, there is a middle-aged bloke dressed all in black. Between them, they are giving Ferguson a terrible time, not even watching the game. It is spiteful, vicious, toxic stuff and Ferguson stirs. He half-turns, as if he is about to have a go back. But then something tells him to break the habit of a lifetime. He stares impassively at the pitch, trying to blank it out. But these guys are close enough for him to hear every word. Two stewards in fluorescent yellow jackets move in but it doesn't make any difference. As soon as they move off, the supporters are back on their feet, yelling abuse. It is a savage, relentless tirade.

There will be supporters of other clubs who cannot believe how spoilt United's fans are. They will not be able to comprehend how this could happen to a man who has brought the club such unprecedented happiness. But football can do this. Ferguson will go down in history as one of the most successful managers of all time and surely deserves better. But this is a hard and unforgiving business. Expectations at Old Trafford are so high that every home defeat represents a crisis.

Managers can suffer from losses of form, as players do, and Ferguson seems strangely out of sorts right now. There is a bad vibe about United and the fans are starting to wonder if this is the Ferguson of old: the guy who used to dismiss every 'crisis' the way the rest of us would swat away a bothersome fly.

Many supporters, Ferguson loyalists, won't have a bad word said against him, but others are querying his transfers and belittling his tactics. They have started to turn against some of the players – Darren Fletcher, John O'Shea, Kieran Richardson – and they have flooded the fans' websites with their vitriol.

Retire Fergie
Fergie Out
Fergie Must Go

Inside Old Trafford it is only a minority, maybe twenty or thirty per cent – but it is a vociferous twenty or thirty per cent.

They are grateful for everything he has done, of course. They want him applauded out the front door rather than shooed out the back. They respect him for his achievements and will always afford him the status of a legend. But it is not the unconditional love that Sir Matt Busby once enjoyed. They have seen Chelsea overtake United as the best team in the Premiership and they have gritted their teeth and watched from behind the sofa as Liverpool, the arch-enemy, won the European Cup. Now they are wondering when the good times are coming back. Losing today leaves them ten points behind Chelsea. For some, it is too much to bear.

'Fuck off Fergie.'

'Fuck off Queiroz.'

It is ridiculous, of course. Manchester United are a big, scary club and they need a big, scary manager. Yet the outpouring of anger is astonishing. Rooney, the crowd's favourite, has been left out and when Blackburn go one up the supporters in the old Scoreboard End are on their feet. Demanding that he is brought on. Demanding an end to 4-5-1.

Rooney! Rooney! Rooney!
Four-four-two! Four-four-two! Four-four-two!

When Van Nistelrooy equalises, everything calms down. But Blackburn score a deserved second, with eight minutes to go, and it explodes again. More swearing, more abuse and then a mass walkout.

There are early leavers at every match, but today they are not fans trying to beat the traffic, or hoping to get a good place in the tram queues. Thousands of people are streaming towards the exits and it feels like a choreographed protest about what they are watching. Ferguson's United, particularly the 1999 team, were famous for the way they could rescue, or win, games with dramatic late goals. But these supporters have lost faith. There are four minutes of stoppage time but Blackburn see out the game with alarming ease. It is only their second win of the season.

Old Trafford is half-empty at the final whistle and when Ferguson makes his way to the tunnel it is the longest walk of his life. Mark Hughes, manager of Blackburn, is in front and the fans stand respectfully to applaud one of their former players.

Hughesy! Hughesy! Hughesy!

Ferguson follows ten yards behind, his head bowed, shoulders hunched. When he flashes his eyes at the crowd, the hostility hits him like a mallet. There are V-signs, middle fingers raised and faces contorted with anger.

There is nothing to prepare you for seeing and hearing Sir Alex Ferguson being jeered and abused by Manchester United's supporters. It is unthinkable. The last time he was subjected to this level of abuse was in December 1989. The crowds were dwindling, Liverpool were champions and Old Trafford was a place of brooding discontent. United lost 2–1 to Crystal Palace and the fans on the Stretford End sang 'Bye bye Fergie'. They chanted for Bryan Robson to take over and they held up a banner that read: 'Three years of excuses and we're still crap – ta-ra Fergie'.

Ferguson went home that night and buried his head in a pillow, confessing later that he was 'feeling uncomfortable' about the possibility of losing his job. There are people at Old Trafford who recognise that same careworn look when they see him today. He looks washed out, with drooping bags beneath his eyes and heavy creases lining his face. He seems emotionally drained. Maybe a little scared.

The only thing going for him is that he doesn't have to face the press and a forensic examination of what has happened. Any other manager would take a deep breath before trotting out some clichés about seeing 'light at the end of the tunnel' and knowing that he could 'look himself in the mirror'. Yet Ferguson has nothing more demanding than his usual interview with the radio reporters – the 'Disc of Doom' – and he gets off very lightly. He is never asked for his reasons for leaving out Rooney, or for plugging away with 4-5-1. Amazingly, he isn't even asked about the crowd's reaction.

SORRY IS THE HARDEST WORD
27.9.05

Manchester United	2
Benfica	1

Champions League, Group D

There are some things you never expect to see. One is journalists and television cameramen stopping fans outside Old Trafford before a game to ask whether Sir Alex Ferguson is still the right man for the job.

The response is interesting. Some of the supporters who booed Ferguson are sticking to their guns. They have legitimate grievances, they say. They pay good money to watch the club and they are entitled to shout and holler if they don't like what they see.

Others are beginning to feel uneasy. They are wondering whether they over-reacted. One or two say they feel ashamed and wish they could turn back the clock. Guilt has set in and they have started to regret all the rancour and hostility.

The request for forgiveness comes sixteen minutes into the game.

> *Stand up if you love Fergie*
> *Stand up if you love Fergie*
> *STAND UP IF YOU LOVE FERGIE!*

It is an outpouring of noise and passion and genuine affection. Ferguson remains impassive, staring intently at the pitch, not a flicker of emotion crossing his face. Yet the hairs must be standing up on the back of his neck. Sixty thousand people are on their feet, clapping and singing, rising as one to applaud him. Old Trafford looks as it always does under floodlights, timeless and seductive, and this feels like a special moment. A stadium saying sorry.

Half an hour after the game, he walks into the pressroom, with his chest puffed out and a defiant stare. He talks about the team's spirit, the contribution of senior players, how important it is to win home games in a Champions League group. He talks of a turning point, of not feeling sorry for himself and, most of all, of the character of his team.

He is asked about the goals, one apiece from Giggs and Van Nistelrooy. Then Oliver Kay, the *Times* correspondent, asks about the team's tactics. 'You seemed to use Paul Scholes in a slightly different role, a little bit further forward perhaps.'

'Different?' Ferguson replies tersely. 'Different from when?'

'Well, from the previous few games. I just wondered if you could explain the thinking behind it.'

Kay is a respected broadsheet writer, one of the best in the business, but Ferguson is eyeballing him ominously.

'I'm not explaining anything to you.'

The Portuguese journalists think he is joking and start to laugh, but they quickly realise that he is deadly serious.

'I'm not explaining anything,' Ferguson continues. 'You've got your own ideas of the game so, please, carry on. I wouldn't want to blunt your imagination with the facts.'

It is weird – United have won yet Ferguson is in a stinking mood, staring us down, looking like he would rather eat broken glass than listen to any more questions. There is not a flicker of happiness on his face and soon afterwards he gets to his feet, looking to the door.

'Thank you,' one reporter says.

'And who are you to decide it's finished?' he shoots back. Then he's gone.

THE ROBOT, THE MADMAN, THE WINNER
29.9.05

Roy Keane has been on MUTV for a question-and-answer session with the club's supporters. He talks about his broken foot, the team's form, the demands of playing for a club like United and, twenty minutes in, a woman from Belfast comes on the line.

'Two questions, Roy. Tell me, from your heart, how much longer you would like to go on here. And then, from your head rather than your heart, how long do you think it will be?'

He barely pauses for breath. 'My contract runs out at the end of the season and I don't expect to be offered another one,' he says. 'Even if they do, it will be too late because I'm looking to sort out something elsewhere. I've still got one or two years left in me but it won't be at Manchester United. Every player has to move on eventually.'

Steve Bower, MUTV's front man, gawps into the camera. In hushed tones, speaking very, very slowly, he asks Keane to spell out exactly what he is saying. Again, Keane doesn't blink.

'It's time to move on. Players come and go – that's football – and it will do me good to experience what it's like at another club, maybe in another country. I've had twelve great years here and I don't think I could stomach coming back to Old Trafford in the away dressing room, but I would like to play for another big club in another country. I'm thirty-five in the summer and I'd like to play on for a year or two, but I've not been offered a new contract and I don't think I will be. My gut feeling is that it would be better to make a clean break.'

In newspaper offices across the north of England, there are journalists staring blankly at the television, saying, over and over again, 'Fuck me'.

Football is a cynical business. There will be people who suspect Keane is simply angling for a new contract, using his best acting skills to try to accelerate the club into action. Tonight, though, it feels very real. Keane looks and sounds deadly serious and if he is being genuine, if he really wants to go, then it is difficult to overstate the importance of this announcement.

Some footballers who leave United are barely noticed: pennies in an arcade, pushed over the edge by the surge of new coins behind. But Keane is a once-in-a-lifetime legend at Old Trafford. He may be thirty-four, in the final phase of his career, but he is still the player who gets everyone else going. The talisman, the captain, the inspiration. The player who lifts the crowd and imposes himself, without fail, in every match. The best player, Ferguson says, he has seen in fifty years of football – and it is not a statement that anyone has ever deemed it necessary to question.

Ferguson's squad is thin enough without losing his most important player and the news from Old Trafford is genuinely shocking: he did not even know Keane was contemplating leaving, never mind on the point of announcing it to the world. Ferguson, it emerges, has been caught completely cold. He may even be angry, quite possibly embarrassed, although it is difficult to know because we have no way of getting to him, or Keane, to find out exactly what is going on.

At times like this, as journalists, it is very easy to feel inadequate. In an ideal world we would be able to phone Keane and write about it from the inside rather than relying on second-hand information or educated guesswork. Yet the days when we can ring United's players have all but disappeared. There are rules in place – Ferguson's rules – and anyone who breaches them is subject to one of the club's banning orders. We can call the player's agent, or his image-rights consultant, or his press officer, but never the player himself.

Not that Keane has ever handed out his numbers, or made himself readily available to the press. He has never had any desire to acquaint himself with the media or with the lifestyle of the modern-day footballer. Keane has never had any interest in what journalists do, or why. In his world, winning football matches is all that matters. The rest, as Harvey Keitel puts it in *Mean Streets*, is bullshit. And Keane belongs firmly to the rest-is-bullshit school.

A couple of Ireland's top writers, Tom Humphreys of the *Irish Times* and Eamon Dunphy of the *Irish Star*, are occasionally allowed inside Keane's world, treated to a snapshot of his life. But it is always on Keane's terms. Nobody is allowed the Access All Areas badge apart from his family and a handful of friends back in Cork, where he grew up. We football writers spend so many hours debating whether he is a genius or a lunatic that we have gradually deluded ourselves into thinking we understand what makes him tick. We talk about his 'demons', but that is just a way of concealing our ignorance about what is really going on behind that dark, impenetrable scowl.

On a rare occasion, maybe once or twice a season, when United play a cup final or a big European tie, he feels duty-bound to speak to us. An audience with Keane is not something to be taken lightly and there is always a pensive air beforehand. We are never quite sure how to handle him or how far we can push him. Some journalists are far too familiar in these situations. Having met someone once or twice, they think it is acceptable to refer to them by their nickname. They nod at Rooney and say, 'All right, Wazza?' Or sidle over to Giggs and go, 'How's the hammy, Giggsy?'

With Keane, the best policy is simply to remember to say 'please' and 'thank you', because he is the only footballer we have ever dealt with who makes a point of pulling us up on our manners.

'Have you got two minutes, Roy?' we will ask.

'Have you got two minutes, *please*?' he will shoot back, not even breaking stride.

So the golden rule is to remember our Ps and Qs – but not to overdo it, in case we come across as fawning and servile. He would see through that as well. We worry and we worry and then he makes his way over, smiling sheepishly. The first thing everyone notices is how surprisingly slight he is, with those sloping shoulders and lean limbs and, no kidding, the blackest eyes you have ever seen.

'How long are you going to need?' he wants to know, looking at his watch.

'Twenty minutes OK?'

'Twenty minutes? Nah, I'm going to be longer than that ...'

He has a nice line in self-deprecating humour. But there is something elusive about him that tells you not to ask a duff question or fluff your lines. Maybe it is the pace at which he walks, as if he is trying to burn off excess nervous energy. Maybe it is the hardwood handshake. Or maybe it is the way he fixes those eyes on you. Challenging you, seeing what you are made of, looking for signs of weakness. You are half a dozen words into a difficult question when his head tilts slightly and his gaze intensifies with peculiar interest, as if you are about to reveal the secret of eternal life. It is like that terrible teenage moment when you realise you have offered a fight to someone twice your size. And it is at that point that you begin to stutter and ramble.

Generally, though, he is a dream of a talker. He never rules anything out. He answers instinctively, he has strong opinions and he refuses to go in for the clichéd claptrap that other footballers fall back upon.

He turned up once with a PR representative in tow and looked mortified when she produced a sheet of paper specifying the three questions she wanted us to ask. He didn't want to offend her but when she left the room he took the piece of paper, screwed it up and shook his head.

'We're all adults, aren't we? Ask me what you like. If I don't like the question I won't answer it. How does that sound?'

It is an attitude that endears him to us. When we interview some footballers, they give us the impression we are eating into valuable MUTV time or that we have pulled them away from an important frame

44

snooker. The best interviewees tend to be those players who can still remember what it is like to turn out
in front of tiny crowds and shower under dribbles of
cold water. Keane doesn't have a diamond earring or
a Louis Vuitton holdall and he prefers to talk in
English rather than in jargon. The modern-day Keane
is a considered individual and a deep thinker, albeit
one with a fuse just as short as Ferguson's – maybe
even shorter.

When Ferguson flies into a temper we know he is
just letting off steam. Whatever is eating him comes
out in an unstoppable torrent. But within a few minutes he might be laughing and joking, poking fun at
his victim but pointing out that it is nothing personal.
Sometimes you get the feeling he is just doing it to
test us, or as a reminder about who calls the shots.
What he says is unpleasant, but he gets himself so
worked up that it is generally harmless bluster. It
seldom makes any sense. In a strange way, that is
comforting when he has just tried to humiliate you in
front of your peers.

Keane is different. He operates by the same hair-
trigger reactions but when he is riled he is more
calculated, perfectly in control of what he is saying.
Not a syllable passes his lips without being vetted by
the censor of his mind first. And what he says is
designed to cut deep. Every grievance or perceived
slight gets an airing. By the time he has finished he
has dealt with everything, in chronological order.
Every insult is impeccably delivered, from A to Z.

His biggest feud was with Mick McCarthy, manager of the Republic of Ireland, before Keane walked
out of the World Cup in 2002 – a story so sensational
that it made the front of the *Delhi Times* at a time when

India and Pakistan seemed on the brink of nuclear war. Yet the list of those who have been publicly savaged by Keane goes way beyond that. Keane has had road rage, air rage, even hair rage.

There is a great story about him laying into Ruud van Nistelrooy after catching him combing his hair before an MUTV interview. What the fuck, Keane wanted to know, was one of his team-mates doing poncing about in front of a mirror? Who wanted to look good for MUTV?

Keane, you quickly learn, is not a man who suppresses his inner thoughts. He has described the team that won the European Cup in 1999 as average. He has complained that a Rolex and fast-car culture exists in the dressing room. In his autobiography he brands Peter Schmeichel, the greatest goalkeeper in United's history, as a 'fannying around poser'.

He once talked of a team-mate trembling with nerves as the team lined up before a big European tie and he was so disgusted it sounded as if he wanted to vomit. But this is Keane, a man who would rather die on his feet than live on his knees. An aggressive ex-boxer who acts impulsively and without regret. Not many footballers feel they are in a position where they can get away with describing former team-mates as 'bluffers, whingers and conmen', as he has. Not many would want to say it, even if they believed it. And you just know he has said worse to their faces. Keane says he has had so many arguments with other players that he never knows from one day to the next who he's talking to.

Gary Neville once sent him a text saying: 'This is Gary's new mobile number.' A few minutes later his phone bleeped with a reply: 'So what?'

After today's MUTV broadcast, it is what happens next that matters. Ferguson will have to be swift and decisive because it is unthinkable that he can let this happen. Keane might not be the gladiator he once was, he might have a bad hip and aching knees, sore joints and a stiff back, but his level of commitment is still awesome. Superbly timed tackles, immaculate interceptions, swiftly delivered passes, a calming presence.

Keane understands precisely what it takes to be a midfielder, coupling this with the ability to bring it into action. He has the capacity to read a dangerous situation before it happens and then go in and prevent it. When things are going badly he will never be the one whose head drops on to his chest, who looks around to blame someone else. He always takes responsibility, always goes for the entire ninety minutes. 'If I was putting Roy Keane out there to represent Manchester United on a one-on-one,' Ferguson once said, 'we'd win the National, the Boat Race and anything else. It's an incredible thing he's got.'

Of all the quotes about Keane, that one probably encapsulates best why today is such a bombshell. Keane has never been one for killer passes, for nutmegging an opponent or sending in raking fifty-yard balls. He doesn't bring a crowd to its feet by trapping the ball with the outside of his boot, dribbling past the full-back with a couple of showy stepovers and crossing from an impossibly tight angle. What he possesses is less spectacular, yet all the more inspiring: presence, control, aura, attitude, desire.

There will be times when a game has gone flat and Keane will lift the crowd single-handedly. He inspires awe, from supporters and opponents alike, and no one else in football can affect a crowd's senses in the way he does. A tackle from Keane is one of the great events of sport.

Journalists and television crews are outside Old Trafford to ask supporters for their reaction. Without exception, everyone describes him as irreplaceable. They talk in the tone that people use when someone has died. They use words such as 'shocked' and 'devastated' and they make it clear United must offer Keane a new deal. This is a big moment in United's season. It is very important that Ferguson does the right thing.

ALL BETS ARE OFF
1.10.05

Fulham	2
Manchester United	3

A press release arrives today from Paddy Power bookmakers: 'Chelsea declared Premiership champs!' It is to announce that they are paying out on the title in record time.

Chelsea are clear of the pack and not looking like they will be caught. Accordingly, we have declared the title race over and decided to pay out seven months before the season is finished. We know, and the punters know, that the Premiership race is already over.

It's a cheap publicity stunt, but a stunning one too. The season is only seven games old – thirty-one to go – and none of the big teams have even faced each other yet. Bookmakers often pay out early in return for easy headlines, but normally in March or April … never October.

And yet it is difficult to see how Paddy Power can lose this particular gamble. Chelsea have won their opening seven games, scoring fourteen goals and conceding one. They are strong and athletic, rich and powerful and totally at ease with their vision of themselves at the top of the hierarchy. The Glazers are promising to back Ferguson in the January transfer window but nobody knows whether to believe them. Even if they keep their promise, the budget will be only a few droplets compared to Abramovich's oil riches.

At least Ferguson shows an appreciation today that things have to change. United go back to basics and, finally, abandon the 4-5-1 system for the old-fashioned 4-4-2. Rooney is moved from the left wing to his favourite position, a roving centre-forward's role, and responds by scoring one of the goals and setting up another. Van Nistelrooy scores twice and looks much happier with another striker beside him. Giggs and Park provide width and penetration on the wings. There is movement, anticipation, speed of thought – everything, in fact, that made Ferguson's teams great in the first place.

It has been a long time coming, but it is a start and it should placate the fans. Things have been getting pretty heavy recently, with supporters calling radio phone-ins and writing to the newspapers. Scapegoats have been sought and Carlos Queiroz, in particular, has become a popular target, partly as a kind of surrogate for Ferguson himself – in the same way people criticise Cherie Blair to get at her husband.

The fans have come to the conclusion, rightly or wrongly, that it is Queiroz, not Ferguson, who decided the team should go with 4-5-1 and that, consequently, he should take the brunt of their anger. The press have started to question whether Ferguson has allowed himself to be guided too much by his assistant. Whether Queiroz is, in fact, responsible has never been confirmed, but it has been said so many times now that it has become generally accepted.

Sky send Martin Tyler to interview Ferguson after the game. When he asks United's manager about the change to 4-4-2 it touches a nerve. Ferguson pulls away, shaking his head with a 'dearie-me' kind of laugh, as though he cannot believe someone in the television industry could have the audacity to question his tactics. Tyler, a respected commentator and interviewer, is so flustered that he completely forgets to ask Ferguson for his reaction to Keane's announcement.

THE ODD ONE OUT
16.10.05

It is the Football Writers' Association's northern dinner at the Portland Hotel in Manchester tonight, although Ferguson has turned down his invitation. Fair enough, he has his own take on what the 'F' and 'W' stand for in FWA right now, but it is still a shame that it has come to this. He used to be a regular guest at FWA functions. It is sad if the biggest name in the business is no longer willing to break bread with us.

Otherwise there is a good turnout of managers – even England's head coach, Sven-Göran Eriksson – but it is never quite the same when Ferguson doesn't turn up and they are just as disappointed as we are. Ferguson is a committee member of the League Managers' Association and, with one or two exceptions, it is difficult to overstate the esteem with which he is held among his fellow managers. He will go out of his way to make himself available if an LMA member needs advice. He will often ring a struggling manager, someone he may hardly even know, if he senses they are going through a bad time. Letters of congratulation are sent to promotion-winning managers. Or a sympathetic note will go to someone who has just lost his job or been relegated. Ferguson may regard Liverpool as a mortal enemy but that did not stop him writing to Rafael Benitez at the end of last season to congratulate him for returning the European Cup to Anfield.

Ferguson, in return, is treated with a starry-eyed reverence not afforded to anyone else in the game. His fellow managers even refer to him as the Godfather. He is the doyen, and they often compete with each other for his affections. They attach themselves to him and hang on his every word. When he talks at dinners and other social functions they listen in complete silence. His success makes it inevitable that there is some professional envy but even his rivals pay him respect. Ferguson is the king of this particular jungle.

It is a good night anyway. An opportunity to spend some time with the managers away from a working environment, update our contacts books with some new numbers and, if there has been any friction with a particular manager, maybe sort it out over a couple of drinks. Ferguson is close to unique in his dealings with the media. There are managers here tonight who clearly want to cultivate a relationship with the newspapers and are as keen to get to know us as we are to get to know them.

Steve Bruce, manager of Birmingham City, is under pressure right now because of a run of bad results. He has been ringing the football writers in the Midlands, offering the odd story, trying to get a few people onside, playing the media game.

Benitez is in Spain but he has asked Ron Yeats, the club's chief scout, to go on stage and apologise for his absence.

Eriksson gets the worst press of all and he would probably rather jump in a pool of alligators than go within thirty yards of anyone with an NUJ card. But he gives a friendly little speech and goes round each table, shaking everyone by the hand.

Allardyce is leaning against the bar, smoking a cigar and blowing smoke rings, like a darts player who has just thrown a 180. His team, Bolton Wanderers, have a UEFA Cup tie against Besiktas of Turkey coming up. He takes the microphone at one point, like some kind of *Phoenix Nights* crooner. 'I hope we kick the shit out of them,' he jokes in that booming gravel voice.

Ferguson is different. He is beyond the stage where he feels he needs to be 'in' with the press. He doesn't want to 'play the game' and he scoffs at managers who flutter their eyelashes at the press.

A few years ago the FWA put on a lunch at Haydock Park for every Premiership manager from the north-west. Allardyce was in his element again. David Moyes, manager of Everton, was on great form too, regaling us with anecdotes about life at the club. But Ferguson achieved the extraordinary feat that afternoon of not saying a single word to any of the daily journalists. Not even a 'hello' or 'goodbye'. In the morning something had appeared in the *Sun* that he didn't like. When he took his place at the top table he could be overheard telling the other managers that we might have laid on his lunch, but there was no way he was talking to us and even less chance that we would get an interview. He had his beef stroganoff, shook the other managers' hands, then got up to go, blanking us on the way out.

We are the losers here. Ferguson must go to thirty black-tie functions a year, and off duty he has a natural desire to entertain. His stories are as funny as those of any after-dinner speaker. His knowledge of the game is encyclopaedic and it is never long before he is rearranging the salt and pepper pots on his table to recreate some tactical move. He can talk about football and make you feel as if you are at the molten core of it. And he is blessed with a sense of humour that not enough people know about, particularly his ability to laugh at himself.

Bernard Manning, the guest turn at one charity dinner, caught him arriving late, trying to slip unobtrusively into his seat. Ferguson had just fallen out with Brian Kidd, his assistant at the time, and Manning could hardly believe his luck.

'Alex, Alex … Brian Kidd's been on the phone. Kiddo says he's got a message for you … Alex, he says you can eff off.'

Ferguson was in trouble and Manning was merciless.

'Alex, I saw a documentary about you on telly the other night,' he continued. Ferguson smiled nervously, waiting for another excruciating punch line. 'Your wife was on it. No wonder you're out every night at these dinners.'

Ferguson had heard Manning use this joke on other unsuspecting guests, including Prince Philip on one occasion. Knowing it was nothing personal, he laughed along, quite happy to have been singled out.

This is the side of Ferguson that people should know more about: his love of laughter and his own quick wit. Outsiders tend to think of him as a man permanently riddled with fury. Yet the truth is that he has a great sense of fun and he can be wickedly funny.

More than once he has interrupted a press conference to question a journalist's weight, shaking his head in sympathy for the reporter's wife and guessing that 'she must be a very understanding lady'. Ferguson, like a lot of men at the top of their professions, prides himself on being able to make other people laugh and he will often bring the house down with one of his barbed one-liners about an opponent or referee. 'That bloody ref,' he joked once. 'He runs like the hairs in his arse are tied together!'

His colleagues at Carrington talk of a man who is never happier than when he is taking 'abuse' from the cleaners or one of the dinner ladies. They remember his training top mysteriously going missing from the changing rooms, taken by person or persons unknown, and then turning up with a picture of Pudsey Bear over the sewn-in A.F. initials. Ferguson never found out who it was but he admired their cheek, whoever it was, and wore the same top every day for a week.

Then there was the time the laundry women accidentally broke environmental regulations by using bleach in their washing machines. Ferguson rang them up, putting on a fake, nasal accent and pretending to be from the local council: 'I wondered if you could explain to me why all the ducks in the nearby pond have disappeared.'

The pity for us is that we generally hear these stories second-hand nowadays rather than from Ferguson himself. The days when he had us in stitches at his anecdotes during a press conference have temporarily disappeared and, in the current climate, none of us can be sure when they will return. The resentment, on his part, seems deep-rooted. He has strong opinions about the game, but recently he seems to have taken a strategic decision to protect himself by saying as little as possible. He has always liked to answer carefully and without ambiguity, but he has started to treat questions with more suspicion than confidence.

When he came down the stairs at Carrington on Friday, bang on time as always, he looked tanned and healthy. He'd had a few days in Malta with his wife, Cathy, and he was singing an old Josef Locke song, playing up to Kath, the receptionist.

Hear my song Violetta
Hear my song beneath the moon
Come to me, in my gondola
Waiting on the old lagoon

But when the pressroom door closed his body language changed.

There were a number of issues we needed to ask him about – the Blackburn defeat, his return to 4-4-2 and, of course, Keane – but as soon as he took his seat it was apparent that it was going to be a difficult press conference. Almost every question was stonewalled with a wrinkle of his nose, a shake of the head or a growled warning to change the subject.

There was some humdrum stuff about the state of the pitch (one of his favourite subjects) and an injury bulletin. Finally, we brought up Keane's MUTV interview. 'Alex, we haven't had the chance to see you since Roy said he would quit the club next summer.'

We had been waiting a fortnight. His reaction to such a huge story was long overdue. Yet we were totally unprepared for his response.

'I don't think he actually said that.'

It was such a strange thing to say it threw everyone. There was a long, awkward silence as we tried to take it in.

'But he could hardly have been clearer, could he?'

'Listen,' he said, more firmly, 'I've got nothing to say about it. Does that help you?'

'Not really, Alex … it's not an unreasonable question, he is your captain.'

'Aye, it's not an unreasonable question and it's not an unreasonable answer. You're trying to create an agenda that's not there.'

ON THE ATTACK
17.10.05

We are back at Old Trafford today for a Champions League press conference to preview tomorrow's game against Lille. The press are given a copy of the programme in advance of European matches and there is a clue in Ferguson's programme notes as to why his invitation to the FWA dinner went in the nearest waste-paper basket. In his column he writes about the abuse he received during the Blackburn game and blames the newspapers for stirring up the fans.

I know the supporters were not happy, but I have to say there has been an awful lot of rubbish in the media trying to blame the shortage of goals on our system of play. It doesn't make me very happy to lose on our own ground, but we should recognise the core of the problem and admit it was simply down to bad finishing. It had absolutely nothing to do with formations, tactics or an unwillingness to attack, but these criticisms were levelled at us by a number of pundits and even a few fans, swayed by press opinion. The fact is we missed fifteen chances. It was nothing to do with playing 4-4-2 or 4-5-1, the line-up that everyone seems obsessed about.

He altered United's formation to 4-5-1, he says, to facilitate Keane as a holding midfield player and he makes it clear he will try to talk him out of leaving:

When Roy was at his peak and worked from box to box we needed only two players in the engine room, but the day came when we could no longer ask quite so much from our captain. Overall, it was worth altering the framework because Roy brings so many other qualities to the team. I want him in midfield for as long as he can get his boots on.

It shows how difficult press conferences have become that these notes are more interesting than anything we can conjure out of him face to face. He is in an OK mood, but Chelsea thrashed Bolton

Wanderers 5–1 at the weekend, having gone last week to Liverpool and whacked them 4–1, the most emphatic victory for an away team at Anfield since 1969. That's nine straight wins and Chelsea are ten points clear already.

'We're only in October so it would be silly to think of them as champions already, but I have to say they are relentless right now,' Ferguson says. 'We're just trying to stay within their slipstream and hopefully they will slip up.'

The problem is that 'hopefully' isn't a convincing word in football. Ferguson has to say the right things and he has to believe that United can get back into it. But he doesn't sound particularly confident. That, for him, is very unusual.

THEY PAY THEIR MONEY
18.10.05

Manchester United	0
Lille	0

Champions League, Group D

The latest *Red Issue* and *Red News* were being sold on Sir Matt Busby Way tonight. And, if they represent the views of the average match-going fan, Ferguson's problems might be worse than he realises. United's supporters come across as cynical and disillusioned and large numbers seem to be turning against him. There are more boos tonight, not as malicious as those during the Blackburn game but still unpleasant, and the fanzine writers have gone for Ferguson. According to *Red Issue*:

That we could be so ungrateful *as to barrack Ferguson during the Blackburn game predictably led to the football establishment filing out to defend his reputation. The old lines were trotted out: 'trophies won ... should have a job for life ... everything he's done'* ad nauseam. *What this has spectacularly failed to take into account is the mantra by which Fergie himself has always judged his players – that medals in the cabinet are only to be admired once retirement dawns. The fact is that United's support has been incredibly patient. The real wonder about the Blackburn hostility is that it didn't occur sooner.*

While *Red News* explains:

The booing was as if United's soul was crying out. It was a release of emotion. And it wasn't because of one poor game. It was a release of everything we've suffered.

The jeers are becoming as familiar a sound at Old Trafford as the Stone Roses and Iggy Pop in the pre-match music. There are 7,000 empty seats inside the ground tonight and you can sense the crowd's disenchantment. The team muddle through. There is no flair, no imagination, no guile, no passion. Rooney is suspended, Keane is injured and it is painful to see how ordinary they look without their two best players.

'How do you spell shite?' an Irish guy shouts as he passes the pressbox after the final whistle. 'S ... H ... I ... T ... E.'

CARLOS QUEIROZ
20.10.05

Manchester United	1
Tottenham Hotspur	1

Some time over the last couple of weeks, Ferguson has received an apology from MUTV. He is talking to them again, although it is difficult to know exactly when the peace summit was arranged, or any more details about what they had to say to persuade him to abandon his boycott. MUTV's bosses have ordered their staff not to say anything about the subject so they can deal with it in-house. Even when the story was reported in the newspapers – 'Fergie bans MUTV!' – it has never been referred to during any of the station's broadcasts.

The whole affair has been intensely embarrassing for the MUTV producers. And it has proved a bruising experience for Paul Anthony, who has looked stiff with horror when journalists have asked him for his version of events. It will be a long time before he, or any of his colleagues, dare to question Ferguson's tactics again.

Ferguson's anger is redirected towards the football writers today. His programme notes are dedicated to a carefully prepared diatribe about the way we operate and, specifically, the way we have been scrutinising Carlos Queiroz's role at the club:

I was under fire not so long ago over the team's tactics and now the media have tired of giving me a hard time they have decided to make Carlos a target. He's next in the firing line because, by now, the press know I'm immune to their sniping. But in answer to a few of the questions stirred up in the media, I'd like to put it on record that I have the utmost confidence in Carlos as my assistant and coach.

Queiroz has certainly been getting a hard time. We have suggested that he has too much influence on the training ground, that his tactics are negative and uninspiring. He is such an influential figure on the training ground that we have questioned whether it would be more accurate to describe him as joint manager rather than assistant manager. The fanzines have nicknamed him 'Carlos Queirozzz' and we have floated the possibility that he, not Ferguson, is to blame for the team's problems.

Ferguson goes on:

Whenever we lose the media want an instant answer, preferably something a little bit different so it makes a good headline. The latest target was our formation and because I didn't respond to the prodding they widened the issue to suggest it was Carlos who was behind the way we were playing and that I was giving him too much authority. I want to make it quite clear that Carlos and I are a team. As for me allowing him too much influence, he has no more authority than any of our previous coaches, but he is allowed to get on with his own job. He knows the theme and gets on without constant interference.

We would be pretty shallow if we thought we could fire a few shots at Queiroz and then take offence when someone aims a few back. The point, though, is that Ferguson would not have to bother with these irritations if the team were doing well, or even threatening to do well. It might not be fair to blame Queiroz for everything, but the fact is that United have won only one league game at Old Trafford in the last three months. They are poor again today, despite taking a seventh-minute lead through Mikael Silvestre. Tottenham equalise, deservedly, with a Jermaine Jenas free-kick, twelve minutes from the end, and there is more booing at the final whistle.

ROCK BOTTOM
29.10.05

Middlesbrough	4
Manchester United	1

It is difficult to believe things can get any worse than sieving four goals against a Middlesbrough side who are sixteenth in the league. This is surely the nadir. The worst Manchester United performance since Ferguson took over, according to the pundits on *Match of the Day*, and he won't be suing. United look like a team whose bad days have all come at once. A tired, depressed side with low morale. A side that is conceding all manner of goals – lucky ones, bad ones, great ones. A side that accepts their fate the first time anything goes against them.

There are mitigating circumstances – a long injury list, no Neville, no Heinze and, most importantly, no Keane – but the facts are stark. And, for a club with the racy glamour of Manchester United, it is numbing to lead this kind of life.

Charlton Athletic are above them in the league. Wigan Athletic are above them in the league. To put it into context, Middlesbrough have scored only three goals at home all season. Their two most experienced players, Gareth Southgate and Ugo Ehiogu, are both injured and an eighteen-year-old, Matthew Bates, is making his debut in the centre of their defence.

It is a game United should win comfortably, yet the standard is set as early as the second minute when Van der Sar drops one in from twenty yards. The goal seems to disorientate United. There are two more before half-time and a fourth, from the penalty spot, after seventy-eight minutes. United's consolation goal arrives in stoppage time, courtesy of Ronaldo, but it scarcely matters. They have been outfought, out-thought, outplayed and, ultimately, outclassed.

Everyone is so flat. Fletcher has been brought into the centre of midfield to compensate for Keane's absence, which is like Will Young taking over from Roger Daltrey in The Who. Silvestre is having a terrible season, a danger to his own team. Richardson has been found out. Scholes looks a shadow of the player he once was. O'Shea is making mistakes as soon as he comes under pressure. Ferdinand is at fault for two of Middlesbrough's goals, an elegant giver of second chances.

United are sixth, thirteen points behind Chelsea, and if anyone sums up the present malaise it is Ferdinand. He plays for England and he cost £30 million when United signed him from Leeds in 2002, but he has been struggling for form and consistency all season. After eighty-two minutes Ferguson has seen enough. He appears on the touchline, all arms and larynx, looking as if he could burst a blood vessel. Even the humblest viewer can make out the F forming on his lips. The substitutes' board goes up and Ferdinand is hauled off for the first time in his United career. Ferguson does not even offer a consoling pat on the arm, expertly blanking him on the touchline.

The players are locked in the dressing room for forty minutes after the game and Ferguson takes his time coming out for his post-match interviews. He is monumentally cheesed off, not even attempting to conceal his disbelief about what he has just seen. His tension shows in his urgent movements and his impatient manner. When he is asked whether he is angry with the players, there is an abrasive edge to his voice.

'It doesn't matter whether I'm angry. The players should be angry with themselves. That was a shocking performance. I expect my players to play with passion and when they get results like that I expect them to search within themselves and accept that it is totally unacceptable.'

He describes it as 'another page in the history of Manchester United'. Typically, he is already turning to the next. 'Middlesbrough have cuffed us,' he says. 'But we'll get a response. That's without question. That's what we've always been good at. And that's my job.'

Yet the next visitors to Old Trafford are Chelsea. Another flash of anger crosses Ferguson's face. 'A lot of people look at us as the team that can stop Chelsea,' he says. 'But not on this showing. On today's form I don't think we could beat anyone.'

UP YER BOLLOX
31.10.05

Football writers can be an ungrateful lot. Friends tell us we have the best jobs in the world, but we say 'puh' and try to explain what it is like asking a pimply nine-teen-year-old for an interview and hear him call over his shoulder 'Speak to my agent'. We get to watch great football from free seats and we travel round the world, staying in five-star hotels, all expenses paid. And yet we still moan and carp about how the game has changed and how football clubs have come to think of us the same way a dog thinks of the fleas on its back. We don't realise how lucky we are.

Football is known worldwide as the 'beautiful game'. But, just as someone who works in a Cadbury's factory will go off the taste of chocolate, many report-ers no longer see the game's aesthetic qualities. They think of it as only a four-letter word: work. Football, in their eyes, has ceased to be beautiful and has turned into a relentless slog. The newspapers have become marginalised and many journalists are embittered. In a few cases, they have turned their back on the sport for good. Others have gone to war with it, barely capable of writing a positive word about a game they once loved. They can no longer see the stars in the sky because they are looking at the mud in the gutter.

But then there are days when you are reminded how grey and bland life might be away from the soap opera, how football can never be classed as drudgery. Days when you cannot sleep because of the buzz of nailing a story that is going to pick up the sporting world by its lapels. Days when you find

yourself switching on Sky Sports' rolling news channel at five to midnight just to hear the sharp intake
of breath when they go through the first editions of
the newspapers. Days when you realise that there
can never be a replacement for football and you can
happily see yourself doing this job for ever.

At six o'clock this evening, every football writer in
Manchester is positioned by a television, pen and
paper in hand, watching MUTV. We are waiting for a
show called *Play the Pundit*, in which a different player
every Monday joins Steve Bower in the studio to go
over the weekend's game and, according to the MUTV
blurb, 'bring you a unique inside view of the Reds'
latest performance from the only people who can
really tell you what happened'.

So we wait.

And we wait.

And we wait.

Something strange happens. There is no announcement about a change in the schedule but *Play the
Pundit* never appears. The information button on our
remote controls tells us it is on, but what we actually
see is a re-run of an old youth-academy match. And
when that is finished, the next programme – a documentary about Gary Pallister – comes on as scheduled,
without a word of explanation.

Any other week we would assume that the show
has been rescheduled. The guest tonight, though, is
supposed to be Roy Keane. And that makes us suspicious. In football, there is usually no smoke without
fire. With Keane, there is no smoke without arson –

and it is normally him holding the empty can of petrol.

We ring MUTV. 'We were expecting a Roy Keane interview but it's been replaced by a kids' match. Can you tell us what's going on?'

'We can't go into details,' says a girl who sounds as if she is going to burst into tears. 'We've been told to say nothing.'

A cub reporter on the *Junior Gazette* would be able to pick up that something is seriously wrong.

Our minds are galloping now. This could be big. It could be nothing – but it could be big, really big.

We ring everyone we can think of – the club, the press office, the directors, the supporters' groups, the fanzines, Keane's solicitor – but for two hours we hit a brick wall. Nobody has the faintest clue what is going on. Or nobody is saying. We get absolutely nowhere. But we're still getting vibes that something has happened.

We ring MUTV again. No answer.

But we persist, in the knowledge that United find it almost impossible to keep a secret. If there is a story to be told, at any major football club, there will nearly always be someone who goes to the newspapers, especially when there might be a few quid in it from the tabloids. There are 500 full-time employees at Old Trafford ... and, sure enough, just as we are on the point of giving up, someone blabs.

Keane has been on MUTV. The show was recorded early in the afternoon, in the MUTV studio at Carrington, and the blood drains from our faces when we hear the words used to describe his performance: 'Explosive ... calculated ... chilling ... X-rated ... dynamite ...'

When he opens his mouth it is as though he has assumed the role of boss. He is brisk, assertive and to the point. He tells it how it is: no bullshit, no fucking about. He uses MUTV to unburden himself. And by the time he has finished he has broken the golden rule of dressing-room conduct. He names players.

It is only football and we really shouldn't work ourselves into such a state of frenzy. But it is difficult to overstate the importance of what has happened. Never in the history of Manchester United has a captain gone public with such cold, sorry anger. Never has someone, other than the manager, named and shamed the players he doesn't think are putting in enough. Keane, though, carries a grudge like a sack of bricks. He didn't even play against Middlesbrough but he is described as 'almost foaming at the mouth'. He had seen a thrashing coming, he says. He is sick of trying to get his message across, sick of being ignored. He is worried the club are never going to catch Chelsea, worried about the dressing room, worried that he is the only one who cares. He feels like he has been banging his head against a brick wall and he has to speak out. He has to because if he doesn't, who will?

It is the kind of story that thuds against a journalist's skull. We spend so much time in this profession droning on about hamstring strains and trying to make 0–0 draws sound vaguely interesting that it is easy to find each news story and match report merging into the next. But this is different. It is a story that should come with flashing blue lights and a government health warning. This is going to be bigger than we can ever imagine ...

... and this is the bit where a huge story turns into a seismic story.

United gag Keane.

They axe the programme on the grounds that it is too inflammatory. They call a top-level meeting, sweat over it, argue whether it could be edited. In the end, they decide they cannot risk it because of the damage it could do. They are frightened about the reaction in the press. They are worried about how the other players will react. They lose their nerve. They panic.

David Gill gives a little speech to the relevant MUTV staff, ordering a cover-up and telling them not to breathe a word about what has happened. The tape is placed in a locked drawer. When he is finally done, he takes a deep breath and picks up his mobile phone.

He stares at it for a few seconds. Then he dials Ferguson's number.

PARIS
1.11.05

When the captain of Manchester United declares civil bloody war on his team-mates it is not something to be squeezed into a single column on an inside page. Every newspaper splashes on Keane today and it will be the same tomorrow, the day after and the day after that. Sports editors are demanding reaction, quotes, analysis, follow-ups, follow-ups to the follow-ups. The tabloids are offering shameless bribes for anyone who can provide them with a copy of the MUTV tape or, at the very least, the transcript.

In ordinary circumstances Ferguson would switch off his mobile, the doors to Carrington would be bolted shut and everything would be dealt with in private. But United play their return game against Lille at the Stade de France in Paris tomorrow and the team have an early-morning flight from Manchester airport.

A jostling scrum of television crews is waiting at the check-in desk and there is a stampede when Ferguson arrives. Fraser Dainton, of Sky Sports, thrusts a microphone under his nose.

'I'll take a couple of questions about the Lille game but nothing about anything else,' Ferguson says, with a look that says he means business.

Dainton weighs up the offer for a couple of seconds and shakes his head. 'I've got to ask you about Roy Keane.'

Ferguson turns and stalks off, five or six brisk paces, but then he turns back and jabs a finger.

'THAT'S YOU FINISHED AT THIS CLUB.'

Dainton's microphone drops limply by his side. There are no follow-up questions.

The story follows Ferguson into the business lounge. Keane is among the headlines on the television news and the newspapers are strewn over the tables, his hard, unflinching face glaring out from the back pages. The players are in little groups, huddled round their copies of the *Daily Mirror*, *Sun* and *Daily Star*. Ferguson has had a late-night call warning him the story is out, but this is the first the players know about it. For years they have worried what Keane, privately, really thinks about them and now they have their answer. They turn the pages in silence.

This lot are not up to it!
Keane gagged by United after TV attack

Keane's blast gagged
United push panic button after Keane's video nasty
Gagged!

The flight is eerily quiet. O'Shea sits alone, staring out of the window. Fletcher isn't talking. Ferdinand isn't talking. Richardson chooses to listen to music, wearing headphones the size of two teacups. Even Smith, usually the loudest player, seems lost in his own thoughts. Ferguson is in his usual seat: front row, left hand side, next to the aisle. He has the look of a man who has just been told a pigeon has shat on his best jacket. He has a book with him but does not open it. He starts the *Daily Express* crossword then gives up. Mostly, he sits in silence.

To Ferguson, the dressing room is the place for airing grievances and pointing fingers, not a television studio or a press conference. A player who goes public with dressing-room secrets is seen as a traitor, and for it to be Keane, his captain, his ally, makes it a hundred times worse. He needs to collect his thoughts, talk it through with Gill and Queiroz and work out what to do. But Keane isn't even on the trip, still injured, and in a few hours Ferguson will have to face the press and somehow put on a brave face.

At the back of the plane we are taking bets on whether he will turn up. We didn't sleep well last night. We still don't know exactly what Keane has said but the more we hear, the more serious we realise it is. The inquest has started already and there is talk of heads being banged together at MUTV. Did nobody at the station realise how ludicrous it was, two days after a 4–1 defeat to Middlesbrough, to ask a loose cannon such as Keane to play the role of 'pundit' in the first place? They weren't to know the captain of Manchester United would start ranting like a demented London cabbie, but even so ...

The press conference takes place in the ballroom of the team's hotel and when Ferguson walks in he is flanked by David Gill, Diana Law and Phil Dickinson, the club's translator. Gill does not normally attend press conferences and he hangs back, trying to be as inconspicuous as possible for a man well over six feet. Ferguson marches to the top table, doing his best to look normal. He lowers himself into his seat, squinting into the flashing camera bulbs, and there is a rush for places.

'Alex, can we ask for your reaction to what Roy Keane has said on MUTV and the decision to pull his interview?'

He gives us his stock phrase of rebuttal, deliberately slow for maximum effect. 'I'm ... nae ... getting ... into ... that ...'

He points out that the purpose of the press conference is to talk about an important match in the Champions League, and not Roy Keane. Not strictly true, but that's all he wants to say about it. He says anyone who ignores him is wasting everybody's time. There are to be no Roy Keane questions. Repeat: no Roy Keane questions.

The story is too big for that. Over and over he is asked about it. Over and over he dodges the topic.

It is put to him that the supporters must be alarmed by the way the season has gone. Does he understand the fans' concerns that United seem to be going backwards?

Finally, he opens up a little. 'Of course I understand their concerns,' he says. 'They deserve better because they are the most loyal fans anywhere. There is no question about that. We have had some disappointing results and I know exactly how they feel. I just hope they know how I feel too.'

We fumble for a way to engage him in conversation but he gives us very little more. At the next pause, he looks to the door and tries to wrap things up.

He is preparing to make his move, but there is something he wants to get off his chest before he leaves the room. 'There's such a fascination with this club, this is manna from heaven for you press guys, isn't it?' he says. Astonishingly he suddenly starts to laugh. 'We're front page, back page, middle page, in the comic strip, the lot. I used to get upset about it but not any longer. I know full well that you're only doing your jobs. I know there is pressure on you and there is no point me getting my drawers in a twist about it. It happens, and in a strange way it's fantastic for us that this attention falls on our club. We are the biggest club ever, in the planet, the universe. Remember that ...'

As he steps off the top table, he stumbles over a French journalist's rucksack, poking out from the front row of seats. For one awful moment it looks as if he is going to fall on his backside. He regains his balance, pretends to swipe the culprit over the head and walks away with a beaming smile, playing up to the television cameras.

On his way out he passes the *News of the World*'s James Fletcher, one of his favourite journalists on the Manchester patch.

'Fletch,' he jokes, 'you're the ugliest fucking journalist I've ever seen.'

'Thanks, Alex.'

THE LEAK
2.11.05

Lille	1
Manchester United	0

Champions League, Group D

The 'Keanegate Tapes' are splashed over four pages in the *Daily Mirror* today, under the two-fingers-up-at-the-*Sun* billing of 'Scoop of the Season'. It is difficult to know where they have got their material from but it was inevitable that this would happen once the story of Keane's gagging came out. MUTV might have been under orders to keep the evidence under lock and key, staff might have been threatened with their jobs and an entire workforce warned to say nothing, but there was always going to be someone with a loose tongue and the telephone number of a tabloid newspaper. It's rumoured to have cost the *Mirror* in the region of £15,000, though it is such a huge story they probably regard that as a snip.

Their back-page splash – 'world exclusive' – is a mixture of awe and self-importance:

Roy Keane has been sitting on the sidelines for six weeks watching Manchester United slip behind Wigan, Bolton and Charlton in the title race. And he has had enough.

We can reveal, in the 'Play the Pundit' slot on MUTV that has erupted in controversy, Keane not only laid into defender Rio Ferdinand's approach, but harshly criti-cised senior players and attacked the younger members of United's faltering team.

The headline says it all:

Keane: we should get rid of under-performers

And inside the first double-page spread …

'Just because you get paid £120k a week you think you are a superstar'

It's explosive stuff. Keane accuses individuals of playing with their reputations, of not trying hard enough, of not understanding the principles of the club. He says it has gone on too long, that there should be a clearout, that United are in danger of becoming a club in decline. He didn't play against Middlesbrough and part of him is saying, 'Roy, stay out of it, it's not your business.' But he can't. He just can't. He says:

There is talk about putting this right in January and bringing in new players. But we should be doing the opposite. We should be getting rid of people in January. There are no characters in this team any more. They've been asked questions and they are not coming up with the answers. I am sick of having to say it and they are sick of listening to me.

He was not surprised by the Middlesbrough result, he says. He watched it in a bar in Dubai and, at 3–1, he walked out, humiliated. He could not stand it any longer: all the people looking over, pointing and smirking.

'I've been expecting something like this to happen,' he says, before laying into his team-mates again.

'These guys think the day they got their new contracts was the best day of their careers. They think they have made it, but they haven't.'

Steve Bower asks him to look at Middlesbrough's goals on a video monitor. Keane goes through them individually, picking out the players he holds responsible. 'The younger players have been let down by some of the more experienced ones,' he says. 'They are not leading. There is a shortage of characters.'

According to the *Mirror* he starts with Ferdinand:

Just because you are paid £120,000 a week and play well for twenty minutes one week you think you are a superstar. Well, it's not enough to play well for twenty minutes. It's a ninety-minute game. You get well rewarded but you have to put in the hard work to earn those rewards. Jimmy Floyd Hasselbaink robbed Ferdinand for the second goal and I have seen that happen before. It's poor defending.

Richardson gets nailed too. This has been his breakthrough season and, already, he drives a Bentley and wears a diamond-encrusted watch. He is a decent player but a bit flash, a bit arrogant, someone to keep an eye on. Keane has spent a lifetime cutting down to size a thousand different Kieran Richardsons. He describes him as a 'lazy defender' and says he 'deserved to get punished'. Richardson gave away the penalty for Middlesbrough's fourth goal and Keane makes himself clear: 'He wasn't doing his job.'

The interview goes on for thirty minutes but it is obvious very early on that it is going to have to be pulled or heavily edited.

Keane releases all his pent-up frustration. 'I can't understand why people in Scotland rave about Darren

Fletcher,' he allegedly says. He blames Van der Sar for the first goal: 'He should have saved that – that was saveable.' He picks out O'Shea for the final goal: 'He's just strolling around when he should have been busting a gut to get back.' He's scathing about Smith's performance in midfield: 'What is he doing there? He is wandering around as if he is lost. He doesn't know what he is doing.'

You wonder whether the players will ever forgive him. But it's not forgiveness that Keane wants. He wants improvement. He wants the mythical 110 per cent. He wants to look into the other players' eyes and know they are putting in as much as he is. He needs to know that he is not alone, that his teammates care as much as he does.

The nub of it is frustration. There is no European Cup winner's medal in his collection and, at this rate, there never will be. He has had his chance to go to Bayern Munich or Juventus but he has hung around, frustration building on frustration, grievance on top of grievance, and now the toilet is flushing on another league season. He is looking round the dressing room, at players he knows have talent, and he is wondering whether they know how to use that talent, or whether they even care. 'At this club it seems to me that you have to play badly to be rewarded,' he says. 'Maybe that is what I should do when I come back: play badly.'

The question is whether his attack has gone too far, and the only person who can judge that is Ferguson. Keane has broken just about every unwritten rule of dressing-room protocol. Yet the fans are on his side and tonight they let Ferguson know about it. There are 4,000 of them at the Stade de France and, three minutes into the game, they are bellowing Keane's name.

Keano, Keano, Keano …

When the first rendition dies down another follows within two minutes. And then another. It is a chant that spreads like fire. As Lille score and take hold of the game, it grows louder and louder.

Keano! Keano! Keano!

Richardson puts what should have been a simple cross out of play for a goal-kick. Instinctively, the cry reverberates round the stadium again. Louder and louder. Angrier and angrier.

KEANO! KEANO! KEANO!

At the final whistle Ferguson blanks the Lille manager, Claude Puel, and heads straight down the tunnel without shaking hands: the classic managerial snub. He doesn't see his players make their way apologetically over to the away end to applaud the United fans, and it is probably just as well. There are V-signs and one-fingered salutes. But the clapping is not reciprocated.

THE FALL-OUT
4.11.05

The *Manchester Evening News*, traditionally a pro-United newspaper, has described the current team as 'shapeless rabble'. The *Daily Mail*, which has a history of getting big stories right, says there have been boardroom talks about whether Ferguson should go. In the

Guardian, a season-ticket holder and freelance writer, Rob Smyth, has explained the reasons for the crowd's disillusionment:

> *Most United fans have had enough. They have had enough of 4-5-1; of an abuse of the traditions of the club that has not occurred since the Dave Sexton years; of the moronic twitter of Carlos Queirozzz; of a gaping chasm where once there was the best midfield in Europe; of the apathy of Rio Ferdinand; of Sir Alex Ferguson.*

It is time, he says, for Ferguson to be sacked:

> *This should not be confused with a lack of respect and gratitude for the unprecedented happiness he has brought to the club but if you love someone you have to set them free and, based on the unforgiving demands of modern football and his performance over the last five years, Fergie does not deserve to be manager of Manchester United. Reputation and gratitude are not enough.*

Mick Hume, another supporter/writer, is equally unforgiving in *The Times*:

> *I would have liked Keane to point the finger off the pitch too. I would have liked to hear him say: 'Fergie out, Queiroz out, Rio out, anybody but Rooney out. Bury the groundsman, hang the DJ, burn the pies.' To lose 4–1 to Middlesbrough is embarrassing but I would take a 14–1 beating by Chelsea if it meant somebody would do something about clearing out Old Trafford before we really do become Who-the-fuck-are-Man-United.*

These are unspeakably bad times if supporters are demanding sackings and openly abusing the players. Ferguson has an outdoor, seen-it-all-before kind of face, but he seemed genuinely shocked by the hostility inside the Stade de France – United's fans traditionally pride themselves on never turning on their own – and the flight back to Manchester after the match felt like an overcrowded lift, airless and bad-tempered.

Ferguson was doodling into a little red notebook when we boarded the plane, scribbling diagrams of tactical manoeuvres where he presumably felt the team had gone wrong. Most of the players avoided eye contact and sat in silence. Van Nistelrooy had his arms folded, his knees hunched up against the seat in front of him, his chin pushed down on to his chest. When we spoke to him in the stadium, in his role as stand-in captain, he told us he had never known the team spirit to be so low.

'This must be the most difficult time I have known at the club,' he said. 'When I came here four years ago it felt like we were unbeatable. It was so enjoyable. I remember games when I was having four or five chances. Good chances. There was constant service, attack after attack. As a striker, it was great. But things are different now, so different, and there's nothing I can do about it. We're not playing well. We have difficulty keeping the ball. It's not fluent that the ball goes from player to player. We're not having flowing attacks. We don't play in the opponents' half, with crosses coming in, second balls won. We're not applying pressure on our opponents. Our confidence is down. Sometimes we hold back when we have to go for it. I don't know what's going on.'

We asked him if United had the resources to turn their season round. He didn't seem at all convinced.

'That's the question. Do we? I really don't know. It's what we all want. But the question is, how are we going to do it? We have to look at everything: the squad, individuals, everything. Each of us knows within ourselves what needs to be done. But when you compare our squad with Chelsea … that says it all. Whether they play team one or team two they are nearly all internationals who have played at World Cups. We just don't have that strength in depth. A lot of our experienced players are injured so there's pressure on the younger ones and, sure, we miss Keano. But that's not an excuse. We don't have any excuses for what's happening.'

RESPITE
6.11.05

Manchester United	1
Chelsea	0

We pack the pressbox today expecting to write football's version of the post-mortem. This is a game Ferguson dares not lose and all the big-hitters are here. Nobody knows what to expect. But, whatever happens, it is going to be huge. We feel like bloodhounds. The fox is in United's dugout.

But we never get our kill.

To see United today is to witness a team that is affronted by their league position and determined to end the descent into despair. At Middlesbrough, their play was dead, untouched by the qualities of overflowing brilliance that have been the hallmark of Ferguson's teams. Yet here, written off as being on the point of professional bankruptcy, they are quick to the ball, strong in the tackle, and when it comes to their intentions there can be no room for misinterpretation. There is a blunt refusal to accept that they are inferior to Chelsea, or that the malaise is fatal. Fletcher heads in the game's decisive goal just before half-time: a moment of supreme irony given Keane's MUTV tirade. United survive a late onslaught and at the final whistle everyone is on their feet, triumphant and euphoric. There are blokes punching the air, clutching each other and bellowing with relief. It is Ferguson's first victory over Jose Mourinho in six attempts and, finally, Chelsea are reminded what it is like to lose a football match. It is their first defeat in the Premiership for 386 days.

United! United! United!

The story has been turned on its head. We arrived at Old Trafford assuming we would be writing long eulogies about Chelsea going sixteen points clear. But the story now is of a possible turning point, of life being breathed back into the title race. And, most of all, of never writing off Ferguson. The decibel levels are cranked up to a volume not heard at Old Trafford for years. Genuine affection pours from the stands and Ferguson waves to the crowd, sticking out his chest, determined to milk the moment.

His eyes are sparkling as he makes his way along the touchline at the final whistle. He pauses a few yards from the tunnel. Then he looks up at the section of the crowd that flashed Vs at him after the Blackburn game and does something he has never done before. He takes a bow and throws his arms in the air, with the palms of his hands upwards. And the crowd roars.

Every single one of us loves Alex Ferguson
Every single one of us loves Alex Ferguson

A few minutes later Sky's pitchside reporter, Geoff Shreeves, stops Ferguson in the tunnel for a quick interview and asks him if he's been feeling under more pressure than at any time in the last decade. Ferguson looks witheringly at Shreeves and tells him live on air that he is talking 'bollocks'.

In the pressroom there are loud cheers and great laughter. Nobody in Fleet Street wants the title to be rendered a *fait accompli* before the leaves have stopped falling from the trees. In fact, most of us have been rooting for Ferguson today. He has been pretty hellish to deal with recently – in fairness, he would probably say the same about us – but there is no point harbouring a grudge. We saw him at Carrington on Friday and he was on great form, full of levity and humour, his demeanour totally at odds with what might have been expected.

He wanted to know if any of the 'miserable so-and-sos' sat before him had brought a present to mark his nineteenth anniversary as manager. He burst out laughing when he saw that some of the chief football correspondents had flown in from London, accusing them of travelling north because they 'scented blood'. Then we started talking about Chelsea and he asked how many games they had gone unbeaten. Nobody knew. His eyes lit up. 'What, you don't know?' he exploded. 'That's classic, absolutely brilliant. Some journalists you are. And you've got the cheek to criticise me when you can't even do your own jobs. Research is the most important thing a journalist should have and you're sitting there, not a fucking clue, any of you. That'll do me. Brilliant.'

It was difficult to believe this warm, humorous man was the same guy who had told a Sky Sports reporter at Manchester airport earlier this week that he was 'finished' for daring to ask a question about Roy Keane. His performance earned some sympathetic press. But none of us honestly thought he would produce his get-out-of-jail card today. Nobody who was in Paris could have believed that his players, with their professional reputations on the floor, would take on and beat the most richly endowed club in the world. Chelsea were unbeaten in their previous forty Premiership games. They did the double against United last season, as well as dumping them out of the Carling Cup. They had already been crowned champions when they came to Old Trafford for their penultimate game, and United's players had to grit their teeth and clap them on to the pitch in a guard of honour.

Today feels like a little bit of payback. Except there is one problem: if United are good enough to beat Chelsea, why can't they do the same against, say, Blackburn Rovers? How can they win 1–0 against the best team in the country yet lose 4–1 to sixteenth-placed Middlesbrough?

No, there's a distinct feeling of 'one-nil-in-your-cup-final'. Every single player gives his all. Even Ferdinand finishes the game pumping his fists and kissing the badge on his shirt. Yet one result does not make a season. United need to play with this sort of passion every week, as they used to – it shouldn't be the exception, as it has become. Because if anyone seriously thinks that this result washes away all of United's problems, both with the team and behind the scenes, it is a blinkered belief.

Mourinho is not fooled. 'I'm not afraid or worried,' he says, chewing his gum and smirking out of the corner of his mouth, as if he thinks he is the Fonz. 'Not at all. Manchester United defended with good spirit but they are not good enough to be champions and there is still more pressure on them than us. If you asked them if they wanted to change positions they would do so in a flash. Chelsea will be the champions this year.'

CLOCKING OUT
18.11.05

Today is the first time for two weeks that Ferguson has held a press conference: there has been a break from the regular 12 noon gathering over the last fortnight for internationals. 'And thank Christ for that,' Ferguson jokes before taking his seat. 'I needed a break from you. Did you know Bayern Munich have a press conference every bloody day? Can you imagine that? I have to summon up every ounce of energy to do it once a week.'

He is jovial, bantering, on the edge of breaking into song. Encouraged, we ask him if he can update us with any news about Keane's future. 'Anything you can tell us about Roy's contract situation? Any developments?'

Putting on his best poker face, he says there is 'nothing going on – nothing to report, it's just like I told you a few weeks ago'. He says Keane is training well, nearly back to full fitness and 'not far away' from returning to the team.

He cracks a few jokes, takes the piss a bit more. He goes over the Chelsea game again, nodding his head in deep satisfaction as he talks through the winning performance. He jokes about Scotland lifting the 'unofficial World Cup' and rocks in his chair when he is asked about England's chances of hosting the 2018 World Cup. 'Dearie me,' he says, 'I'll be seventy-six by then – if I'm still alive!'

It is a pleasant little session. He ushers us out at 12.25 p.m. and goes straight into the same routine with the Sunday guys. And we do what we always do when it looks like being a relatively quiet news day – we leave the training ground and drive along Isherwood Road to get a round of bacon sandwiches from Gail's snack bar.

And there we are – innocent, naïve lambs.

Just before 1 p.m. someone's mobile rings. Bang! – newsflash!

ROY-KEANE-HAS-LEFT-MANCHESTER-UNITED

Pandemonium. Shock. Horror.

It feels like a bad joke. By the time we arrive back at the training ground everyone is swearing or jabbering into mobile phones. Press releases, still warm, are being handed out in reception. They say it is an amicable decision. There is a line from Ferguson, thanking Keane for his twelve years of service and describing him as a fantastic servant, and a couple of quotes supposedly from Keane: 'Whilst it is a sad day for me to leave such a great club and manager, I believe that the time has now come for me to move on.'

The whole thing stinks, but we will have to worry about that later. It is Friday afternoon, which tends to mean one thing to newspaper journalists: early deadlines. And we are sweating, bursting with tension, desperate for the facts. We need the precise sequence of events, a blow-by-blow account of what really happened. This is a huge story by any standards. Yet there is no way of dressing it up: none of us had the faintest clue it was on the cards.

There is a maze of fairground mirrors to navigate. Everyone has a slightly different story, every phone call muddies the water a little more. There are wild rumours that punches have been thrown. Speculation mingles with fact and guesswork. It is difficult to know what to believe. All we can really think is that this could be the single most dramatic sports story of the year.

What we hear is that Keane arrived at Carrington at 9 a.m., went up the stairs and knocked on the door marked 'Manager'.

You can call Keane what you like, but not stupid. Going into that meeting, he knew. He had cleared out his locker the previous night. He had his solicitor with him and the final meeting was solemn, brief and to the point. Ferguson told him there would be no new deal at the end of the season and that the club wanted to come to a financial arrangement about the rest of his contract. His testimonial was still on the table because he had been made a promise, but he was no longer deemed a part of the club. He had crossed the line. He had to go.

The two men shook hands and said their goodbyes. David Gill said he would take care of the relevant paperwork. Keane left at 9.20 a.m. for the final time, carrying his belongings. He had a gaunt, sulphurous stare, as if a contract killing was his next job of the day.

Ferguson went into the canteen and asked everyone to be quiet for a minute because he had an important announcement to make, something that would affect everyone at the club and mean that things would never be the same again. When he broke the news to the players there was an audible gasp. Nobody had expected this.

Van Nistelrooy put his hands on his head. He couldn't hide his disappointment. 'Shit.'

Whatever happens now, Manchester United will be a quieter, less tempestuous and much more boring football club to cover.

The official line from Old Trafford is that it's 'mutual consent'. All grown up. Keane gets the kids, Ferguson keeps the house. Everybody lives happily ever after. The truth is entirely different.

People at the club say there was an almighty shouting match at Carrington a couple of weeks ago. It was the first time Keane had seen his team-mates since MUTV took *Play the Pundit* off the air. The players were studying his body language, looking for a sign of contrition – anything to break the ice.

Keane being Keane, his demeanour was of a man who had not once thought: 'Shit, what have I done?' He didn't seem to have had a single moment when he thought it would be a good idea to build bridges. The players were treating him like an unexploded firework, pretending everything was normal, pottering about and exchanging small talk. But the atmosphere was driving Keane mad. He couldn't stand all the fake bonhomie.

He exploded. 'If they aren't going to show you the tape then, fuck it, I'll tell you what's on it. I would have been happy for it to be played. In fact, I think it *should* have been played. I judged your performances honestly and if you are not criticising yourself in the same way then you shouldn't be at this club anyway.'

Keane was throbbing with fury by the time Ferguson walked in. He had nothing to be ashamed of, he said. He had told the truth and it was nothing he wouldn't say to the players' faces. If the club, the players, or anyone else couldn't cope with a few verbals then, Christ almighty, what kind of people was he dealing with?

He got no joy out of Ferguson. There was a brief exchange and a standoff before a decision was made that everyone should watch the *Play the Pundit* tape. Ferguson switched on his video recorder, pushed in the cassette and the players sat in silence while thirty minutes of car-crash television unfolded in front of their eyes. Keane stood throughout: arms folded, unshaven, unapologetic.

The tape was nothing like as bad as the players had imagined. At one point Keane even said he knew Ferguson would 'put it right' and made it clear that he was totally behind the manager. But Ferguson was as angry as Keane by the time it had finished. He accused Keane of ranting, of bringing the club into disrepute. Keane listened, took it in and returned fire.

It has been tough for Ferguson, tougher than we could ever imagine, and it has taken him a fortnight to make up his mind. But, in the end, he has decided that Keane is no longer good for the club.

It's clear that he remains absolutely The Boss. Ferguson has made his career from being braver than any manager before him and, in all probability, any who will follow. He has never shirked the idea of discarding loyal servants if he felt it was his duty to do so, no matter how strong the emotional attachment. Keane has become a pebble in United's shoe and Ferguson has decided they cannot hobble on any longer. 'Anything we do at this club should remain indoors,' he said after the Lille game. 'We can't allow United players to be demolished by criticism. Young lads like Darren Fletcher are the future of our club and we do not want to destroy them. These lads have not cried off and they have not deserted their posts. They have wanted to play every game and carry us through. We need to help them, not destroy them.'

There are reporters outside Old Trafford and supporters milling around, shaking their heads, talking as if they have seen a plane going into the Arndale Centre. One woman, in her forties, looks as if she has been crying. Keane played through injury for the shirt. He suffered for the cause that took fans to loan sharks to pay for pre-season tours. He may have black edges to his heart but the supporters worship him. Even on the occasions when he acted like an idiot, he somehow emerged with his immortality enhanced. As a player and a man, his contribution was so enormous that he helped to define what the very words 'Manchester United' mean.

His downfall, ultimately, was that he was a 24-hour-a-day obsessive and couldn't understand why he was the only one. When he looked around the dressing room he was convinced that some of the players were coasting, hugging the shores when the high seas offered so many new adventures. He couldn't see the team winning another European Cup and it wounded him that they didn't seem to hurt like he did. He grew bitter and resentful, and when he turned on his team-mates he knew he was taking on Ferguson too. And players who do that always come off second best.

Problem dealt with, Ferguson will move on. The popular belief is that United without Keane is a car without petrol, but there is a long line of distinguished players who have crossed Ferguson and been expelled from the payroll. Eventually, the club will always get over it. Norman Whiteside and Paul McGrath were sacrificed because Ferguson grew intolerant of their boozy all-dayers. David Beckham was sold to Real Madrid because Ferguson hated his showbiz lifestyle. Jaap Stam was abandoned after writing an autobiography that embarrassed Ferguson with its revelations of dressing-room secrets. After twelve years on the payroll, Keane can hardly claim he was unaware of the history.

The next step, in theory, is that Ferguson owes the fans a proper explanation. Not the day-trippers who come along once or twice a season from the Home Counties, or the businessmen whom Keane once derided as the 'prawn-sandwich brigade', questioning whether they could even 'spell football', but the diehards who follow the team to bear-pits in Istanbul and iceboxes in the eastern bloc. The supporters certainly deserve an explanation, although whether they will get one is another matter. Ferguson can be a cold-blooded so-and-so sometimes and Keane, it seems to us, is already a part of the Old Trafford history, someone to let go and forget about. Ferguson has made his decision. Once that happens, he never allows himself any regrets.

It has been bugging everyone. How, today of all days, could he come into the pressroom at Carrington looking so bright and breezy and making jokes about Scotland's record in international tournaments? Keane's world had just turned upside down and one of the strongest manager–player relationships in the game had disintegrated into dust. Yet as Keane was breaking the news to his wife, Theresa, and their five kids, Ferguson was full of bonhomie and good humour. It is difficult, in fact, to remember him in a better mood at any time in the last year, and that is just crazy.

THE FIRST DAY OF THE REST OF THEIR LIVES
19.11.05

| Charlton Athletic | 1 |
| Manchester United | 3 |

And so the great Manchester United soap opera rumbles on, minus one of its most entertaining characters. Ferguson turns up at The Valley grinning broadly, signing autographs, ruffling a ballboy's hair. He appears determined to make it clear that it is business as usual, even though it patently isn't. He looks totally at ease and with an hour to kick-off, there is only one thing on his mind: finding somewhere to watch the horse racing. The Charlton manager, Alan Curbishley, lets him use his office. They have a glass of wine, and Curbishley finds his old friend 'as happy as can be'.

The world keeps turning, of course, and one view today (the cynical one) is that the team play as though a weight has been lifted from their shoulders. Van Nistelrooy scores twice, there is a first of the season for Smith and Ferguson tells MUTV it is their most impressive away performance of the season. Whether that has anything to do with Keane it is impossible to tell, but Ferguson's theory seems to be that the other players should feel liberated by his expulsion.

The logical step for Keane is to find new employers, and there will be no shortage of high-profile clubs wanting to take him on. The other option would be to retire from playing and try his hand at management, but it is unlikely he will go down that route just yet. Television crews have been camped outside his house in Hale Barns, a village for Mancs-done-good, on the edge of the city. They have followed him through the meadows as he walks Triggs, his golden Labrador. They have knocked on his door and they have been ordered off his land. Everyone is desperate to hear his side of the story but, as yet, he has refused to say anything.

Ferguson has also adopted a policy of *omerta*. MUTV's post-match questions are structured sympathetically to touch upon Keane only very briefly. Sky Sports are obligingly reluctant to press the issue and journalists waiting by the team coach are cold-shouldered.

All Ferguson offers are bland fudges ('we wished each other well … pleased to hear the fans pay tribute'). Then he is gone, joking with the bus driver, patting Queiroz affectionately on the back.

GAME, SET AND MATCH
21.11.05

Villarreal are at Old Trafford tomorrow and we sit down for today's press conference determined to get some proper answers. Pathetically, we even try to bribe one of the Spanish journalists to ask about Keane, employing the logic that Ferguson is more likely to entertain questions from a foreign reporter than from one of us. Our tactics are becoming increasingly desperate.

We still haven't heard anything from Keane, despite rumoured six-figure offers from the tabloids. He is still walking Triggs but, that apart, the only sighting has been at a chippie in Altrincham. Good luck to him. Under the transfer window regulations, he cannot register for another club until January anyway. He is entitled to a bit of mush in a tray.

The supporters are grieving but Ferguson seems like he would be happy if Keane were temporarily airbrushed from the club's history. He takes his seat, scanning the room, and the first question lands like a stick of dynamite round his toes.

'Alex, can we ask you about Roy Keane's departure?'

The shutters go up immediately. 'What has that got to do with the Villarreal game?' he says, reminding us that it is a press conference to talk about the Champions League.

'Alex, this is clearly a massive story. Could you please explain some of the reasons behind Roy's departure?'

His face is hard. 'I've already given them.'

Really? A proper explanation?

'Well, that's all you're going to get from me … nice try, though.'

Groans.

Thirty-nine out of forty newspaper, television and radio reporters give up. One presses on. Surely, Alex, you would like to offer some thoughts? Surely you realise there are United fans waiting to hear from you?

'I'm sure they are,' he replies, and we know he isn't going to buckle.

He stares at us, we stare back.

He stares harder.

We lower our eyes. General Zod couldn't beat Ferguson in a staring contest.

Emergency action is required. The programme is sold in Manchester city centre the day before every game. So we drive in convoy to Deansgate, pick up a copy from the *Evening News* stand outside Kendals and turn to page four – Ferguson's column.

It is in his programme notes that Ferguson feels most at ease to get his message across without fear of a mischievous headline or a careless sub-editor twisting what he says. Surely, we assume, he will offer some explanation to the supporters. What else could he possibly write about?

> *As you are well aware, Manchester United and Roy Keane have parted company, a decision we consider to be in the best interests of club and player. As I said at the time of the announcement, Roy has been a fantastic servant for Manchester United. The best midfield player in the world of his generation, he is already one of the great figures in our club's illustrious history.*
>
> *Roy has been central to the success of the club in the last twelve years and everyone at Old Trafford wishes*

him well in the rest of his career and beyond. It's always sad when a great player departs the scene of his triumphs but football doesn't stand still and I know Roy will be the first to agree we must all focus now on tonight's match as a crucial moment in our bid to reach the knockout stage of the UEFA Champions League.

And that is it. That is all Keane merits. His life and times, his leadership, his longevity, his part in winning all those trophies, condensed into two measly paragraphs. No explanations, no reasoning, no promises of replacements. Just some cop-out line that 'football doesn't stand still' and then he moves on.

A HUMDRUM TOWN
22.11.05

Manchester United	0
Villarreal	0

Champions League, Group D

The front cover of the new *Red Issue* fanzine depicts Ferguson next to Keane, with a speech bubble saying: 'You shouldn't be saying things like that about the players.'

Keane's reply is: 'No – *you* should.'

Mutiny is in the air. Before kick-off Ferguson accepts an award from UEFA for his 'services to the Champions

League'. There is a polite cheer when he steps on to the pitch but, within seconds, a smattering of boos and the first defiant chant of the evening.

Keano! Keano! Keano!

Too much can be read into a song. There are probably fans chanting Keane's name solely as an act of gratitude for what he did for the club and to let him know, if he is watching on television, that he still has a place in their affections. Others, though, have less innocent motives for bellowing his name. It feels rebellious, their way of making it clear that they do not agree with what Ferguson has done and that they will not tolerate Keane being consigned to history.

It is the theme of the evening. Everywhere you look there are shirts bearing Keane's now-obsolete number sixteen. Irish tricolours flutter from the stalls on Sir Matt Busby Way. High up, in the old Scoreboard End, there is a banner carrying the words: 'Keano, 1993–2005, Red Legend'.

One *Red Issue* contributor writes:

As much as we love Roy, and while many of us have genuinely come to despise Fergie, the boss should always be the boss. But once the dust has settled Keane will be forever remembered and adored, with the affection and respect of all Reds. As for Fergie, it's too late. Too many errors of judgment, too many wrong decisions, too selfish and too greedy. Too bad, Alex. This latest balls-up will be added to the growing list of this old man's mistakes.

Emotions are dangerously high if there are now supporters claiming to 'despise' Ferguson. It seems very unfair – but we should not be totally surprised. The atmosphere surrounding the club has been poisonous all season, starting with the Glazers, going on to the Blackburn game and now Keane. The fans are angry and disillusioned, even those who have remained loyal to Ferguson, and with every bad result it gets worse. Tonight is another lousy performance, full of misplaced passes and lacking any sense of guile or creativity. The supporters drift away at the final whistle in the queasy knowledge that there is now a serious danger United won't even make it through the qualifying stage.

Champions League football after Christmas is something the fans assume they are buying into when they pay for their season tickets. But United have managed only one win and two goals in their opening five group games and it is playing havoc with the crowd's nerves. To qualify now, United will have to go to Lisbon in their final group game and beat Benfica on their own ground, the famous Stadium of Light. A draw might just squeeze them through, depending on other results. But a defeat will feel like a plague of locusts is on its way to Old Trafford.

PUNCH AND JUDY
25.11.05

The tone is set today from the moment Ferguson comes down the stairs at Carrington and orders everyone out of the pressroom except Dave Anderson from the *Daily Mirror*. Ferguson has a long and acrimonious history with the *Mirror*, going back to when Piers Morgan was editor and the newspaper was openly and aggressively anti-United. Morgan was sacked in 2004 but Ferguson is convinced the *Mirror* still have an agenda against the club. He has decided to ban them for a week to give them something to think about. Anderson gets the full hairdryer treatment and is ordered out with a message for his sports editor that the newspaper is risking a permanent ban.

The door is swung open. Anderson shuffles out and we nervously make our way in. The door slams shut and Ferguson bursts into laughter. 'Right, that's one down – who's next?'

He is a bit cranky at the moment. He is worrying about the Benfica game and the way we are hyping it up as a make-or-break moment for the club's season and, possibly, for Ferguson too. Some of the newspapers have started speculating that the Glazers will move him on at the end of the season if United fail to qualify. The *Sun* reckon Glasgow Rangers want him as their next manager.

'I'm not going anywhere,' he says. 'Can we get that clear? I shouldn't have to respond to this nonsense just because some idiot has written a stupid story.'

The person he is calling an idiot is sat on the second row. 'Actually, Alex, Rangers have confirmed that story is true.'

'They have not. They've confirmed nothing.'

'They confirmed it to reporters in Scotland.'

'They did not.'

'They did.'

'You're lying.'

'I'm not lying.'

'YOU'RE A LIAR!'

'No, I'm not.'

'Yes, you are.'

'I'm a liar? This time last week you told us Roy Keane would be staying, thirty minutes before announcing that he'd gone. Who was lying then?'

This is possibly the most courageous thing any journalist has said to Ferguson in the last ten years.

'YOU'RE STILL LYING! RANGERS HAVE NOT CONFIRMED THAT STORY TO ANYONE.'

'Yes, they did.'

'No, they didn't – you wrote a story knowing fine well it wasn't true.'

'No, I didn't.'

'Yes, you did.'

'No, I didn't.'

'Yes, you did.'

'We could go on like this for hours.'

Ferguson is semi-shouting, semi-laughing. 'I'll go on for as long as you want – it was a ridiculous story.'

'It wasn't ridiculous at all.'

'Yes it was.'

'No it wasn't.'

'Yes it was.'

'No it wasn't.'

Everyone is laughing now.

Diana Law: 'Right, I think we'll call it a day there. Thank you everyone.'

LISBON
6.12.05

An early-morning flight to Lisbon and the press are out in force. Television cameras follow Ferguson through passport control at Manchester airport and he stops for a couple of interviews. He looks confident, really up for it, as he always is before a big game. He has been upbeat all week: 'People outside the club must be loving this situation but we'll get through, don't worry about that. I'm not even thinking about failing to qualify.'

When we thump down on the tarmac at Lisbon airport he has some good news. We had all assumed he would never do airport briefings again, but Diana Law comes over to say he has had a change of heart and that we should wait for him by the carousel. After a few minutes Ferguson strolls over, claps his hands together and smiles broadly.

'Right lads, ready to do some work for once?'

We take this as a minor breakthrough. But a flight carrying 300 supporters has landed at the same time and trying to get Ferguson by himself is hopeless. They spot us, mid-interview, and suddenly they are all around us, singing and cheering and snapping with cameraphones. Beery and boisterous. Shouting 'Well done' and 'You tell them, Alex' every time he says something positive. Then breaking into the old chant, arms in the air.

Every single one of us loves Alex Ferguson
Every single one of us loves Alex Ferguson

These few minutes are an ordeal for Ferguson. They smother him, slap him on the back, shout how much they love him. When he tries to break free – the interview is impossible – there are so many of them that he has to fight his way through the scrum. They chant his name and try to carry him shoulder-high towards the exit, grabbing at his arms and legs. You would think this is a man who has just won the European

Cup rather than someone on the verge of climination.

It is an outpouring of tribal emotion, genuinely good-natured, but it is interesting to see how he copes with it. He is smiling, trying his best to look happy and appreciative, but you do not need to know him well to see he just wants to collect his case and get out of there as quickly as he can. He doesn't want to be jigged about, hoisted in the air and bounced up and down in an airport full of holidaymakers. Not at his age. He is bright red, looking about him for help, but none is forthcoming.

He makes it to the exit and his first words are, 'Jesus Christ!'

The next time we see him he is sitting between Queiroz and Ronaldo behind a long table, in the ball-room of the team hotel, for his pre-match Champions League press conference. He has straightened his tie and smoothed down his hair. Once again he looks happy and relaxed, back in control. UEFA's translator has phoned through to say he is stuck in rush-hour traffic and Queiroz, who speaks five languages, has volunteered to help out.

Everything is very good-humoured. Ferguson responds to some harmless questions with equally harmless answers. He is bright and positive, and at one point he starts to tease Queiroz for not keeping up. Queiroz is very apologetic and a little embarrassed. Ronaldo is having a fit of giggles.

Everything is ticking along. Then comes a moment that no journalist in that room will ever forget.

Oliver Holt, the *Daily Mirror*'s award-winning chief sports writer, asks The Question. 'Alex, if the team were not to get through, and we all hope that's not the case, would it be valid to speculate about the ramifications for your own future?'

Ferguson blinks, as if he can hardly believe what he has just heard. He tilts his head, squinting to make out where it has come from, working out how to respond. It is a question that goes against every rule he has put in place in his dealings with the press. A question that tramples over the Ferguson etiquette about what we should and should not ask.

It feels like we are in that moment of a cowboy film when the wind is whistling and the tumbleweed blows past.

'I'm not even going to respond to that,' he says.

But Holt carries on. 'Is it not a legitimate question?'

'Listen,' says Ferguson, much more fiercely, 'I'm here to talk about the game, not my future.'

'But are the two not linked?'

Ferguson's mood can usually be gauged by the colour of his cheeks. Now he is flushed with anger. He changes the subject but is clearly distracted. He glares at Holt again. It is a glare that reaches across the table, grabs Holt by the collar and suggests they take it outside, the old-fashioned way.

GOODBYE TO ALL THAT
7.12.05

Benfica	2
Manchester United	1

Champions League, Group D

Classical music is being played on MUTV. For the first

time in ten years United have been eliminated from the Champions League before the knockout rounds. They are bottom of their group, which means there isn't even an escape route to the UEFA Cup. By the standards of any top European club, it is failure. By United's, it is cataclysmic.

The inquest will be long and painful and we take care to look suitably morose as we file past Ferguson on the flight home. Our match reports are going to hurt him tomorrow. Football can be brutal sometimes, and victory over Chelsea is quickly forgotten in the context of a December exit from the Champions League. One of the fans' websites is already running a feature entitled 'Ten Reasons Why Fergie Must Go', accompanied by a mock-up of his P45, bearing the signature of Malcolm Glazer.

Sir Alex Ferguson sacked?

It feels strange even typing those words. Strange and surreal. Yet it is very clear some supporters want Ferguson out, as long as there is a dignified way of doing it. There have already been headlines this week such as 'End of the line?' and 'Fergie on the brink'. Glazer, like most multi-millionaires, has a reputation for being ruthlessly unsentimental and tonight has cost him a minimum £10 million in terms of the prize money and gate receipts that United will be missing out on. As a businessman, does he grin and bear it? Or does he make changes at the top?

This could be the end, this really could be the end.

The press conference takes place in a downstairs room full of chain-smoking Portuguese journalists and officious-looking women in Benfica blazers and short skirts. Ferguson comes in through a side door, looking like death warmed up. His eyes flash round the room, working out who's there, which newspapers, which faces. But he avoids eye contact.

He says he is 'waiting for players to mature'. He promises that the 'rebuilding job' will eventually pay dividends and he asks us to be patient with his team, which is a clever piece of bargaining. When managers request tolerance for players it is usually because they want to siphon off some of it for themselves.

One big question has to be asked. It's not a question that anyone particularly wants to ask, but it has to be put to him, all the same.

'Alex, you've spoken about a rebuilding job but given the financial implications of this defeat, and everything that it stands for, are you certain you will be allowed to oversee that rebuilding job?'

It is the second time in twenty-four hours he has been asked about getting the sack.

'Listen,' he replies, trying his best to sound in control, 'there will always be a profile on me, whatever I do. But I am not going to answer those type of questions. I'm sure you will have plenty to say about it yourselves in the press. But I've got a job to do, a good job, and I'm confident in my players. OK?'

He probably expects worse. But nobody – and there are a lot of us packed into the room – takes a cheap shot. Our questions are constructed sympathetically and put to him in a solemn tone. There is no interrogation, no *schadenfreude*. We recognise greatness and we know that is what we are dealing with here. Without greatness, there is no fall, no tragedy. We are not going to trample over greatness when he is sitting before us, looking thoroughly miserable.

We are entitled, however, to ask whether he has taken his eye off the ball.

Managers in the Champions League are supposed to know every detail about the opposition. But when United played Maccabi Haifa in 2002 Ferguson spent his entire pre-match briefing, a day before the game, talking about the wrong team. 'We've watched their videos and we know Israeli football has improved a lot over the years,' he told a roomful of Israeli journalists. 'They have beaten Lokomotiv Moscow, Parma and AC Milan so we know we can't underestimate them.'

There was an awkward silence before Lilach Sonin, the presenter of Israel's Sports Five Plus, tried to correct him. 'I'm sorry, but I think you're talking about a different club.'

'They've made changes?' Ferguson innocently replied.

'No, you are talking about a different team. You are telling us about Hapoel Tel Aviv rather than Maccabi Haifa.'

Ferguson went bright red. 'I'm sorry,' he said, looking genuinely appalled. 'I must have got it wrong.'

'I'm embarrassed for him,' Sonin said afterwards. 'He didn't seem to know which team Manchester United were playing. Yet he's the manager, isn't he?'

This might have nothing to do with what has happened this season but, all together, it creates the impression of a man who has let things slip. Ferguson didn't seem to have any answers tonight. He sat forlornly in the dugout, strangely inert, as Benfica recovered from Scholes's early goal to equalise, move into the lead and take a grip of the match. At the final whistle he headed straight for the tunnel without a backward glance. He looked absolutely knackered and when we board the plane we can see the strain is getting to him. His fingernails give him away. They are bitten to the quick.

THE BLAME GAME
11.12.05

| Manchester United | 1 |
| Everton | 1 |

Carlos Queiroz began training yesterday by announcing: 'Let me introduce a new player, a young man from Norway …' before presenting Ole Gunnar Solskjaer, fit again after a knee injury that had threatened to end his career. The squad gave Solskjaer a round of applause before he began his first full session in nineteen months.

So there are still good times to be had at Manchester United. It is just that good-news stories tend to be ignored by the newspapers when there is a crisis howling like a gale. United have become 'Crisis Club Manchester United' since the defeat in Lisbon and some of us have been chasing a tip today that Ferguson has already been persuaded to leave at the end of the season. We haven't been able to stand it up – it is probably just the usual mischief-making – but it is typical of the rumours that are doing the rounds. This is what happens when a club of United's stature goes out of Europe before Christmas. Fingers are pointed and blame apportioned.

Today is another bleak day, a Groundhog Day. Everton are an average side and the match ends with more shouting and booing. Football is a fickle business. Earlier this week the supporters tried to carry Ferguson shoulder-high through Lisbon airport. Today, one of the fans' websites describes United as football's equivalent of the Conservative Party, their performance against Benfica being 'the fading wheezing of a dying beast'. There is no harmony whatsoever between crowd and team and, yet again, the roads around the ground are clogged with early leavers. It has become as much a part of life at Old Trafford as the neon sign outside the stadium.

To Ferguson, the press cuttings have begun to read like hate mail. Alan Smith, the *Daily Telegraph*'s footballer-turned-journalist, has described the performance in Lisbon as 'a shambles, a headless chicken charge relying on a crash-bang-wallop approach'. Scapegoats are being demanded and, almost without exception, the newspapers have come to the conclusion that Ferguson will be politely ushered towards the door at the end of the season. 'His quitting will be sudden,' according to the *Sunday Times*. 'A small statement on the club website, a brief press release will appear, probably as media outlets are closing down late on a Friday, perhaps on the eve of England's opening game at the World Cup.'

It is a big assumption to make and Ferguson has a bee in his bonnet about it. He was at a funeral on Friday, meaning Queiroz took over media duties and there were strict conditions attached. Queiroz would not take any questions relating to Ferguson and the club let us know beforehand that if the warning went unheeded the conference would be abandoned immediately. We were not even to mention Ferguson by name and told that if we did, Queiroz would walk out without saying another word. The orders had been passed down by Ferguson, it was explained, and they were non-negotiable.

Ferguson's belief is that we are taking a malicious sense of pleasure from what has happened and 'seeking to make it personal'. A rumour has reached Old Trafford that we ordered champagne to toast Benfica's victory on the flight home from Lisbon. Complete nonsense, but hugely damaging anyway. 'There are people,' he says, and we think he must mean us, 'who are trying to drive me out ... but they've been trying that for the last ten years.'

He is a proud man and it is probably only to be expected that he has such a downer on the press right now. It cannot be very pleasant for someone of his achievements to pick up the newspapers every morning and read that a large chunk of the Alex Ferguson magic has died. But it is a mistake for him to think it is vindictive on our part. The only fact that matters, from our perspective, is that it is a big story. Just about everyone has an opinion on Ferguson. He provokes a response, often a strong one, and even his closest journalistic allies are debating whether his departure could be forced upon him.

'Restoring true greatness to Old Trafford threatens to be a dauntingly wearing, long-term project,' Hugh McIlvanney, his old friend, observes in 1,500 words dedicated to Ferguson's predicament in the *Sunday Times*:

> *His warrior spirit abhors the thought of ending his managerial career in any way but on a crest of triumph, but*

his achievements are already so monumental that recent events could not conceivably cast a shadow on them. A personally choreographed exit would be bathed in the dignity and honour that are his due. He must never run the risk of being dispatched by remote control from Florida. Eventually there comes a moment when the best and bravest of fighters shouldn't answer the bell.

Coming from a man once known among United supporters as the Voice of Fergie, that is an elegant piece of advice many of us thought we would never see. But these are strange times. If Ferguson had switched on his television tonight he would have seen Jose Mourinho win Coach of the Year in the BBC Sports Personality of the Year awards. Rafael Benitez was runner-up, having won the European Cup for Liverpool. On Radio Five Live's phone-in, meanwhile, United fans were calling time on Ferguson's professional life and questioning whether he still has what it takes to be a successful manager. An Arsenal supporter rang in to defend him, saying he could hardly believe what he was hearing, that United fans were either stupid or just didn't appreciate how lucky they were. Strange times, indeed.

TRAGICOMEDY
13.12.05

The bee in Ferguson's bonnet is beginning to buzz out of control. Today's press conference is a classic.

'Morning, Alex.'

'Right, injuries. Silvestre has got a slight groin strain, should be OK. Other than that, everybody is fit. John

O'Shea's fit again. Then, looking at tomorrow's game, Wigan have been fantastic this season. I'm really pleased for their chairman Dave Whelan and everyone else. He's a straight talker. He's had a few managers but he's struck up a terrific bond with ...'

He cannot find the right name so Bill Thornton, of the *Daily Star*, helps him out.

'Jewell?'

'Aye, Paul Jewell. That's refreshing and that's the reason why they are there. So that's all I have got.' He's rising to his feet. 'See you later boys. I'm busy.'

It lasts seventy-four seconds. Eighty-six words, and he is gone. Out of the door, up the stairs, along the corridor, into his office.

Some of us laugh. We laugh and we laugh. Others swear and get angry, really angry. One guy has driven ninety miles for a press conference that's lasted less time than it takes to boil an egg. Or even to get the egg out of the fridge. At England press conferences, where the journalists often have more control than the manager, some of the *questions* last longer than seventy-four seconds.

There are television crews at Carrington and, very quickly, Sky Sports hear about it. Sky can be more sensationalistic than the worst tabloid. They announce on their rolling news channel a 'newsflash' claiming that Ferguson stormed out and refused to answer any questions. Press Association and Reuters pick up the story and suddenly it is buzzing through wire services all over the world.

Well, here's the truth. He didn't exactly storm out. There were no tape recorders scattered across the floor. No expletives. No slamming the door off its hinges. He didn't even raise his voice. He simply got up and marched to the door before we had time to realise what was going on. His body language was tense but he was only seventy per cent angry, at most, and there was even the flicker of a smile as he closed the door behind him.

He went straight into an interview with MUTV, and his motives quickly became clear. The press, he said, were the real villains. Going out of the Champions League had hurt but the criticism had been disproportionate to the scale of disappointment. He was sick and tired of picking up the newspapers and reading personal attacks.

'The press have a hatred of Manchester United. Any opportunity and they will have a go at us. Right now, they are trying to fragment the club, the players from the supporters and the supporters from the players. I suppose it goes with the territory, us being a high-profile club, but they go over the top. They make it personal.'

The supporters, he said, should disregard everything they read in the newspapers. 'I think our fans are aware of it and I don't think they will fall into the trap of believing what the press say. I make the point, and I make it strongly, that we are at our best when the fans are right behind us. That is the only thing that should matter right now. We have to stick together.'

AGGRO
14.12.05

Manchester United	4
Wigan Athletic	0

Sky Sports have been cranking up the story all day. James Cooper, their Manchester reporter, has been positioned outside Old Trafford to find out what the fans think about the press. Some of us have been on television to put across our side while various pundits have been wheeled out to analyse whether we have, as alleged, got it in for United.

Our message, in essence, is that we should be talking about the headline makers rather than the headline writers. The whole business is slightly embarrassing. Those aren't notepads stuffed in the pockets of the people who have been barracking Ferguson, but season tickets. It wasn't a reporter or a splash sub who suggested he signed misfits such as David Bellion or Eric Djemba-Djemba or Diego Forlan. We cannot refrain from publishing scores or Champions League tables because results are not going well. We cannot conveniently go on sabbatical because there are supporters calling for his head. Making a monster out of the media isn't going to solve the club's problems.

It's funny though. The fans have been laying into Ferguson, getting right on his back, but they don't like it when the press become involved. After twenty minutes, Scholes tries his luck from thirty yards out and the goalkeeper spills the shot. Fletcher follows in and puts away the rebound. The crowd are roaring but the linesman has his flag up for offside and a bald chap, probably in his fifties, turns round in front of the pressbox and starts pointing and chanting.

Blame the press! Blame the press! Blame the press!
Fuck the press! Fuck the press! Fuck the press!

Ten minutes later Ferdinand scores for real. This time another guy, a pillock in a tie, comes up really close, giving it the middle finger, screaming abuse. The woman he's with, his girlfriend or wife (or carer?), is trying to pull him away, but he has really lost it, threatening all sorts of GBH.

This is unusual but not unprecedented. Journalists, rightly or wrongly, are disliked more than anyone bar estate agents and traffic wardens, and there have been many times when this has led to confrontation, even violence. One night out in La Coruña with Neville Neville (Gary's dad) ended badly when someone in the same bar realised who he was drinking with and started shouting the odds about the 'anti-United press'. Other reporters have been told to leave certain pubs and restaurants for their own safety. One guy, on England duty, was whacked over the head with an ashtray.

Sometimes it can be very sinister. A *Daily Telegraph* reporter once opened his mail at Canary Wharf to find a jiffy bag containing human faeces. The accompanying letter came from a Millwall fan and said: 'You talk shit – you might as well have some.' Opening an envelope on another occasion, the same journalist suddenly realised his hand was pouring with blood. A razor blade had been taped to the inside of the flap.

More recently, a *Daily Mail* journalist picked up the phone to hear some crank accusing him of being a 'nigger-lover' and making all sorts of threats, using the worst kind of racist language imaginable. It later came out that the man responsible was the father of a Premiership player (unrelated to United), upset because his son had been given a lower mark out of ten than a black team-mate.

It is unusual, though, for the hostility to surface inside a stadium. The only other time it's occurred in Manchester was at Maine Road, in 1998. On that occasion a gang of big, hard-looking blokes invaded the pressbox looking for a *Daily Mirror* reporter called Steve Rogers, who had written something they didn't like about City's attendances. City, who were in the old Third Division at the time, had had a record low crowd of 3,007 for an Auto Windscreens Shield first-round tie against Mansfield Town, the day before United had a sell-out against Bayern Munich in the Champions League. The *Mirror* had some fun with it, comparing the fortunes of the two clubs. At the next City match there were people hunting for Rogers.

What they couldn't grasp was that the story had been written by a freelance agency and that 'Steve Rogers' was a cod by-line. Threats were made, things got out of hand and the police were called. It took six of them to get Lindsay Sutton, the *Mirror*'s local stringer, out of the stadium before he was lynched.

CHANGING THE RULES
16.12.05

It's an odd place, Carrington. A huge, sprawling development secluded behind farmland and trees on a private country lane five miles west of Manchester, the type that only horse-riders or loving couples would normally frequent. We call it Fortress Carrington because it is so difficult to locate or get into, because it seems specifically designed, as Ferguson once allegedly put it, to 'keep those fuckers from the media out'. It is like one of those rural hideaways in a James Bond movie where the villains hatch bomb-making experiments. There are no signs, while three sets of electronically operated barriers and a stubbled security man in the front cabin make sure nobody gets in without permission.

Stopwatches at the ready, we head there today not knowing what to expect and, quite frankly, more than a little worried. It is the first time we have been invited to see Ferguson since the seventy-four-second press conference and it is difficult to grasp what might happen. We have got wind something is brewing and we are mentally prepared for a sustained attack.

These briefings take the form of a series of question-and-answer sessions in a room to the side of the reception area. It is a pretty nondescript place, with a couple of rubber plants, a coffee machine and four rows of seats. First he speaks to Sky. Then it is the turn of the radio reporters. The daily newspapers go next and, finally, he sees the Sundays. It is a set routine, replicated at every Premiership club, and it takes about an hour out of his week.

Today, though, he drops his bombshell. There is to be a new venue and a new format – an all-in press conference with every arm of the media squashed into an upstairs room at the youth academy building, 100 yards the other side of the car park.

He is blaming the coverage of the seventy-four-second conference, the way it has been reported throughout the media as a sign that the pressure is getting to him. He says he is no longer willing to satisfy our different requirements and from now on he will see the lot of us in one go and for no more than ten minutes per week. There will be no press conferences whatsoever before midweek games, no one-on-one player interviews for the rest of the season. And, in addition, the *Evening News* will no longer be allowed to ring him or send reporters to

Carrington separately, a privilege that has always been granted to them exclusively in the past. It is described as a 'trial', but everyone who is there knows the rules have been set in stone. Diplomatic relations have been suspended, as they say in countries on the verge of war.

We are genuinely shocked. We think he has over-reacted, that he should have had it out with the individual journalists and sports editors who have upset him rather than punishing everyone together. But Ferguson's argument is that no other manager in the country has to put up with the crap that is thrown in his direction. There have been too many times, he says, when we have ganged up on him. He is tired of worrying about what he says being twisted. Tired of our two-facedness. Tired of the way we smile and then stab. He has been falling out with journalists all his adult life and he is tired of the same old arguments. Tired of falling out, making up, falling out, making up.

'Why should I talk to people who have been slaughtering me?' he asked David Meek, the former *Manchester Evening News* reporter and one of his closest journalistic friends, recently. 'Going out of the Champions League has triggered not just criticism, which I can accept, but personal abuse aimed at my position as manager.'

Diana Law explains his grievances to us and we gather in a little huddle, digesting the implications, suitably disheartened. This is a very bad day in our professional lives. Everything newsworthy from his press conferences will now go straight out on Sky Sports's rolling news channel. In newspaper terms, it will look dated by the time it appears in print the following day. Nor will we be able to go off the record with him – not with half a dozen television cameras filming everything he says. Visiting Ferguson for his Friday briefings has always been the highlight of the working week. It is never going to be the same again.

The weird thing is that Ferguson drives. At 11.59 a.m. he comes out of the double doors of the main Carrington building, climbs into his Audi S8, swings out of the car park, puts it into second gear, bears right past the groundsman's hut and pulls into the nearest parking spot (the disabled one) to the youth academy. Then, once his ten minutes is up, he makes the same John Prescott-style journey back. It is a round trip of no more than 200 yards.

In happier times, we would be able to tease him a little, ask whether his legs were giving up, how long it would be before he was eligible for free bus travel. That is out of the question today. His press conference is humourless and bland, devoid of friendly interaction. Ten minutes of strained questioning, with television and radio interviewers desperate to be heard and frequently talking over one another. No flow, no spontaneity.

Ferguson is sour and unhelpful. He takes his seat and pours a glass of water. It's sparkling, he prefers still.

'What the hell is this?'

BUGGED
24.12.05

Throughout history there have always been intermittent problems between managers of Manchester United and the press. Dave Sexton never made any secret of his distrust of newspapermen and Tommy Docherty once declared: 'There's a place for journalists, they just haven't dug it yet.' Yet nobody can remember a manager's relationship with the press completely breaking down and it doesn't make us feel very good that the first time might be on our watch.

What we have today is a man who comes into his press conference with the expression of a vegan going into TGI Fridays. Ferguson drives again. He parks in the disabled bay and we can tell, as soon as he gets out of his car and we see his face, that it is going to be another waste of time. He might as well make a W for 'Whatever' with his fingers.

Ole Gunnar Solskjaer is fit again and a reporter from the *Sun* asks Ferguson what it will mean for the team to have him back.

'You tell me,' comes the reply. 'You're supposed to be the expert.'

Another reporter asks for an update on Gabriel Heinze's fitness, saying he has 'read somewhere that he might be back for the World Cup'.

'Where did you read that?' Ferguson replies. 'A comic?'

After the Chelsea game the *Sun* ran a front-page story – 'What a cheeky bugger!' – about the dressing rooms at Old Trafford being secretly bugged. The newspaper claimed to have been offered the tapes of Ferguson's team talk by 'a middle man demanding tens of thousands of pounds' but said it had refused to pay, handing them over to United instead. The club held an internal investigation and the local CID was called in. Between them, they worked out that someone must have planted the bug on one of the organised tours of the stadium. But Ferguson had a different theory. 'It was the *Sun*,' he said. 'I'm convinced of it. They did it all right. They bugged us. They were behind it.'

When the *Sun*'s correspondent tried to object, Ferguson cut him dead. 'Don't even think about telling me it's not true. I know exactly what happened and it won't happen again, believe me.'

Ferguson, it seems to us, is on the brink of refusing to do any more press conferences at all. There are voices telling him he is not getting any younger, that he no longer has the magician's touch. He is trying to ignore them – but it has reached the point where he feels the volume of criticism has become intolerable. He is blaming the supporters' criticism of him on what they read in the newspapers rather than what they see on the pitch.

'I take exception when the press try to drive a wedge between the supporters and the team,' he says. 'It has been reported, for example, that the crowd booed the team at the end of the Everton game, suggesting that our supporters had seriously turned on us. Certainly there were a few boos, but what else would you expect after a disappointing performance?'

The press, he says, have blown it all out of proportion. 'It's the fans' way of expressing their feelings when we fall below expectations. Supporters don't like losing and a few are always going to let us know exactly how they feel. I can live with that. It's a reminder that we have to do better. Our home form has been pretty poor and it has blunted our attempt to challenge Chelsea. So I can understand the frustration showing itself in a few boos.'

If only it were that simple. The Christmas issue of *Red News* is out today and it is as festive as a snowball in the face. In fifty-two pages not a single contributor advocates that Ferguson should stay beyond the end of the season. The fanzine describes him as having 'nothing left to offer in terms of tactics, changes or inspiration'. It talks about him leaving at the end of the season as if it were a *fait accompli*:

> *It will be gut-wrenchingly sad, especially for those of us who have only ever known Sir Alex as manager. But maybe that's just emotion stopping us from saying what needs to be done. The heart can't rule the head if it's the right thing to do for the club's future. After so much motivating, after working his magic on so many players, on so many magical journeys for so many supporters, he looks unable to conjure like he once did. In a world full of hungry young managers he seems no longer able to fight back. Fergie looks old and that's because he is now. He looked a beaten man on the bench against Benfica. A forlorn figure, slumped back in his chair, looking lost.*

BURTON
8.1.06

Burton Albion	0
Manchester United	0
FA Cup third round	

Peter Schmeichel has been offering his thoughts about where things have gone wrong.

'From where I'm looking,' he says, 'the players seem interested only in cars and who has the biggest diamond. The team lacks personality. They had that in Roy Keane but the only one with that kind of personality now is Wayne Rooney. I'm thinking about players who could take the club forward. Ronaldo? No chance. Park? No chance. Ferdinand? No chance. Without Rooney, United would be a very ordinary team.'

Burton have been building up to this game for weeks. When we collect our press passes from a little window in the main stand we get a free gift, a jar of Marmite from the local factory, as a souvenir of 'the biggest day in the club's history'. The programmes are handed out and when we run our fingers down the list of Burton's previous matches it is easy to see why they are so excited. One fixture in particular stands out – a Birmingham Senior Cup tie at home to Romulus FC, of the Midland Football Alliance, in front of 119 people.

Burton have a shiny new stadium and a familiar manager in Nigel Clough. They are a touch more refined than the traditional non-league side – but only just. The club has a sponsorship deal with Bovril, a captain who doubles up as a builder and a ground named after a tyre factory. Today is only the third time they have reached the third round of the FA Cup. When Clough pops into the pressroom an hour before kick-off to say hello to all the journalists and thank them for coming – most unlike his father and, indeed, the opposition manager – he admits to fearing the worst. He doesn't expect to win or anything silly like that, but he hopes they give a good account of themselves. 'We don't want to get thrashed,' he says, 'but there's a chance it could happen.'

What happens next is the classic David and Goliath cup story.

When the game gets under way, it is immediately obvious something is wrong. The pitch is bumpy and gloopy and covered in sand and there is a bad vibe about Ferguson's players. He has picked a deliberately weakened side, promoting Richie Jones, Gerard Piqué and Giuseppe Rossi from the reserves, leaving out the likes of Ferdinand, Giggs and Van Nistelrooy, and there is a lazy vibe. They are playing as if they just have to turn up to qualify for the next round.

Burton have a shot that is cleared off the line. Then another one. They start getting hold of the ball, knocking it around, left and right, and as the players in yellow and black start to gain in confidence, there is gallows humour in the away end.

We're being outplayed by Burton
We're being outplayed by Burton

Lots of teams start games sluggishly. Except that United's bad start becomes a bad half and then a bad hour. Suddenly seventy minutes have gone and they still haven't had a chance of note. Ferguson is starting to look seriously agitated, out of his dugout, and the humour in the away end is slowly making way for anger.

Fergie, Fergie, sort it out!
Fergie, sort it out!

The final twenty minutes are fraught. It dawns on United that they are in danger of being made a laughing stock and they pile forward. But Burton have their chances too. Back come United, trying to save face, but time is up. Too late, too late.

Photographers are haring on to the pitch to get their celebratory pictures of these strange, unfamiliar, non-league heroes.

Clough describes it as a 'miracle'. The club's grounds-man, a stocky guy in a blue parka, is weeping with joy, blubbing into a soggy handkerchief. As United's players trudge apologetically towards the away end, we sit in stunned silence in the row of seats that passes as a temporary pressbox, trying to take it all in and saying 'Unbelievable' over and over again. A chant sweeps round the ground and we realise we might never witness another moment like this in our lives.

Are you Tamworth?
Are you Tamworth?
Are you Tamworth in disguise?

When Ferguson comes out for his interviews he looks baffled and embarrassed by what he has just seen. He knows it is going to make the headlines on *News at Ten* and that the shit is going to hit the fan – again. He is smiling, but it is the smile of a man who has just been punched in the face and is pretending everything is all right.

He talks to MUTV and Sky about how great it is for a Conference club to get a replay at Old Trafford. He is desperate to put some positive spin on it, however much his face betrays him. 'I didn't expect a replay,' he says. 'The whole nation probably expected us to win, but we were up against committed opponents on a difficult pitch and these shock results can happen. It's the FA Cup, I suppose, and fortunately we didn't get a more severe shock. At least we've got a second game to put it right. We're still in the cup, that's the main thing.'

He heads back to the dressing room and we sincerely doubt whether he is so philosophical and understanding with his players. United will win the replay, of course, but the point is that a replay should never have been necessary. Not against a side that is fourteenth in the Conference. Not against a team that gets 119 people for some matches. Goliath should really be kicking David's ass.

Ten minutes later there is a knock at the dressing-room door. A queue of Burton players has formed and, very politely, they ask if they can get some souvenirs, in particular Rooney's autograph. They are giggling like nervous schoolboys, as if they can't quite believe what is happening. Rooney comes out, freshly shampooed, and they nudge each other and thank him profusely. They do their *Match of the Day* interviews, staring nervously into the television cameras. Then it is time to celebrate properly and they arrange to meet at a pub on the outskirts of town. The cry goes up: 'Everybody who wants a drink, head for the Beacon.'

By the time the first journalists arrive the players are already getting stuck into their third pint. There is a plate of corned beef sandwiches, with dry cucumber slices on the side. A golden Labrador is asleep in the corner, with a yellow and black Burton scarf tied round its neck. It is a typical scene from a pub team's Sunday lunchtime. The air is thick with cigarette smoke and there is beery talk about where United went wrong.

The captain, Darren Stride, says it is a question of desire. 'You could sense their lads didn't fancy it. You could tell a few of them didn't want to be out there. It was as if they didn't want to get hurt. We were getting the ball down, passing it and creating chances. It was them, not us, who resorted to knocking it over the top.'

Burton is a brewery town and a specially commissioned pint called Fergie's Fury will be on tap in the next few days. There is talk about printing T-shirts for the replay carrying his quote: 'The whole nation expected us to win.' Tomorrow, news crews will be on their way from all around the world. This is what happens when United leave themselves exposed to embarrassment. Everyone wants a piece of it.

UNKNOWN PLEASURES
24.1.06

Manchester United	2
Blackburn Rovers	1

Carling Cup semi-final

The Carling Cup is the ginger stepchild of football trophies. To Ferguson, this competition used to be an afterthought, cluttering up an already congested fixture list and getting in the way of more important matters. He would play his reserves, they would lose in the third or fourth round and, unblushingly, he would move on. Even when York City knocked them out, winning 4–3 over two legs in 1995, there was no sense of prolonged anger or disappointment. United had other priorities, and he would never apologise for playing his kids – even when an MP once complained about it in the House of Commons.

This season, Ferguson cannot be so choosy. United have beaten Barnet, West Bromwich Albion and

Birmingham City to get to the semi-finals and tonight they put out their strongest team in an effort to reach the final. Ferguson is not going to make the same mistake he made against Burton. It is his most attacking line-up, with Giggs and Rooney playing as advanced midfielders, and Louis Saha partnering Van Nistelrooy in attack. Wigan Athletic, sixth in the Premiership, will be the opposition at the Millennium Stadium, six months into their first-ever Premiership season, and suddenly, almost freakishly, Ferguson is talking about the Carling Cup as if everyone has misjudged it all these years. 'It is a great cup competition, one we have always enjoyed,' he says. 'The Carling Cup represents a great opportunity to mark this season as a successful one. I'm delighted to be in the final.'

The club certainly need a lift after the embarrassment of Burton. It is still strange, though, to hear Ferguson banging the Carling Cup drum. The fans seem genuinely appreciative of a good performance, with Saha and Van Nistelrooy getting the decisive goals, but it doesn't alter the fact that the season has come down to a battle for the consolation prizes. Or that the Carling Cup, to quote one of the fans' websites, is 'a $50 hooker compared to the supermodels we used to date'. The internet messageboards have become a battlefield for pro- and anti-Ferguson factions recently. The phone-ins have been crackling with angry callers and the fanzine writers have been bitingly, and increasingly, cruel. *United We Stand*'s new-year edition bore the front cover: 'Goodbye and good riddance to our annus horribilis'.

This is where Ferguson could do with some better PR. He never speaks to the fanzines these days and it has become rare for him to attend official supporters' functions. Yet when he joined the club in 1986 he went out of his way to identify with the fans. He was a regular guest at meetings of the Independent Manchester United Supporters' Association and his message was one of unity. He wore a gold ring with the club's Red Devil motif and spoke of his concerns that working-class supporters were being priced out of the game. He described himself as the 'bridge' between the club and the fans.

His attitude these days seems to be that it is no longer worth the hassle. The fanzines have become increasingly personal and he had a bad experience when he attended his last IMUSA meeting. Apparently he made a throwaway remark, responding to a question about Rooney's temperament, about the player's Liverpool origins, saying that 'They've all got chips on their shoulder.' Despite an unwritten rule that whatever he said should remain private, the quote turned up in the *Daily Mirror* and the headlines caused a lot of embarrassment.

His last appearance at the club's AGM, in 2002, was another chastening experience. Ferguson had agreed to a question-and-answer session and the first shareholder to raise his arm told him he had stayed on too long: 'I've got the greatest respect for you and I will forever be indebted for what you have done at this club, but I wish you had retired when you said you would. You're wearing Rock of Gibraltar's blinkers and I've got news for you – you need to go back to the stable, have a clear-out and start with the biggest cart-horse of them all, Juan Sebastian Veron.'

Ferguson earned a smattering of sympathetic applause when he said he would 'not respond to that

idiot', but the grilling was not over. The next shareholder to ask a question accused him of allowing Roy
Keane to become 'bigger than the club'. Rio Ferdinand
was described as 'an average defender who cost £30
million'. United were fifth in the league at the time
and Ferguson was accused of taking the club
backwards.

Some supporters are never happy, of course. United
won the league that year by five points, with Veron
playing a bigger part than he was ever given credit
for. This season, though, with the bulk of the league
fixtures completed, Chelsea are so far in front that the
chasing group comprises nineteen stragglers. United
managed only three goals in the six games that mas-
queraded as their Champions League challenge and
they have just been held to a scoreless draw in the FA
Cup against a club 104 places below them in the
ladder of English football. Set against that, the supporters are entitled to be sceptical when Ferguson
says winning the Carling Cup would represent a successful season.

MICE
17.2.06

Old Trafford has mice, a whole family of them. The
players have seen them running around on the pitch.
Then the photographers spotted them scurrying
about in the centre circle. After the newspapers had
had some fun with the pictures, the *Sun* sent someone
to ask Ferguson if the club had a problem.

'Mice?' he said, heaving with huge cackles. 'I don't
know about mice, but we've got a bloody big problem

with rats.' He pointed at the packed pressroom. 'And you walked straight into that one, son ...'

Boom, boom.

There are signs that he might be loosening up. There has been a lot more laughter recently, a lot less aggro. The period from August to December was pretty unpleasant but he has reined in his temper now that his press conferences go out, uncut, on television and radio. He can't swear. Not when it would be on Sky Sports within an hour. He can't say anything that might offend the PC brigade. He has to think carefully about everything he says, has to be on his best behaviour.

Today, though, he gives Adam Leventhal, one of Sky Sports' reporters, a blast for pestering him with questions about finance. Real Madrid have overtaken United as the club with the highest turnover in the world and Leventhal, who is at his first United press conference, is asking question after question about revenue and shirt sales.

Ferguson hates being bogged down with this kind of stuff. 'I don't know what you're thinking of,' he says. 'Why are you coming to a football press conference and asking all these bloody business questions? Talk to David Gill if you want to know about facts and figures. But not me, OK? These other guys' – he points at us – 'are proper sports journalists, football fans, you understand? So let them ask about football for a change and let them get on with their jobs. Because if you're after some kind of rare bloody interview, you're not getting it here.'

For a few moments it looks as though he has forgotten he is being filmed. But he quickly regains his composure and he is fine for the rest of the press conference, full of good humour, smiling warmly and generally being jovial and frivolous.

Towards the end, he even starts an impromptu quiz to test our football knowledge. 'Come on then,' he says, picking out Tim Rich of the *Daily Telegraph*, 'name the last team from outside the top division to reach an FA Cup final?'

'Millwall, 2004,' Rich replies instinctively.

'Before that?'

'Sunderland, 1992.'

'And before that?'

'West Ham, 1980.'

'And before that?'

Rich is not only one of the finest writers in Fleet Street but also a human football encyclopaedia.

'Southampton, 1976 ... Fulham, 1975 ... Sunderland, 1973 ... Do you want me to carry on?'

Ferguson is impressed, nodding appreciatively.

'You're OK, son.'

CITY OF CULTURE
18.2.06

Liverpool	1
Manchester United	0

FA Cup fifth round

They despise Manchester United on Merseyside. Hate them with a passion. Yet strangely Ferguson never seems fazed by the hostility. Ask him to list the clubs he truly dislikes and he will say it is at Leeds, not Liverpool, that he actually feels the atmosphere is dangerous. At Anfield, he says, it is usually 'good-natured stuff, never any problem'. He has a certain respect for Liverpool and the way they conduct themselves. He likes the way their crowd appreciate opposition teams that play good football and he laughs about the time he went to one match at Anfield as a spectator. 'You Manc bastard, come to see the champions?' was the greeting as he parked his car.

Leeds, he says, are different, because 'They give us the impression that lynching would be too good for us.' He tells a story of Eric Harrison, then his youth coach, being punched and spat at during a crowd invasion at Elland Road one year, and hot tea and other drinks being thrown over United's directors, including Sir Bobby Charlton and his wife, Norma.

Another time, Ferguson was caught at traffic lights outside the ground. 'This bunch of supporters, skinheads, twenty or thirty of them, they see me and go "Ferguson!" and start running across the road. The lights are still red. I'm almost shitting myself. They're getting nearer, then the light goes to amber and' – impersonation of a tyre-squeal – 'I'm away.'

It is doubtful, though, whether even Leeds can replicate the hatred that is unleashed at Anfield today. Relations between Mancunians and Liverpudlians have never been very good but, as regards football, they have taken a sudden turn for the worse over recent years. There is a violent, almost evil, atmosphere. Objects are thrown on to the pitch – a couple of coins at Steven Gerrard and the same, plus a half-eaten burger, at Gary Neville. There are chants about the Heysel and Hillsborough disasters, outstretched arms to mock the Munich plane crash, plus songs about Harold Shipman, George Best, Michael Shields and Emlyn Hughes – anyone, in fact, whose death or crimes can be used to score points. And for the *pièce de résistance*, Liverpool fans in the top tier of the Anfield Road toss plastic cups of piss and shit on to the United fans below.

Incessant hatred is a fact of football life, particularly where United are concerned. It's out there, it's unshakeable and anyone who cares about the club is obliged to live with it. Yet legitimate rivalry is lost today. When Alan Smith breaks his leg, blocking a shot from John Arne Riise, the Liverpool fans celebrate it like a goal. They clench their fists and punch the air, and when it is obvious he is not going to get up they dust off the old Monty Python song.

Always look on the bright side of life
Da-dah, da-dah, da-dah, da-dah

When Ferguson's eyes flash towards the crowd, they cheerfully wave back. They make ambulance noises – *nee-nah, nee-nah, nee-nah* – and they change the words of the old Bruce Channel song.

John Arne Riise
I wanna know-oh-oh
How you broke his leg

By the time the ambulance sets off for hospital, Smith's ankle jutting out of his sock like a broken cricket stump, the final whistle has gone. Ferguson is a picture of professional misery, leaning against a wall, hands in pockets. He is reflective and solemn, and every bit as depressed as he was after the Benfica game. 'Alan has broken his leg and dislocated his ankle,' he says. 'It's a bad one, very long term. The ligaments have come right out too. He's such a brave lad I'm sure he will be back, but it's one of the worst injuries I've ever seen. It sums up our day. It's eighty-five years since Liverpool last beat us in an FA Cup tie and I wish it had been another eighty-five years. But our first thoughts are with Alan because he's got a bad one, a really bad one.'

Some days in football are golden, others are plain horrible. There is little doubt about which category this falls into. The FA Cup could have rescued United's season, but Ferguson cannot even claim they have gone out of the competition with great dignity. United give the ball away with bewildering frequency. They don't chase back. They lose the 50-50s. There is a strange going-through-the-motions vibe. They are behind from the nineteenth minute and, late on, Van Nistelrooy gives up on an overhit pass he could probably have caught with a bit more effort. Suddenly Ferguson is on the touchline, swearing at the player, throwing his arms up in the air in disgust.

He looks up at the Kop, where a large banner is being unfurled: 'Look Alex – back on our *****ng perch'. The asterisks are in gold, to signify Liverpool's five European Cups.

FERGIE AND THE CARLING CUP
24.2.06

Tim Rich, our resident quiz master, was invited to Carrington earlier this week to interview Ferguson for a commissioned piece to be published in the Carling Cup final programme. As he waited outside the players' lounge, nervously wondering what mood Ferguson would be in, he was disconcerted to hear a Glaswegian voice the other side of the door.

'Jesus Christ, what time is it? WHERE THE FUCK IS THIS TIM RICH?'

The music from *Jaws* was playing in Rich's head as he knocked tentatively on the door. Yet Ferguson greeted him like a long-lost friend, offering him drinks and biscuits and asking him how his journey had been. Ferguson, he says, was 'absolutely charming', giving him a brilliant interview, full of good humour – until a little exchange with the photographer as he posed for some promotional pictures.

The photographer was after the classic Ferguson shot: gruff and confrontational, glowering like a pitbull. 'Can you look just a little bit more moody?' he was asking. 'Come on, Sir Alex, a little bit more fierce, perhaps?'

Ferguson's patience was wearing thin: 'I've been stood here for ten minutes already and you're asking me to look moody…'

Today is Carling Cup final press day and Ferguson is on great form again – witty, thoughtful with his answers, obviously excited about the prospect of a final at the Millennium Stadium.

'Everyone's fit,' he announces, not even waiting for the first question. 'We don't have any injury problems, apart from Alan Smith of course. It's a big occasion for us. Wigan are bringing a bit of romance to the day because of what they've achieved over the years. The whole country will be behind them, and I understand that …'

James Cooper, of Sky Sports, interrupts him in full flow. 'You must be desperate to win the game for Alan Smith ...'

'Jesus Christ!' Ferguson splutters. 'I hadn't actually finished what I was saying. You're like a Rottweiler, aren't you, James? Are you on an early deadline or something?'

'No,' Cooper shoots back, 'but we've got only ten minutes – I thought we'd better be quick.'

It is a good press conference. When we question Ferguson about United's troubles, he is unusually expansive. Yes, he says, it has been a disappointing period for the club, but a manager has to be strong in times of adversity and he has no time for self-pity. He is still convinced that the club are heading in the right direction and that next season they will be able to challenge Chelsea properly. He still has reason to be optimistic when he looks round the dressing room and sees formidable young players such as Ronaldo and Rooney.

'I've been watching the Champions League,' he says. 'At least not being involved has taken away the threat of a heart attack. But it does remind me of the level I want us to get back to. I just hope we can come back as a force next year.'

Winning the Carling Cup, he says, is a chance to salvage some pride. 'There are only four trophies available every year and we set out at the start of each season with the intention of winning one. No matter what that trophy is you've got to take that as a successful season, because there are plenty of clubs who won't win anything. Not world-renowned clubs like Manchester United perhaps, but big, big clubs.'

'Do you think the fans will agree with that?' someone asks. 'When the Carling Cup was known as the
Worthington Cup, didn't the supporters nickname it
the Worthless Cup?'

He is taken aback by that question but it doesn't
put him off his flow. He says, again, that the Carling
Cup is an important competition. His line has been
the same ever since he reached the final: 'We know
it's not the Champions League but it's still a competition that means a lot to this club. Winning the Carling
Cup would make it a successful season.'

It's debatable. To the average fan, winning the
Carling Cup might not even represent a successful
month, bearing in mind what happened at Liverpool
in the FA Cup. But Ferguson has turned on the cool-
ing sprinklers recently and there is no point
antagonising him when we are in this period of rec-
onciliation. He seems to be over that spell, just before
Christmas, when he treated every question as though
it were our explicit intention to dig up every little sin
or defect. We want to keep it that way.

The only reminder of any underlying friction is that
The Times and the *Daily Express* have been barred from
his press conference because he is unhappy with their
coverage of the club. *The Times* has offended him by
questioning why United paid £7.2 million for Nemanja
Vidic during the January transfer window when,
according to the paper's sources, he had a get-out
clause in his contract at Spartak Moscow that meant he
could have been signed for £4.8 million. Ferguson has
taken exception to the wording of the story.

Similarly, he has taken issue with the *Express*
because of a couple of paragraphs in Matthew Dunn's
diary column. Ferguson has a habit of fiddling with

our tape recorders, probably without even realising it, while he answers questions, and he accidentally turned one off during a recent briefing. Dunn made a joke about press conferences being 'sabotaged' but his attempt at humour has backfired. Ferguson wants an apology printed and the *Express* is out in the cold in the meantime.

CARDIFF
27.2.06

Manchester United	4
Wigan Athletic	0

Carling Cup final

Some of the Sunday newspapers were reporting today that Ferguson might be sacked if United lost this match. It isn't the first time he has faced such headlines, and it probably won't be the last, but it can't be nice waking up to them on the morning of a cup final. 'You haven't got a clue,' he berates us before leaving the pressroom at the Millennium Stadium. It is the first time this season he has come to a post-match conference, with the exception of Champions League matches, and it ends with him walking out in disgust.

Our sin is to ask him about his future and, specifically, whether he has felt his position was under threat. There is a time and a place for these things. One guy in particular is given a crash course in how to deal with Ferguson when he starts asking him whether winning this trophy may have saved his job. Ferguson still has the taste of champagne in his mouth and is genuinely shocked. The red mist comes down and he lets us know exactly what he thinks of it.

He is probably entitled to be angry. This is the seventeenth trophy he has won for United and at the final whistle he is on the pitch, arms raised, triumphantly punching the air. He wants to embrace every single player, every single coach. It has been a good day and he is determined to make the most of it, striding across the playing surface in his full-length overcoat, waving to the crowd, smiling from ear to ear.

To watch him after a victorious cup final is like peering through your fingers at a wedding as a tipsy uncle takes to the dance floor demanding more Jive Bunny or 'YMCA'. Ferguson is certainly not one of those managers who prefers to stand to the side and let the players milk the moment. He is right in the thick of things, jubilant and euphoric. When MUTV grab him for an interview he treats them to an impromptu chorus of 'Flower of Scotland'. Fatboy Slim booms out and he starts swaying to the thump, thump, thump of the beat. He does a one-man Mexican wave with the trophy and enfolds Queiroz in a bear-hug.

He is led to the media centre by an entourage of stewards-cum-bouncers wearing yellow blazers. The place is packed and he marches through the door like a newly elected senator, his winner's medal round his neck. The cameras flash and his face shines.

He says he wants to congratulate his players. He never devalued the Carling Cup, he says, and it is a wonderful day for everyone at the club.

Not quite everyone. Ferguson dropped a bombshell today by playing Saha instead of Van Nistelrooy

– an astonishing decision, given that Van Nistelrooy has been a fixture in the team, averaging thirty goals a season, since he joined the club from PSV Eindhoven five years ago.

He is the club's top scorer again this season, with twenty-one goals in thirty-five appearances, and when the team-sheets are brought to the pressbox an hour before kick-off we cannot help wondering whether Ferguson has taken leave of his senses. Saha plays magnificently, scoring one and setting up a couple more. Rooney gets two, Ronaldo one, and Wigan are completely overwhelmed. Nonetheless, it is a remarkable snub, one which Van Nistelrooy doesn't seem to have taken well. His body language as he sits on the bench is sullen and aggrieved. He is clearly in a huff, and he is conspicuously isolated when the celebrations begin at the final whistle.

The other players seem oblivious to his torment. They bob up and down on the winners' podium and pull on T-shirts that say 'For You Smudge', in honour of Alan Smith. They kiss their medals and take turns raising the cup before linking arms and belting out 'We are the Champions'. At first, Van Nistelrooy tries to join in, but it is a half-hearted gesture. When it is time for the lap of honour he gives up the pretence. He is detached from the group, hands on hips, head bowed. He puts on his T-shirt and queues for his medal, but he cannot raise a smile to pretend everything is OK. Eventually, when he has seen enough, he leaves everyone to it and heads to the tunnel.

His medal is stuffed in his pocket when he leaves the stadium an hour later. He is alone, utterly dejected, and he doesn't want to talk to the media. When he passes through the interview area and we ask him to stop he completely blanks us, which is out of character.

Ferguson, wearing his poker face, tells us that Van Nistelrooy accepted the decision that he should be left out. But we are not sure whether to believe him. The team was leaked beforehand to the *Daily Mirror*, whose Manchester reporter, David McDonnell, is convinced there has been a major fallout and, potentially, an irreparable rift. Ferguson, it is said, doesn't like Van Nistelrooy's attitude. Van Nistelrooy is alleged to have reacted badly to the news, angry enough to challenge his manager in front of the other players. There are rumours of a huge row in the dressing room. But Ferguson denies everything. Nothing sinister should be read into it, he insists. His explanation is that nobody can take a place for granted at a club such as Manchester United, not even the most prolific goal-scorer in the country. Van Nistelrooy is disappointed, he says, but he cannot please everyone. Saha deserves his chance because he has scored in earlier rounds of the competition. That, he insists, is all there is to say on the matter.

'I've explained my reasons to Ruud. It's not about who the best player is or who has scored the most goals. It's about who deserves to play. And how could I leave out Saha?'

Soon afterwards things go pear-shaped. A guy in the front row changes the topic to bring up Ferguson's future.

'Alex, there has been a lot of talk in the build-up to this match about you being under a lot of pressure,' he says. 'Do you think this victory buys you some time?'

'Buy me time?' Ferguson says incredulously. Suddenly his mouth is twisted and his eyes have narrowed into ominous slits. 'Buy me time? Dearie me … that's a good one, son.' He is smiling, shaking his head as if he finds it hugely amusing. But his eyes scream: how fucking dare you?

'Let me tell you something,' he says, his voice steadily rising. 'The problem you press have got is that you don't get any titbits out of Manchester United any more. The Glazers are in America and won't speak to you. David Gill gives you nothing, absolutely nothing. All your wee sources have been cut off at the very top of the club. And because of that, you invent stuff in your own minds. Your imagination is amazing. But listen, you haven't got a clue! Not a bloody clue! And on that note …' He rises from his seat.

'Congratulations anyway,' someone pipes up.

'Bye bye.'

THE COMEDOWN
6.3.06

Wigan Athletic	1
Manchester United	2

When you win eight Premiership titles in eleven seasons, as United did from 1992 to 2003, the bar tends to be set rather high. 'Thanks, Sir Alex, but now go,' is the headline on the United Rant fans' website. 'Take this trophy as your last hurrah and let the club make a fresh start. It's a trophy – not an important one – but some silverware nonetheless. Go with your head held high.'

It is no way to say thank you. When Ferguson took over at Old Trafford the club had not won the league for nineteen years. Since then, they have won seventeen major trophies compared to Arsenal's twelve, Liverpool's ten and Chelsea's five. They have won the double twice, an unprecedented treble and they had their boot on the head of English football for a decade until Abramovich stepped off his helicopter. At the height of Ferguson's powers, a full-page advert for MUTV in the matchday programme showed a skip outside Old Trafford overflowing with empty tins of silver polish.

And yet this year the facts are stark. No Europe. No Premiership. No FA Cup. No open-top bus parades. If they close Deansgate to show off the Carling Cup, can you imagine supporters shinning up lamp posts and hanging over balconies to get a better view?

Chelsea fans are getting merry on *las Ramblas* tonight ahead of a glamour tie against Barcelona and Champions League billboards are being bolted into place at Arsenal and Liverpool. All United have is a Monday night game on a soulless industrial estate on the outskirts of Wigan. They win again, courtesy of a late own-goal and with Van Nistelrooy once more on the bench. But the JJB Stadium is not the Nou Camp or the San Siro. The Champions League feels a lifetime away as we look across the pitch at hoardings advertising Poolies Pies and Uncle Joe's Mint Balls.

Cardiff was a good day out and the supporters inside the Millennium Stadium seemed genuinely happy, but tonight the reality sinks in. United usually have the loudest away following in the country, yet they watch long spells in virtual silence. This is not where they want to be.

MOVING ON
12.3.06

Manchester United	2
Newcastle United	0

Ferguson skipped his press conference yesterday but popped up later in Salford, opening a new sports centre and generally charming everyone – until he realised a small group of journalists had been invited. He agreed to take a few questions, but couldn't resist having a little dig first. 'Do you have to follow me everywhere?'

He has been sore since the Carling Cup final because of the negative reaction in the newspapers. *The Times*, for example, has described it as 'a significant trophy only to those who haven't got a pot to pee in'. The final was not sold out and some of the United fans did not even stay to see the presentation of the trophy. The *Daily Mail* has likened the crowd to 'a suburban father whose daughter had just married an anarchist with a bolt through his nose – it wasn't the one they wanted but they did their best to look delighted and not to wince when the champagne started flowing'.

Ferguson has taken it personally. 'Some bright spark might have dubbed it the Worthless Cup but we have never regarded it in that light,' he says in his programme notes today. 'I find it irritating when people suggest we changed our tune when it became our last chance of a trophy. Nothing of the sort. We've never regarded it with anything but respect.'

He has been banging this drum ever since United reached the final. But it is not an argument he is going to win. Before kick-off today, souvenir stalls on Sir

Matt Busby Way are selling T-shirts commemorating the 1999 treble, along with photographs and posters of past cup finals and victories over sworn enemies such as Liverpool and Manchester City. But there is nothing to commemorate the Carling Cup – no T-shirts, no flags, no banners. Inside the stadium it is the same. The trophy isn't paraded before the match, the public announcer doesn't introduce the team as the '2006 Carling Cup winners' and there are no chants of 'Championes' or photo opportunities beside the silverware. It isn't even the main picture on the front of the programme. United play some outstanding football, with Rooney scoring twice and twenty-one efforts on goal, but this is no victorious homecoming.

'This is Manchester United we are talking about,' according to *Red Issue*. 'This is a club whose fans christened that trophy the Worthless Cup. Will our win in Cardiff be talked about for years to come like so many fantastic finals in the club's history? Not a chance. A lot of Reds have probably forgotten about it already.'

THE GOOD COP
17.3.06

There are still two months of the season to go but at Carrington it feels as if preparations for summer are already under way. The car park is virtually empty today, there isn't a single truant or Japanese tourist hoping to snatch a glimpse of the players from behind the electronic barriers and the guy in the security cabin waves us through without lifting his eyes from his copy of the *Daily Star*. Ferguson is in Glasgow for the funeral of Jimmy Johnstone, the former Scotland international, so Carlos Queiroz takes the press conference.

Queiroz is a polite, intelligent man and it is difficult not to warm to him. He has kind eyes, a genuine smile and time for everyone. He has become an object of ridicule to some supporters but Ferguson won't hear a word said against him. He has worked on four continents, he is multi-lingual and, at Real Madrid, he was in charge of three former World Footballers of the Year. Queiroz, more than most, knows what it takes to be a top player.

This is his second stint at Old Trafford. During his first spell the media had even begun to talk of him as manager-in-waiting. Queiroz was the approachable half of a good-cop/bad-cop partnership. He frequently lost us with his funny little sayings – 'it is not right to sit behind the tree and spit' – but there was something endearing about his long, rambling speeches and his Tony Ferrino accent. We appreciated the fact that he was generous with his time and happy to pass his numbers to journalists he trusted. We liked him and we genuinely thought he liked us.

But earlier this season he fell out with us. And it was a silly row, totally avoidable.

Queiroz was interviewed by the Portuguese newspaper *O Jogo* after the home defeat to Blackburn. When the interview appeared in print, a Lisbon-based freelance journalist by the name of Victor Vago sent the English newspapers a transcript. 'People have been crying out for us to use a 4-4-2 formation but in the Blackburn game we tried the system the fans have been demanding and we lost,' he quoted Queiroz. 'That's why football is a game in which imagination and, on many occasions, stupidity has no limits.'

Supporters were furious at the use of the word 'stupidity' when it appeared in the English newspapers. Football fans tend not to appreciate being described as stupid when they are spending fortunes following their club. Outraged messages were posted on internet chatrooms and angry emails sent to the newspapers before a statement appeared on United's website: 'Carlos Queiroz says comments attributed to him in the English press were falsely translated. "The fans of Manchester United deserve more than this blatant attempt to divide the club," Queiroz commented.'

Quotes can often be misinterpreted from foreign newspapers. But this was all rather odd. One by one, we started ringing journalists in Portugal and every time the same message came back: that Queiroz had been quoted accurately.

'Por isso é que o futebol é um jogo em que a imaginação e, muitas vezes, a estupidez não têm limites.'

He was waiting for us at Carrington the next day, shaking his head and wringing his hands, extremely agitated.

'After thirty-five years in the game I shouldn't be surprised by what football can throw up but sometimes it is hard to believe these things can happen,' he told us. 'Thanks to you, this has been a very uncomfortable period for me. You are trying to create factions between the club and the supporters.'

'But Carlos, we've double-checked and triple-checked that quote and we've been told it's word perfect. Maybe if you could explain exactly what you said we could look again to see if there was a misunderstanding.'

This was the only time we have seen him lose his temper. He didn't pin anyone up against a wall, he didn't rant or rave and he didn't swear. But we could detect his anger. We let him say his piece about being misquoted and treated unfairly and then we left.

SUNDAYS
25.3.06

Another no-show from Ferguson today, although he has sent a message that he will see us for ten minutes on Tuesday, his first midweek appearance since the 74-second walkout in December. The official line is that we are being rewarded for our good behaviour. United have won five in a row and words such as 'shoddy' and 'dismal' have stopped appearing in our match reports. Ferguson no longer has to pick up the newspapers with industrial gloves and metal tongs.

The twist is in his relationship with the Sunday newspaper journalists.

These guys are, on average, a few years older than us and, traditionally, they have always got on better with Ferguson than we have. They have been on the circuit longer and he knows their faces better, so he feels that he can trust them more. He's willing to debate with them delicate subjects that he refuses to discuss with us. They are older and greyer and he feels safer in their company.

Except that Ferguson has been in a foul mood with them since a 3–1 defeat to Manchester City in January, after which they reported that he had flown into a rage with the referee, Steve Bennett, at half-time. Ferguson thought Ronaldo was being kicked out of the game and, according to the Sundays, he allegedly screamed in Bennett's face: 'You fucking cheating bastard. You're going to need a police escort to get you out of here.'

There was talk of the FA getting involved and of Ferguson facing a fine, maybe even a touchline ban. But the FA's disciplinary department didn't think it necessary to do anything when they looked at Bennett's match report. What's more, Ferguson says the quote about needing a 'police escort' was invented. He has admitted having a go at Bennett but categorically denies making the threats that appeared in the newspapers. He says there was libellous spin attached and he has demanded a letter of apology, signed by all the reporters and stating, unequivocally, that their stories were exaggerated and inaccurate.

The Sundays say they have nothing to apologise for and that their source is impeccable, but they are under the impression that if they do what he asks he will call a truce and go back to giving them separate briefings rather than all-in press conferences. Desperate to reopen their best lines of contact, they have swallowed their pride and drafted a request for forgiveness that does not admit to any serious wrongdoing. There is something along the lines of 'we're sorry if you have taken any offence', but nothing that amounts to an admission of guilt. Nonetheless, it is an apology, which is what Ferguson asked for.

All that is left is for the relevant journalists to sign it and deliver it to Old Trafford – but then Ferguson has a sudden change of mind.

He has decided that he has been far too easy on everyone. An email has been sent to the reporters, via United's press office, explaining that he has been thinking it over and now wants an apology printed in every newspaper that carried the offending quote.

We daily reporters have been watching this affair unfold with a mixture of relief and bemusement. Relief because it is not us in the firing line, bemusement because Ferguson understands our industry well enough to know he is asking for something that will never happen. No national newspaper is going to print an apology for a story they believe to be true – and they are definitely not all going to do it simultaneously.

An impasse has been reached. The best the Sundays can hope for now is that Ferguson, in time, will be able to put it behind him. Everything is so fast-moving at Old Trafford that these arguments eventually get brushed under the carpet.

THE LOCALS
13.4.06

Ferguson gives a reporter on the *Manchester Evening News* a blast at the end of his press conference today. Stuart Mathieson is a really good guy and a respected journalist but Ferguson is notoriously suspicious of the *Evening News* and takes offence to a question about FC United of Manchester.

FC United have divided opinion in Manchester and they are high on Ferguson's list of taboo subjects. They

were set up by a splinter group of supporters so disen-
chanted with the politics at United after the Glazers'
takeover that they decided to form a breakaway club
and since then they have gone from strength to strength,
developing a loyal following and becoming recognised
as having the best away support in non-professional
football.

It has started to irritate a few people at Old Trafford.
Little United, as they have become known, have
attracted bigger crowds in the North West Counties
Football League than some professional clubs get in
League One and League Two and their aim is to be in
the Football League before 2012. After they won their
first promotion this week, the *Evening News* had
visions of carrying a back-page story about Ferguson
offering the 'Rebels' the hand of friendship.

'Alex, do you have any words of congratulation for
FC United and their manager, Karl Marginson?'
Mathieson asks.

He has waited until the end, just as Ferguson is
preparing to leave. But it is immediately obvious that
the *Evening News* has made an error of judgement.
Ferguson's eyes narrow and he peers menacingly
over the table.

'Who?'

'Karl Marginson, and the job he's done at FC
United?'

'You're joking, right?' says Ferguson, instinctively
rising from his seat.

The press conference finishes abruptly and he is
still muttering about it as he marches to the door. 'Not
interested! Not interested!'

The *Evening News* has a tough time with Ferguson.
Most football managers regard the local newspaper

correspondent as a confidant and ally, granting him or her special treatment. But the *Evening News* is not afforded anything like the same access at United that they get at Manchester City, or that other regional newspapers are allowed at their respective clubs.

Ferguson's opinion of the *Evening News* has never fully recovered since the newspaper conducted a phone-in poll in 1995 asking whether he should resign. The club was going through a difficult period in the league and Ferguson had expected more support because of the preferential treatment he'd given to David Meek, the newspaper's United correspondent at the time. Ferguson thought it was a kick in the teeth and the *Evening News* has suffered ever since. 'I don't think our local paper does us any favours,' he said once, 'so I'm reluctant to do it any in return.'

The irony is that Ferguson's relationship with Meek was strengthened by what happened. 'He was having a hard time and the majority of people who responded to the poll said he should be fired,' Meek recalls. 'The figures were presented to me to write the story but my view was that he didn't deserve to be sacked, so I questioned how many Manchester City supporters had voted and how many United fans simply couldn't be bothered to pick up the phone because they were happy with him in charge. I presented it as an overwhelming vote of confidence and, in his eyes, that cemented me as a Fergie man. I'd proved to him I wasn't against him. You have to do that with Alex, because he can be implacable if he thinks he has an enemy.'

Meek, who is still on the scene in a freelance capacity, remains that rare thing: a journalist whom Ferguson admires. He worked for the *Evening News* for nearly forty years, from the Munich air crash in

1958, and he has gradually become an unofficial extension of the club's PR department. He and Ferguson have had a few barneys in their time. Ferguson gave him an almighty dressing down one Christmas Eve. 'Happy bloody Christmas,' Meek shouted back. Yet he never writes anything about Ferguson that could be construed as critical. He ghost-writes Ferguson's programme notes, collaborates with him on books and frequently rails against his critics in the fanzine / internet world.

Ferguson, in turn, shows Meek a side of his personality that the rest of us glimpse only occasionally. He gives him his phone numbers and is always available. Meek, he says, is 'entirely trustworthy' and 'part of the fabric of the club'.

SQUEAKY-BUM TIME
14.4.06

Manchester United	0
Sunderland	0

It is that point of the season when newspapers start referring to 'squeaky-bum time'. It was 2003 when we first used this odd little phrase and, to our disbelief, it is now recycled every Easter. Disbelief because the truth – the awful truth – is that we don't know for certain that Ferguson ever said it.

We'd been interviewing him during one of those epic title battles with Arsenal. Ferguson was using the media to unnerve Arsène Wenger, questioning whether Arsenal's players had the mental strength to hold out, and when we played back the tape to transcribe his quotes we couldn't make out whether he had called it 'squeaky-bum time' or 'squeeze-your-bum time'. He speaks in a drawling rasp, with that broad Glaswegian accent, and there are times when it sounds as though he is talking in a different language. So we ended up taking a vote. Four went for squeaky-bum, three thought it was squeeze-your-bum and two could not decide.

The majority ruled and 'squeaky-bum time' is now an accepted part of the football lexicon. Other managers have started using it as if it is an everyday phrase and it has even reached the *Collins English Dictionary*, where it is defined as 'the tense final stages of a league competition, especially from the point of view of the leaders'.

It is difficult to imagine that Jose Mourinho's bum is very squeaky right now, and we certainly aren't going to find out this season. United have been on a good run of form recently but any hope of catching Chelsea disappears tonight. The gap has come down to six points, having been eighteen at one stage, but United have only four games left and if they were going to stand any chance of making up the difference they really had to beat Sunderland, the Premiership's bottom club. Chelsea have two games in hand and in Ferguson's words, it is the 'killer blow'.

Sunderland are a very poor side. They have had the chilly fingers of relegation around their throat all season, with only eleven points from thirty-two games. They have scored twenty-one goals and conceded fifty-seven and Ferguson describes them, a little uncharitably, as possibly the worst team there has ever been in the Premiership. But when the final whistle goes they have deserved their point and might even have nicked it with a late winner. The Sunderland fans can be heard in the corner, while Ferguson looks dead on his feet. 'We need a miracle now,' he says. 'We won't give up but it's going to take a miracle.'

A manager in his position cannot accept defeat. Deep down, though, Ferguson knows it is all over. All that is left now are the formalities, with one last twist of the dagger when United go to Stamford Bridge in their final away match of the season. Either Chelsea will have won the title by then, or possibly they will clinch it against United. Either way, the trophy will be presented at the final whistle and for Ferguson, it doesn't get much worse than that. This is one party to which he doesn't want an invitation.

BLUE IS THE COLOUR
30.4.06

Chelsea	3
Manchester United	0

It has been a long, difficult season and Ferguson's eyes are red-rimmed as he leaves Stamford Bridge. The worry lines jump out of his face, the bags beneath his eyes are even more super-sized than usual. There is only a week of the season left and then he is off for a five-week holiday with Cathy on the French Riviera. He looks as though he needs it.

He handles himself with dignity. An upright back, a thousand-yard stare. The trophy is adorned with blue and white ribbons and, as far as Ferguson is concerned, out of reach. He grits his teeth and puts on his war face, determined not to be a sour loser. He makes a point of shaking Mourinho's hand as well as those of all the Chelsea backroom staff, and he is generous in his praise: 'It is not easy winning the league and Chelsea deserve it. They don't lose games at home and their record this season has been sensational. I would like to congratulate them because they are worthy champions.'

But he is long gone by the time the Chelsea players embark on the champions' lap of honour, hugging and high-fiving and taking turns to give each other piggybacks. The Chelsea Pensioners form a guard of honour, Mourinho crosses his heart and Stamford Bridge rocks to the sound of 40,000 gloating Cockney voices.

Who the fuck are Man United?
Who the fuck are Man United?
Who the fuck are Man United?
As the Blues go marching on, on, on.

There is a sad, mournful look about Ferguson as he leaves the stadium. A street party is under way – lots of bare-chested blokes swigging plastic cups of beer, sprawled all over the pavements – and he has a lot to think about as the bus inches its way through the celebrating throngs. What has gone wrong, what needs to be put right, who should stay and who has to go.

United have some great players, but a smattering of world-class talent isn't always enough. Too often this season their tactics, especially away from home, have been no more refined than getting the ball to

Rooney and hoping he does something to win the game. Rooney is certain to win the club's Player of the Season award, but he cannot always be expected to scintillate on demand. You cannot operate a team to rely solely on one player, however brilliant that individual might be.

If Ferguson is going to wipe that smile from Mourinho's face there will have to be changes. And they might have to be significant changes, because maybe only Rooney, Ronaldo, Giggs, Neville and Van der Sar can legitimately argue that they have played to their best form throughout the season. Scholes is exempt, having missed half the campaign with an eye problem, and Van Nistelrooy's confidence has not been helped by being left out of the team. Others, though, will reflect on a difficult year. Ferdinand's form has been so erratic that he lost his England place at one stage. Park has been in and out of the team, unable to make a serious impact. The same applies to Patrice Evra and Nemanja Vidic, who were signed in January for a combined £11 million. Before his injury, Smith had taken over Keane's role, and that is exactly what he looked: a centre-forward playing in midfield. Heinze has been badly missed because Silvestre, once a mainstay in defence, is no longer good enough for the highest level.

As for Ferguson, he deserves better than to be lambasted. Equally, though, there have been times when he has sounded like the captain of the *Titanic*, waving away all warnings and ordering full speed ahead. He has described it as a 'transitional period' and he likes to argue that the current side is a young one lacking maturity and experience. Yet anyone with a calculator would know that is simply not true. The average age is older than that of the 1999 team and the only two players below the age of twenty-four, Rooney and Ronaldo, are established internationals with experience of major tournaments.

The truth is that United are ending the season in no-man's-land: too good for the vast majority of the Premiership, yet no longer strong enough to challenge for the league or the European Cup. In 1991, Nick Hornby wrote in *Fever Pitch* that fans of Manchester United were 'imbued with frustrated grandeur' and now, after a period of great joy and success, Old Trafford is once again engulfed in a grey blanket of negativity. Chelsea have the title sewn up, Liverpool are in the FA Cup final and when Arsenal and Barcelona walk out on to the Stade de France pitch for the Champions League final next month it will have been seven long years since United triumphed in Europe. It's four since the club even made the semi-finals.

The answer is not to get rid of Ferguson – the Glazers would be foolish if they even thought of it. True, Ferguson might not be the autocratic presence he once was, and, yes, he has made a bit of a pig's ear of this season. But he still has the complete respect of the players. And the point is: who could do a better job? That is the question the Glazers have to ask themselves. Because when a man with Ferguson's force of personality is involved, finding someone who is equipped to take the job and able to shift the club forward will be fiendishly difficult.

This might be Ferguson's *annus horribilis* but he is still powerful enough to control great swathes of the Old Trafford workforce. He can still silence a room when he walks through the door and, when he does finally retire, whoever fills his shoes will have to possess unbreakable self-belief. Every trophy, every memorable achievement, every European campaign will be set against his predecessor's medal count. Every defeat or substandard performance will be greeted with sniping that he is 'not a patch on the last guy'. A new appointment will have to work against a backdrop of endless comparisons, in a stadium lined with photographs of Ferguson's greatest achievements. History has shown that it will require a man of exceptional qualities, if such a man exists. Take Nottingham Forest, post-Brian Clough. 'All I ever got was the history of the club rammed down my throat,' Joe Kinnear once said, reflecting on what it was like to be Clough's seventh successor. 'I couldn't fart without someone bringing up the European Cups he won.'

All that matters to Ferguson is going out on a high, whether it is in two years, five years or ten years, and that can mean one of only two things: recapturing the Premiership or the European Cup. Either achievement has seemed unreachable this season and will continue to be so unless he makes some courageous decisions.

His career has been distinguished by clear thinking and instinctive decision-making, but if one thing has badly let United down it is the absence, since Keane, of a truly exceptional midfield. Once, the quartet was Beckham, Keane, Scholes and Giggs. Ferguson must realise he will not outdo Abramovich's millions by packing his midfield with players such as Fletcher, O'Shea, Smith and Richardson. He has even tried Ferdinand, a centre-half, and Rooney, a centre-forward. Both times the experiment predictably failed.

Perhaps Scholes can come back next season and show he is still a player of authentic brilliance, the most stylish English midfielder of his generation. Ronaldo has demonstrated that he may be on the point of making a significant mark. Giggs is still a beautifully ingenious player and Park may find his second season easier. But the problem is that Chelsea have the money and the players to dominate English football for years to come. Some people think what Chelsea are doing is great, others think it is boring. But nobody questions the inevitability of it. Chelsea are that much better, that much richer, that much more powerful.

Twelve minutes from the end, Rooney goes down under a heavy tackle and breaks a bone in his foot. He is carried away on a stretcher and, after that, United lose hope. Chelsea are already 3–0 ahead, winning from the fourth minute, and they start to showboat, juggling with the ball, keeping possession, lapping up the crowd's approval. Little flicks here, little flicks there. The fans start the celebrations early, chanting 'Olé' whenever a player in a blue shirt touches the ball, thundering 'Easy, easy, easy' in the manner of the old wrestling chant. It is a party. Ferguson watches grimly from the sidelines, hardly uttering a word.

Mourinho comes over to the United dugout with two minutes to play to offer an outstretched arm. Ferguson will not have liked that when the game is still going on, but he chooses not to make a scene and shakes hands respectfully. He stays on his feet to wait for the final whistle, raises a dutiful arm in the direction of the United fans and then he is down the tunnel and out of sight. The rest, he does not want to see.

RUUD VAN NISTELROOY
7.5.06

Manchester United	4
Charlton Athletic	0

In happier times, the final game of the season at Old Trafford would be a riot of flags, banners and general redness. The players' wives would totter on to the pitch after the final whistle. Ferguson would walk out to the centre circle, take the microphone and thank the fans for their support. The trophies would be paraded on a lap of honour and the players' kids would join them on the pitch for a kick-about.

Not this year. United have ended the season as football's equivalent of the Rolling Stones. Struggling to find their old magic, a little frayed round the edges. No satisfaction. Everybody's tired, looking forward to a break. Not only tired physically, but emotionally. There is nobody milling about on Sir Matt Busby Way trying to blag a ticket. All the touts are in position but business is slow. The season is drifting into anticlimax and there are other, more significant stories going on elsewhere. Relegations, promotions, Arsenal's final game at Highbury, the battle for the fourth Champions League spot. For once, Old Trafford isn't the place to be.

And yet they still manage to make News at Ten.

Ferguson has asked the players to arrive early for a team meeting and a spot of lunch. When they start drifting in he is waiting for Ruud Van Nistelrooy. There is an exchange of words and Van Nistelrooy is told, in no uncertain terms, to go home. On his way out he passes the other players.

'Good luck with the match,' he says. 'I'm off.' The whole thing has taken no more than five minutes.

When the rumours start to filter through to the pressroom Van Nistelrooy is already at Manchester airport, booked on the first flight to Amsterdam. The team-sheets are handed out forty-five minutes before kick-off and Giuseppe Rossi, a teenager from the reserves, is playing in attack. A one-line statement is passed around to say Van Nistelrooy has left the stadium and won't be coming back. Keane has already been fed to the sharks and now it is Van Nistelrooy's turn. Today, in this stadium, we know it is all over for him.

Old Trafford is in a state of shock when the game gets under way. The news spreads like a Mexican wave and for long spells the fans hardly seem to be paying attention to what is happening on the pitch. Winning confirms second place above Liverpool and it is Alan Curbishley's farewell match after fifteen years as Charlton's manager, but there is only one point of discussion in the stands. The supporters are barely able to take it in.

First Keane, now Van Nistelrooy. Who next?

The mood at the final whistle is strange: polite applause mingled with confusion and disillusionment and a desire to get a proper explanation. Yet none is forthcoming. Ferguson, as always, ignores the post-match press conference, while on MUTV all he offers is a couple of ambiguous sentences. 'There have been a couple of issues that have concerned me in terms of the team spirit,' he says. 'It was such an important day I wanted everyone to be together and because of that I felt Ruud should be left out. But that's all I want to say about it at the moment.'

His voice is hoarse, but his words are clear and emphatic. He says he will discuss it with the club's directors and he briefly refers to an incident in training. We later find out that Van Nistelrooy had a shoving match with Ronaldo because he hadn't passed him the ball. Van Nistelrooy is twenty-nine, Ronaldo twenty-one. A manager has to respond to something like that and Ferguson chose to side with Ronaldo.

So much doesn't make sense. It was obvious that there would have to be changes, but nobody thought the clearout would begin with the club's most prolific striker since Denis Law. Van Nistelrooy has been a truly great player for Manchester United. Only eight strikers in the club's history have scored 150 times or more and he did it in just five seasons. Clinical finishing, anticipation, the nerve of a bomb-disposal expert. His goals in Europe alone have repaid his £19 million transfer fee. Yet it is this one-man goal machine – not Richardson or Fletcher or O'Shea or any of the other United players who would struggle to get on Chelsea's bench – who has been sacrificed.

Reliable sources at the club say he and Ferguson have stopped communicating since he was dropped for the Carling Cup final. Ferguson has started to think of Van Nistelrooy as a threat to team morale. He has been studying Van Nistelrooy's body language, grievance building on grievance, and has started to feel that his authority is being challenged.

The newspapers have picked up on it. Van Nistelrooy has been linked to a new club every week – Tottenham, Newcastle, AC Milan, Roma, Inter Milan, Bayern Munich and, in the last few days, Real Madrid. Publicly he has said very little but, in private, he has made it clear he cannot accept Ferguson's reasons for not including him in the biggest match of the season. Inter's president, Massimo Moratti, has described it as an open secret that Van Nistelrooy is 'not happy in Manchester'.

Nobody, however, expected this and the supporters are entitled to be angry. Ferguson even went on MUTV to deny reports of a rift, telling viewers to ignore 'all this stupid talk in the papers'. David Gill went further, saying that the fans should pay no attention to 'mischief-making' and insisting there wasn't a word of truth in it. 'If you are looking to improve your squad you are not going to sell a player who can deliver twenty-five to thirty goals a season. Ruud is very much part of our plans and we are looking forward to him playing a part in what should be a successful next season.'

Somehow it feels appropriate that the season should end on a note like this – controversial and shocking.

United may have won the Carling Cup but Ferguson will still remember this season with all the affection reserved for appendicitis: early elimination from the Champions League, the abuse he suffered during the Blackburn game, humiliation against Burton Albion, the breakdown of his relationship with Keane, the unwanted takeover by the Glazer family, the near-incessant speculation about his future and, now, a parting of the ways with Van Nistelrooy.

This is supposed to be the autumn of Ferguson's career but it has felt more like its winter, harsh and unforgiving. It has been the season when fans have called for him to be sacked, the press have parked their tanks on his lawn and his relationship with the media has hit an all-time low. It has been the season of Chelsea, Jose Mourinho, Frank Lampard, John Terry ... and FC United of Manchester.

Winning today at least guarantees an automatic place in the Champions League and a little more Premiership prize money, which will not go unnoticed by the Glazers. But it has been three years since United could call themselves champions. The mentality of this club is that second is first-last, that nobody remembers who finished second. Ferguson began the season wanting to fight the world. He has ended it looking solemn and depressed and in need of a holiday. The beautiful game can seem very ugly when seen through tired eyes.

2006–07
Annus mirabilis

GODZILLA
18.8.06

We asked Ferguson once whether he had mellowed. We wanted to know about his temper. How did he sustain that blowtorch of a personality? And was it true, as some of his old Scottish acquaintances say, that he had lost some of the harder edges? One of the things that is often said about Ferguson is that he operated on a shorter leash when he was younger and that he is more of an avuncular figure now than twenty or thirty years ago. It is said he does not shout at his players with the same ferocity or regularity. 'I'm a pussycat compared to what I used to be like,' he told us.

He found it all rather amusing. He said he had lost some of that inner rage and, teasing him, we rolled our eyes disbelievingly. But he insisted it was true. He said he was far more aggressive when he was younger and he told us a story about when he was St Mirren's player-manager, in 1976, and took them on a pre-season tour of the Caribbean, where the games included a 'friendly' against the Guyana national team.

'They had this one guy at the back and he was absolutely huge,' he said. 'He was built like Godzilla and he was kicking the shit out of one of our strikers. I was watching from the touchline, getting more and more wound up. I wasn't even a sub but I got my boots on for the last fifteen minutes and I was going: "Let me at him." I had to do something about it.'

He was clearly very fond of this story, laughingly confessing his shame, as if he could scarcely believe it was himself he was talking about.

'I can remember my assistant, big Davie Provan, pleading with me: "Don't do it, don't, I know what you'll do, I know what you're like." But when you're younger you've got that stupid courage, haven't you? I couldn't help myself and, first chance, I took him out.'

We were all laughing now. 'Oh, I was sent off,' he continued, 'but it never got out. I made sure of that. I went into the dressing room afterwards and I told the players: "If anyone ever talks about this I'll find out who it is and I'll kill you."'

He can laugh about this side of himself sometimes: the way others see him with devil horns and steam coming out of his ears. On other occasions, though, it gets on his nerves. Drives him barmy. 'How do you want me to be?' he will ask. 'Why can't you just accept me for the way I am rather than constantly analysing my manner and temperament?'

What he doesn't seem to grasp is that there is nobody like him anywhere else in football. Television may have sanitised his press conferences but we are still wary around him. It's all in his eyes. Testing you, checking you out, looking for vulnerable areas. Trying to put you on the back foot. Always probing. They may be a touch rheumy these days but one injudicious remark or question and those eyes will be screaming 'don't go there'. Or the demons will overtake him and Lord help you if you are in his way.

One interviewer once asked him if he ever regretted it and he said, yes, sometimes he 'wished it had been with somebody six foot ten. Sometimes it's a small guy, sometimes it's a medium-sized guy. I've no discrimination that way. Sometimes there's guilt. Sometimes you say to yourself, "Why did I do that?"

But if someone argues with me I have to win the argument. So I start heading towards them. That's where the hairdryer comes in. I can't lose an argument. The manager can never lose an argument.'

And the hairdryer tag? 'It was started by Mark Hughes. I can understand it because of my policy in the dressing room. When somebody challenges me in there, I have to go for them. That's me, you know. I believe you cannot avoid the confrontation.'

There was nothing wrong, he said, in losing your temper. 'You still have to create a little spark sometimes. If it's in your nature to lose your temper, let it out. Don't keep it bottled up otherwise you can end up growling and kicking doors and not getting across what you actually feel. I've thrown more teacups across the dressing room than I can tell you. But as far as I'm concerned, anger is not a problem. Losing your temper is OK – as long as you do it for the right reasons.'

Fair enough. Yet Ferguson once complained to another interviewer that the public perception of him was flawed. The truth, he said, was that he didn't shout half as much as people made out. 'I've lost my temper over the years, but every manager has lost his temper at some time. There's a lot of myth. The hairdryer and the teacups are just a couple of examples.'

He blamed the press for creating the monster. 'I read one article, it was in a supposedly responsible, quality newspaper and it said that when I started in management I used to go behind the stand at East Stirlingshire to practise losing my temper. I was going to say you couldn't make it up, but somebody obviously has! Have you ever heard such nonsense?'

It is certainly difficult to imagine that those explosions of rage are rehearsed in private or planned with strategic motives. Equally, though, it isn't always easy to believe he has mellowed. At times last season he lost his temper so often that it became almost monotonous. When journalists questioned him he resorted to confrontation as if it were his default position. The more he felt under threat and struggled to get his own way, the more combative and sour he became. He accused us of hating Manchester United, which was simply untrue.

This is a new season, possibly a new start. A new season brings new hopes. Yet it has been another summer when the fault lines have cracked open and he has kept us a very long arm's length away. On a pre-season tour of South Africa, Ferguson was the guest speaker at a charity dinner at Turffontein racecourse, where he apparently accused Chelsea of being 'hell-bent on ruining football' because of the way they threw money around. Unbeknown to him, a news reporter from the *Johannesburg Star* was taking notes in the audience and Ferguson's comments appeared in print the next day. It was blown up into a huge row and he had to issue a statement saying he had been misinterpreted. 'It's unfortunate,' he said, 'that you cannot go to a dinner these days without someone sneakily reporting everything you say.'

That particular argument has had repercussions for everyone in the Manchester press pack. It had nothing to do with the English newspapers and many of us actually sympathised with him. But it has felt as though we are getting the blame anyway, just for being part of the same industry.

On the same tour, a reporter from the *Daily Mirror* asked him whether after three years without the league title he felt under increased pressure.

Ferguson exploded.

He has drawn a firm demarcation line between himself and us. The press-conference restrictions he brought in as a 'trial' last season are to remain in force. What's more, he has stopped his players from having newspaper columns because he is unhappy about the number of stories coming out from the dressing room, predominantly the spat between Ronaldo and Van Nistelrooy. Ferdinand has had to tear up his contract with the *Sun* and Neville has severed his ties with *The Times* (though neither player was responsible for the leak). Rooney's people have been speaking to the *News of the World* but that is dead in the water now.

Today, though, we see other layers of Ferguson's personality. When he comes through the double doors at Carrington he is smiling and has his arm draped around David Meek's shoulder. He answers all our questions with long, considered responses. He is bubbly and confident, happily talking up United's chances.

'We're disappointed about what happened last season but we think we've got a great chance this year. We've got some fantastic players at this club. If we get a bit of luck and keep the players injury free there's no reason why we can't do it. We know the target we must aim for this season. We have to hit the ground running and keep it that way.'

It has not been an easy summer, though. In the World Cup, Rooney was sent off after stamping on Ricardo Carvalho, a Chelsea player, before England went out on penalties against Portugal in the quarter-finals. The winning kick was taken by Ronaldo, who has come back to England to find his windows smashed and enough hate mail to fill a freight train.

Ronaldo was caught on camera winking to the Portuguese bench after telling the referee that Rooney deserved a red card and, among other indignities, the *Sun* have superimposed his face on a pullout dartboard. It has been a shabby campaign of vilification and Ronaldo has spent much of the summer trying to engineer a move to Spain, openly confessing that he did not want to return to Old Trafford and had made up his mind that he wanted to play for Barcelona or Real Madrid. Ferguson has had to pick up the pieces and he has done so brilliantly, not only persuading Ronaldo to change his mind but making sure there are no lingering problems between him and Rooney. Even so, it is a delicate situation and Ronaldo will have to show immense inner strength to survive the coming season. He was never the most popular player with opposition supporters and wherever United play from now on, great flows of invective will be unleashed on that gelled quiff.

The other headline news is that Van Nistelrooy has been sold to Real Madrid for £10 million, which seems an extraordinarily low fee and has gone down badly with the supporters. There has been lots of propaganda and promises about possible signings but the only new arrivals are Michael Carrick, a midfielder, for £18 million from Spurs and Tomasz Kuszczak, a goalkeeper, on loan from West Brom. Chelsea have added half a dozen new players, including two former European Footballers of the Year in Andriy Shevchenko and Michael Ballack, and a lot of United fans are thinking the worst already. They have been singing Van Nistelrooy's name in the pre-season games, showing their support for a player they always appreciated. But when we asked Ferguson in pre-season about the fans being unhappy he refused to accept that was the case, snapping that there was no evidence whatsoever.

A NEW BEGINNING
20.8.06

| Manchester United | 5 |
| Fulham | 1 |

There is always something therapeutic about the first game. When we leave in May everyone is knackered, maybe a little disillusioned, but those three months off are like balm and today there is a buzz of excitement again. The sun is shining and Old Trafford looks magnificent, with a new roof and a new capacity. Seventy-six thousand faces. Four vertiginous stands, all packed.

And United, minus Van Nistelrooy, make a statement of intent today. They look confident, purposeful and determined and they play a brand of football so exhilarating it is at total odds with the image we have conjured up in our minds, that of a team in need of rehabilitation and nursing bruised egos.

It is only one game and we should not be sucked into that classic journalistic trap, the knee-jerk reaction, yet it is difficult not to feel a surge of genuine excitement. Rooney plays as though he is on first-name terms with the ball. Scholes radiates confidence, showing United what they missed last season. Giggs shimmers and dazzles and Ronaldo dances past the Fulham defenders as if they were no more of an obstruction than a set of training-ground cones. Old Trafford holds its breath every time he collects the ball and sets off on one of those mazy yet penetrative runs and it is evident that the summer's controversy has been overstated. Rooney scores twice, Ronaldo gets one, and they bear-hug after each goal as if the World Cup was nothing more than a playground game of marbles. The Fulham fans boo Ronaldo's every touch, but it seems to inspire him to greater heights of excellence.

Ferguson surveys all this from a new seat – a red, leather-padded seat the size of a throne and complete with an in-built heater – and he is nodding his head in satisfaction, fond of his players, happy to be back. He had talked to us about the importance of getting off to a good start, but even he seems taken aback by the elegance of their play and the blitz of goals. It is first-touch, pass-them-to-death football and four goals arrive in the opening nineteen minutes. United settle for just one more and Fulham get one back but, even so, it is a performance of stunning quality, the club's biggest opening-day win since 1966.

The sting comes at the end. Fulham are so comprehensively outplayed that their manager, Chris Coleman, refuses to come to the pressroom to talk about the game. His press officer goes down to the dressing room to see what is wrong. She is gone for ten minutes and then she comes back looking embarrassed and very, very apologetic.

'I'm afraid he's getting on the bus. There won't be any interviews today.'

And so a small piece of history has been made: the first-ever top-flight match in England in which neither manager talks to the press.

Ferguson has not attended post-match conferences in the Premiership since a 3–1 defeat against Liverpool in November 2001. The nineteen other managers in the Premiership will usually set aside time to speak to the dailies, Sundays, radio and television in separate briefings and Coleman, in fairness, is usually very media-friendly. Today, however, he is so angry with his team's performance that he says he cannot trust himself not to say something he might later regret.

FERGIE AND THE BBC
26.8.06

Watford	1
Manchester United	2

Fraser Dainton of Sky Sports put in his first appearance at one of Ferguson's press conferences for nine months yesterday. He hasn't dared show his face since Ferguson told him he was 'finished' for daring to ask about Roy Keane when everything blew up last season. He was never officially banned but he has been on a 'self-imposed exile' to take the heat out of the situation, with his colleague James Cooper taking care of United's briefings.

These things have to be treated with a certain delicacy and Dainton timed it well. It has been an immaculate start to the season. All wins. No problems yet, no battles. Ferguson narrowed his eyes and gave him a knowing look, as if to say: 'I remember you, son.' But that was all. Dainton eased himself in with a couple of deliberately uncontroversial questions. Afterwards he stood in the car park and blew out his cheeks like a man who had just heard the judge utter the words 'not guilty'.

The BBC have had no such luck. BBC Radio Manchester wrote to Ferguson at the start of the season asking if there was anything they could do to persuade him to lift his boycott of the station. Writing a letter was, in their words, a final act of desperation. But he has written back to confirm it is a lifetime ban. He makes it clear he doesn't want to hear anything more about it. That life means life.

A lot of people who are not *au fait* with the way Ferguson operates might not understand why he should freeze out a local radio station that generally gives him nothing but positive publicity. But the history relates to his grievances with the BBC in general. Radio Manchester has never done anything to upset him but the BBC has been Ferguson's least favourite media organisation for many years – and he punishes every arm of the corporation as one.

The list of his grievances would fill a book but, in short, he cut off all contact in 2004 after BBC3 ran a *Panorama*-style documentary probing his son Jason's dealings as a football agent. He also took legal action in 2000 after a profile of him appeared in *Match of the Day* magazine. The article was written by the editor, Tim Glynne-Jones, a United supporter who started one of the club's earliest fanzines, *The Shankhill Skinhead*. Ferguson's solicitor described it as 'character assassination'. The BBC agreed to pay out £10,000 and publish an apology.

Ferguson has a long memory and these are offences he is prepared neither to forgive nor to forget. He still remembers, having lost 6–3 to Southampton during a difficult period in the 1996–97 season, switching on Radio Five to hear the presenters say it had made their weekend because of their dislike of United. He tuned in on another occasion to find an entire programme dedicated to the 'demise of Manchester United' and he has fallen out spectacularly with the commentator Alan Green, who now freely admits to longing for the day when Ferguson retires. 'Bluntly,' Green says, 'he is someone I would have preferred not to deal with. Football will undoubtedly miss him. But I won't. I will toast his departure.'

As feuds go, Ferguson versus Green would make one hell of a *Celebrity Deathmatch*. What many people don't realise, however, is that they once regarded each other as friends. Green says he learned how to drink 'copious amounts' of vodka on long nights out with Ferguson while covering Aberdeen in Europe in the early 1980s. When Ferguson came down to work in England, Green would let him into New Broadcasting House on Oxford Road in Manchester so he could watch live feeds of Scottish teams in action. He remembers Ferguson being 'great company, witty and charming' as they sat together, drinking wine and eating sandwiches. But Ferguson's success made him less tolerant of Green's outspoken commentary style and the relationship gradually disintegrated. They haven't spoken since 1992 and they probably never will again. Green describes Ferguson in his autobiography as 'foul-mouthed', 'arrogant', a 'control freak', whereas Ferguson chooses silence as his form of weapon. The feud with Green isn't mentioned once in Ferguson's autobiography, as if it doesn't even register.

The bad blood can be traced back to a typical Ferguson story. Jimmy Armfield, the Five Live match summariser, had sat in on a Friday press conference in which Ferguson said Mark Hughes was carrying an injury and wouldn't be fit for the game the following afternoon. Armfield had previously arranged an interview with Hughes, and when he bumped into him in the car park he suggested they postpone it if he were unable to play. 'What are you talking about?' replied Hughes. 'I'm fine.'

Green then went on air to say he didn't pay attention to the news emanating from Old Trafford and that he preferred to see for himself who actually ran out on the pitch rather than listening to spin.

'I don't mind if a manager says nothing,' he later said. 'That's his prerogative. But giving out wrong information is something else. Too many managers try to use the press in this way and I object to it, whoever it is.'

The fuse was lit. Green was despatched to the Dell to commentate on United's next game at Southampton. And Ferguson was waiting for him.

'YOU DON'T PICK MY TEAM, YOU BASTARD ...'

Relations deteriorated rapidly thereafter although, on reflection, Green believes there had been persistent signs before that of a terminal breakdown.

To begin with, Ferguson had heard that Green was a closet Liverpool fan. In April 1988, United drew 3–3 at Anfield after being two goals down, despite playing most of the second half with ten men after Colin Gibson had been sent off. Green was chatting to Liverpool's manager, Kenny Dalglish, outside the dressing rooms when they heard Ferguson complaining to a local radio reporter that he was 'choking on his vomit' because of the way referees never gave visiting sides anything at Anfield. Dalglish was so annoyed that he went into his office and came back out with his young daughter in his arms, telling the Merseyside reporters they would get more sense out of her. Green, taken aback by the way Ferguson had blanked him, followed him up a flight of stairs to the directors' lounge to ask what was wrong. 'I'm not talking to you,' Ferguson shouted. 'You're a Liverpool fan. You are just like all the rest.'

Green knows how to defend himself. He stood in front of Ferguson, looked into his eyes and told him he didn't know what he was talking about, that there was absolutely no reason to refuse to speak to him.

Others are not so courageous. In October 1995, Ferguson reduced the *Match of the Day* commentator John Motson to a gibbering wreck after he couched a question, in the mildest possible terms, about whether the club were worried about Roy Keane's disciplinary record. Motson had been asked to get some reaction after Keane had been sent off for the third time in fourteen games, but Ferguson went bananas as soon as it was brought up.

'John, you've no right to ask that question. You're out of order. You know full well my ruling on that. Interview finished. I don't want to fucking watch it. Cancel it! Fucking make sure that does not go out!'

Motson, who is no Jeremy Paxman, spluttered something about being under orders to ask it. 'You fucking know the rules here,' Ferguson yelled back. Every word was picked up by *Match of the Day*'s microphones, and the presenter, Des Lynam, wanted to use it, with the swear words suitably bleeped out, but he was overruled by the programme's editors.

For the record, Green does support a club whose name begins with L, but it is the Irish club Linfield, not Liverpool. He did himself few favours by describing Keane once as a 'lout' but it is crazy to think he is waging a personal vendetta against United, as some United supporters now believe. He may have a soft spot for Liverpool, and he admits disliking Ferguson intensely, but he was also one of the first broadcasters to argue that winning the treble of European Cup, Premiership and FA Cup in 1999 warranted a knighthood. He has tried to bury the hatchet by making generous remarks on air and he snubbed an unofficial 'Farewell to Fergie' dinner that had been planned by some of Ferguson's media enemies when he seemed about to retire in 2002. A table had been reserved at Belle Epoque, a restaurant in Knutsford, just a few miles from Ferguson's house, but Green turned down his invitation, believing it to be disrespectful and unprofessional.

He also wrote Ferguson a letter saying what a shame it was that two men who cared passionately for the game could not have a civil relationship. Ferguson simply replied: 'I have said all I wish regarding Radio Five Live and all those associated.' His letter was not even signed.

Green is now a pantomime villain to some supporters at Old Trafford and he has been threatened and abused outside the ground. At times, Ferguson has seemed convinced that the BBC is not just biased against United but strongly pro-Liverpool, with a Scouse mafia in the sports department. He is said to question how *Match of the Day* can get away with filling the pundits' couch with so many ex-Liverpool players. And he finds it strange that, when Brian

Barwick was the BBC's head of sport, the double-winning United sides of 1994 and 1996 never won Team of the Year in the Sports Personality of the Year awards. Barwick, an ardent Liverpool fan, left the BBC in 1999 to take up a similar position with ITV. Later that year United's treble-winning side won their first Team of the Year award.

'There was never any doubt that the award had to go to United and the whole team plus Sir Alex turned up to collect it,' Greg Dyke, director-general of the BBC at the time, later wrote in a column for the *Independent*. 'So I was rather surprised a week or so later when I got a call from Alex, who thanked me for making sure United had won. I hadn't done anything and was puzzled. Alex explained there was no way United would have won if "that bastard" Barwick had still been there.'

Was it true? 'I said I was sure Brian would never let his hostility to United stand in the way of the right decision,' Dyke continued. 'The next time I saw Brian I relayed what Alex had said. "Too bloody right," he said. "They'd never have won if I was there." I think he was joking ... but it wouldn't be going too far to say that he hates United and all they stand for.'

Barwick subsequently became chief executive of the Football Association. When we asked Ferguson about the appointment his face dropped. He said, very bluntly, he would not talk about Barwick, and his expression told us not to push it any further.

And so we have the situation where the BBC's *Match of the Day* cameras are at Vicarage Road today and when it comes to the post-match interviews Ferguson marches straight past them to where Sky

and MUTV are set up. It is a weekly ritual and the BBC reporters don't even bother asking any more. There is too much history. Queiroz does all the BBC interviews.

Gary Lineker, presenter of *Match of the Day*, used to complain about the situation during the show and apologise to the viewers, hoping to embarrass Ferguson into changing his mind. But he was wasting his time. Ferguson's grudge with the BBC makes his quarrel with Fraser Dainton look like a playground squabble and there is nothing Lineker or anyone can do about it. It is so historic and deeprooted, in fact, that it is difficult sometimes to remember exactly where or how it started. All we can be certain of is that it is an argument that will never be resolved.

CEASEFIRE
13.9.06

Manchester United	1
Tottenham Hotspur	0

It is amazing the difference it makes when the team are doing well. We have not witnessed one angry word so far this season. Ferguson's briefings have been placid and humorous and, increasingly, good fun to attend. He has stopped treating every question as though it was a carefully laid trap. He no longer looks at us as if we are intruders. He smiles a lot more. He stays behind after press conferences, passes on horse racing tips, tells us he is going to make us rich, that we'll never need to work again.

The fear factor is still there – his press conferences are still far more guarded than those of any other Premiership manager and he still controls what happens with those glacial eyes, that piercing stare – but he is definitely treating us more like human beings. He has started to tease us again, poking fun at our questions and addressing us as 'the plebs'. He is a natural mickey-taker and he is talking to us in a softer, friendlier tone, as if we are the bane of his life but, hey, he cannot help secretly liking us. In the way you might talk about an annoying younger brother. Or a loyal, yet incontinent, dog.

The obvious conclusion is that he is a very different person when he is winning from when he is losing. Yet we are also starting to think someone close to him might have had a strategic word about how to deal with the press this season. Maybe someone high up at Old Trafford, David Gill or Sir Bobby Charlton. Or possibly someone from outside the club: his friend Alistair Campbell, Tony Blair's former media minder, or one of the Ferguson boys, Jason or Darren or Mark. Cathy even. Someone who knows him well enough to say it is time he stopped picking so many fights, that life is too short.

This time last year, media relations with Ferguson were at an all-time low. He was arguing with everyone, at war with the press, refusing to speak to MUTV. One crisis after another, one war after another. Every question was viewed with suspicion, every press conference an ordeal. His answers were clipped and resentful, his body language rigid and defensive. Arms folded, back pressed against his chair. There was something eating away at him. Something destructive. Us.

This is a different Ferguson. The team have hit the ground running. Giggs scores the winner today, making it United's best-ever start to a Premiership season. Ferguson, in turn, seems to have forgotten what happened in South Africa. We are daring to think the relationship might not be terminally poisoned after all, that last season's ructions can be put behind us. We like this Ferguson. We respect him. Even if the line between respect and fear is as thin as Rizla.

When we saw him at Carrington yesterday, we knew it was going to be a fun press conference from the moment he bounded into the room, cheerfully murdering 'The Rose of Tralee'.

He passed James Fletcher of the *News of the World* in the doorway and looked him up and down, eyeing his suit.

'I thought I'd make an effort,' Fletcher volunteered, anticipating what was coming.

'Well, son,' Ferguson shot back, 'you could have started by getting yourself a decent suit.' And he heaved with laughter.

We'll enjoy it while we can. Because, with Ferguson, nothing can be taken for granted. Something might be written that he doesn't like. Or the team will have a bad result, someone will ask a question that's slightly too daring and, bang, we'll be back to square one. We are still the Back Row Kids in his eyes, too demanding, too egotistical, too damn young. But for now, everything is so much better – and this is the way it should be all the time.

RIO FERDINAND
27.9.06

A grey chauffeur-driven Bentley pulls up outside Old Trafford and out steps Rio Ferdinand. He is bringing out an autobiography, so the publishers have asked him to devote an afternoon to press interviews. Ferguson has given his blessing and, one by one, we are ushered into a private room where Ferdinand is sitting on a leather couch, waiting to present us each with a copy. He has autographed them 'Rio 5' and we are genuinely grateful – not for the book, but because he seems happy to talk to us with none of the usual restrictions.

Most footballers these days insist on copy approval for interviews. This is a hidden shame for many newspapers, one that has grown to epidemic proportions in recent years. We need player interviews but the clubs don't really trust us, so they will grant us access only if we allow them to 'approve' the finished article, and sometimes the photographs and headlines too. It's a showbiz thing the clubs have picked up. In the worst cases, they tape the interview and vet the questions. Quite often someone is in the same room to interrupt the conversation if it veers in a direction they don't like. They want to know exactly what has been said, and they will insist that anything remotely controversial is removed. It is censorship, and it sticks in the throat.

The exception is when the player has something to sell or advertise. Then the PR companies usually make sure everyone gets roughly what they want and most of the restrictions are lifted. But it comes at a

THIS IS THE ONE

price. We are duty-bound to write something along the lines of 'Wayne Rooney was speaking at the launch of his new computer game'. Or carry a photograph of the player with his sponsor's logo clearly visible. Product placement, they call it. A lot of us don't feel comfortable about it but the alternative is simple: nothing.

So today we are allowed half an hour with Ferdinand – a man who has had so much bad press during his career that he dedicates a page in his book to a montage of the worst tabloid cuttings.

Rio Butted
Rio Hotel Rampage
Rio's Binge
Rio's Drugs Test Shock
Rio: I'm Gutted
Video Sex Shame Of England Stars
Here We Rio Again
Rio Hit In Bar Brawl

The public perception is that he is a bit of a bird-brain, with too much money for his own good and brains in his feet. He forgot a drugs test once, going shopping instead. He was banned for eight months as a result but still received £2.5 million in wages. Then he became involved in a very messy contract row, despite being offered a record-breaking salary of £120,000 a week, and was photographed dining out in London with Chelsea's chief executive Peter Kenyon, a man with a reputation (whether or not deserved) for tapping up players. Ferdinand claimed the meeting was totally innocent but some supporters have never forgiven him. Thirty of them went round to his house one night, wearing hoods and balaclavas, and made it very clear what would happen to him if he carried on rubbing them up the wrong way.

But when you meet him, you wonder whether he would have had so much negative publicity if we had been permitted to get closer to him. Ferguson's restrictions prevent us from forming a proper bond with the players. There is no relationship, in the true sense of the word. Nobody we feel we should protect. So we demonise those who make mistakes when we don't really know what they are like.

The truth is that Ferdinand is probably smarter than many people imagine. He isn't scared to speak his mind and when he is encouraged to drop all the vaporous clichés he is a good talker, passionate about the game and full of opinion. He is willing to admit he has made mistakes and he has a dry sense of humour that makes you warm to him.

He tells a story about when he played for Leeds, on the way to the Champions League semi-finals in 2001. The players had a secret game which involved passing a coin round during the match.

'If a team-mate came up to you and offered you the coin you had to take it, and the one who was left with it at the end had to do a forfeit. We scored a goal in one game and, while we were celebrating, Gary Kelly slapped the coin in my hand. You could see me on the telly going, "Oh fuck!" That was one of the best passing games. It had gone round the whole team twice. We did it for five or six matches without the manager [David O'Leary] knowing. It didn't affect our play at all, but he'd still have gone bananas if he'd found out. We'd finish a game and the first thing on my mind was: who's got the coin?'

Ferdinand is open and expansive, good company, generous with his time. Some footballers have a special face they show to journalists, as though they dare not show their true character. They are reluctant to open up in the way that a cricketer or rugby player would. But Ferdinand doesn't just want to be interviewed. He wants to chat. He wants to know whether we like his book and why we give him such a hard time. Interestingly, he reckons the *Mirror* got the transcript of 'Keanegate' wrong and that his salary was never mentioned. 'We watched the tape together. Roy highlighted the goals and said: "Rio should have done better there. I've seen him make that mistake before. He should have dealt with it and got the ball away." It was just football analysis. I didn't have a problem with it. He couldn't have criticised me any more than I did myself anyway. After that match I couldn't get to sleep until five in the morning.'

By the time the interview is finished we have been reminded why we went into this business in the first place. To see football from the inside. To meet the players, to hear the stories and to feel involved, albeit in a very modest capacity. Interviewing the footballers is one of the most rewarding parts of our job. Yet a lot of them have grown to dislike us. One of their mates might have been turned over by the *News of the World*'s kiss-and-tell team. Or they might have had a five out of ten in the player ratings. Ferguson is forever telling them we have it in for the club and when we meet them it can be an uncomfortable experience, for them and us.

In another era, Manchester's football writers were on first-name terms with the players. They would enjoy nights out, drink and socialise together, swap stories and share secrets. Peter Batt, who covered the club for the *Sunday People* during the Sir Matt Busby years, can remember admiring Paddy Crerand's right hook on raucous Saturday nights out in Manchester city centre. Sunday lunch would be spent at the home of George Best's parents. Then on Monday morning he would collect Noel Cantwell to take him into training.

Mike Morgan, formerly of the *Sun*, shared a house with Sammy McIlroy, the last of the Busby Babes, when he started working in Manchester in the early 1970s and David Meek, correspondent for the *Manchester Evening News*, was allowed to travel on the team coach for his first fourteen years. Meek was considered 'one of the lads' until 1972, when he criticised the sacking of Frank O'Farrell, after a barren run of results, under the headline 'Be Fair to Frank'. United regarded this as treachery and the club secretary, Les Olive, wrote a stiff letter to Meek to inform him he would have to make his own arrangements in the future.

The process now is one of tactical isolation, not just at United but at all the big Premiership clubs. The players are fenced off like A-list actors on a Hollywood film set. To a different generation of journalists, footballers were people to protect as well as admire. Now, apart from a few exceptions, they are simply celebrities we write about and struggle to identify with, television personalities we sometimes bump into at airport check-ins. They travel in coaches with blacked-out windows. They are flanked by security guards, along corridors where nobody else gets in. They play. Then they go back the same way.

The general rule at Old Trafford is that Ferguson doesn't like his players doing in-depth interviews with anyone apart from MUTV, Sky (occasionally), the match-day programme or *Inside United*, the club's in-house magazine. We still find ways to quote the players but very often the comments that appear in the newspapers are second-hand recycled as new. The modern-day journalist has to be resourceful, because even the club's favourite reporters can go three or four seasons without being granted an interview.

This is a shame because there are some outstanding interviews to be had at Old Trafford. Gary Neville is a dream of a talker, bursting with opinion and not afraid to tackle any subject. Alan Smith is the same. Ole Gunnar Solskjaer is polite and unassuming. Ryan Giggs is witty and sharp, though strangely uncomfortable in front of the television cameras. Edwin van der Sar, like most Dutchmen, is never slow to speak his mind. Put a microphone in front of Paul Scholes and he looks as uncomfortable as a man putting on wet swimming trunks but, generally, the players are confident enough to handle a few questions.

The interview everyone wants, of course, is Ferguson – but that really is like asking for a sitting with the Pope.

Even when his relationship with the press was at its strongest he would limit himself to two or three big interviews a season. Only on one occasion, with Robert Crampton of *The Times*, has he allowed a journalist to visit him at home.

Crampton remembers being driven to Wilmslow by Jason Ferguson: 'I kept expecting us to arrive at a really big house, something at the end of a very long drive, quite possibly with iron gates. So when we drove on to a new-ish, private estate – nice houses, but nothing out of the ordinary – I thought we'd go through it. Then, when we turned into the drive of one of these houses, a short drive, I thought Jason was turning round for some reason. But then I saw that the house – mock-Tudor, leaded lights, lantern-style illumination by the door – had a name-plate which read Fairfields.'

Inside, Crampton remembers a beautifully kept house – named after the dockyard where Ferguson's father, Alex senior, worked in Govan – with the stripes and swirls from a recent vacuuming still visible on the carpet. Cathy was in the lounge, watching a Martin Kemp drama on UK Gold, and Ferguson led the way to a snooker room, complete with a tartan carpet and small busts of John Wayne, Stan Laurel and Oliver Hardy. 'I'm unbeatable on this table,' he boasted. 'Unbeatable.'

There were books along one wall, hundreds of them. Tony Benn. Mandela. Elvis. Terry Waite. Vince Lombardi. Bob Monkhouse. Books about the Alamo and Rorke's Drift. Biographies of Eamon de Valera and Michael Collins. *Parker's Wine Buyers' Guide.* Sinatra. Ali. Thatcher's memoirs. 'Never read it,' Ferguson hastily pointed out. 'It was a present.'

Crampton's memories are of a man who was pure Dr Jekyll, all twinkle-eyed merriment, bouncing his newest grandchild on his knee. 'On occasions, however, his face would settle into a harder shape, his eyes locking on to mine, and I would catch a glimpse of what Mr Hyde might be like. This change, I came to realise, always preceded him saying something he wanted me to remember, some part of his creed.'

Meeting Ferguson for a prearranged interview is certainly very different from seeing him at a run-of-the-mill Friday press conference. He has an extraordinary mind and, quite often, he will have a little nugget stored up for the interviewer, something that he knows will make a good headline.

His last one-on-one with the *Guardian* included the immortal quote that his greatest achievement was knocking Liverpool 'right off their fucking perch', in response to comments that Alan Hansen had made in his *Daily Telegraph* column. Ferguson gave a dramatic pause that Al Pacino would have been proud of, then turned to his interviewer, Michael Walker, and exclaimed: 'And you can print that.' Journalistic gold dust.

WAYNE ROONEY'S BLIP
13.10.06

Today is the first time we have seen Ferguson for a month. There was an international break last week and he didn't turn up for the previous two Fridays because of 'other commitments'. Carlos Queiroz stepped in but it was difficult not to feel slightly underwhelmed. Queiroz is a nice guy, with the air of an affable old vicar, but in newspaper terms there is nothing about him that is Hold The Back Page. And we have been waiting to ask Ferguson a very important question – what is going on with Wayne Rooney?

Questioning a player of Rooney's gifts can feel like a pointless exercise, like taking Tiger Woods to task about his backswing or criticising Roger Federer for his serve, but something has malfunctioned recently. His touch has deserted him and his head has gone down. Simple things like trapping the ball or the execution of a short pass have seemed beyond him. He has been giving the ball away, missing chances he should really score, allowing defenders to get the better of him. For a player of such immense self-belief, he looks riddled with insecurity.

Lots of strikers go through periods when they are struggling for their best form. When we asked Queiroz about it he made it clear he wasn't overly concerned, that it was just the kind of blip that young players occasionally go through. Our prodding, however, is getting on Ferguson's nerves. 'You know his heart is in the right place, you know his desire is right, you know his attitude is always good, so why create problems?' he asks us today, and it is obvious we have pricked his temper glands. 'Are you hoping I'm going to tell you, "That's the end of Wayne Rooney?" Because I really think you are. Wayne's your number one seller and, without him, you wouldn't sell half as many papers. So you want me to say something to make you a good headline, don't you? But you know deep down, and every defender in the country knows deep down, that the lad is going to be fine.'

A braver group of reporters would point out that it is still a legitimate talking point. Yet we know Ferguson too well. His face says 'stop' and 'danger'. And when he has that kind of aggressive mien, what is the point of challenging him? He never tolerates any media criticism of his players. He always stands by them in public. Never questions them, defends them to the last.

Even now, he won't talk about why he felt he had to get rid of Roy Keane, how it hurt him to hear what his captain had said on MUTV and know that things would never be the same again. He still speaks about Diego Forlan, one of his least successful signings, with dewy-eyed affection, as if he has forgotten about the days when the Uruguayan's shots were more of a danger to low-flying pigeons than they were to opposition goalkeepers. And he won't hear a bad word against Juan Sebastian Veron. He will never admit that Veron's form was erratic or that, for £28.1 million, it caused him a great deal of embarrassment.

His argument at the time was classic Ferguson, a mixture of spin and deflection to make it look as if United were the victims of some elaborate jingoistic plot. England had been drawn against Argentina in the World Cup and Ferguson said the press had set out to persecute Veron for the simple reason that he was Argentinian. 'Seba is a marvellous player but ever since England drew Argentina the press have turned on him,' he said. 'It's a witch-hunt. I don't know what the agenda is, but I don't like it.'

He has stuck to his guns ever since and in the opinion of many Manchester-based journalists, the Big Veron Debate was an important factor in shaping how he has come to see us. He grew so protective of his player, so sensitive about any criticism, that the muscles round his eyes would tighten ominously every time it was brought up. This period coincided with some of the older journalists retiring or moving on and younger ones coming through. And it was here that his press conferences went into a tailspin.

At one briefing, only a single question had been asked when he threw his hands in the air, as if he had suddenly decided he should never have agreed to see us in the first place. 'That's the end,' he shouted, pointing to the door. 'Get out! I've had enough of you already.'

He turned to Diana Law. 'Get the Sunday papers in. This lot are done.' The whole thing had lasted less than a minute.

Veron was a beautiful passer of the ball, full of subtle touches and elegant flicks, but there were also moments when he disappeared in important games. And, excruciatingly, he pulled his foot out of a tackle when United were behind in a Champions League semi-final against Bayer Leverkusen. His price tag meant that every poor performance was highlighted and, at the end of his first season, Ferguson threw us out again after a reporter from the *Sun* asked him whether he was disappointed with the player's lack of consistency.

At first, Ferguson wanted to know what the reporter thought. When the reporter said he did not think Veron had been worth the money, Ferguson erupted.

'On you go. Out of my sight. I'm not fucking talking to you any more. Veron's a great fucking player.'

We headed for the exit, his eyes scorching holes in the back of our heads.

'Youse all fucking idiots.'

TOTAL FOOTBALL
28.10.06

Bolton Wanderers	0
Manchester United	4

Everything is clicking. Rooney looks a lot happier today. The team play brilliantly and he scores the kind of hat-trick that demonstrates two things. The first, to borrow Ian Botham's phrase, is that form is temporary and class is permanent. The second is that we might be witnessing the start of something very special indeed.

At the very least United have restored a genuine sense of intrigue to the top of the Premiership. In their opening ten games they have won eight, drawn one and lost one, scoring twenty-three goals and conceding only five. They are three points clear of Chelsea, squatting defiantly in first place and daring to believe, for the first time in a long time, that maybe they can mount a serious challenge for this league.

Bolton away is a tough fixture, one that most teams approach with equal measures of dread and caution. Yet United's football is the type usually seen only on a PlayStation – one-touch, fast and incisive. It's Manchester United playing the Manchester United way: 4-4-2, picking off their opponents like flies. 'The best we have played for years,' Ferguson says proudly. 'No other team will come here and get a result like that. We were outstanding from the first minute to the last.'

There are still three-quarters of the season to go, so this is no time to be making rash predictions, but United certainly look like a side who believe they can be champions.

Their football has rippled with intelligence and purpose. They have played with touch and life, in the fashion of a real team, and their big players all have the bit between their teeth. Ronaldo, in particular, is in show-stopping form, silencing the boo-boys wherever he plays. Scholes is passing the ball as if he has a computer device in his boots. Saha is slick and athletic, determined to show he can lead the attack in Van Nistelrooy's absence. Rooney has been the weak link since the first few weeks of the season, but today he looks like the player with whom we are all familiar. The one who could fall into the Manchester Ship Canal and come up with a salmon in his mouth.

United's only defeat so far this season has come at home to Arsenal but, since then, they have beaten Newcastle at home, Wigan away, Liverpool at home and now Bolton away. They have won at Crewe in the Carling Cup and they have beaten Celtic, Benfica and FC Copenhagen in their first three Champions League group games. All they need now is a point from the next three, starting in Copenhagen next week, and they will be through to the knockout rounds and can start forgetting about what happened last season.

The average supporter is still wary, concerned about the strength of the squad, worried that thirty-somethings such as Scholes or Giggs might not last the pace. For now, though, it's championship form. And, if we are being truly honest, not many people can genuinely say they expected this.

COPENHAGEN
1.11.06

FC Copenhagen   1
Manchester United   0
Champions League, Group F

Grim scenes tonight. Everyone expected United to qualify for the Champions League's knockout stages

– a draw would have been enough – and Ferguson looks thoroughly fed up when he comes into his press conference. The standings in Group F haven't dramatically altered, but he is in one of those moods when any reporter who has dealt with him over a certain period recognises the danger signals and knows to give him a little space.

We saw this expression yesterday when we had our five minutes with him at Copenhagen airport. A girl in a United top, maybe eighteen or nineteen, came too close as she was snapping away with her camera and he reacted: 'Can you please leave us alone? Bloody hell!' and tonight he takes exception again when a Danish journalist starts to quiz him about his team selection.

Ferguson has chosen an odd, unbalanced side. Older players such as Giggs, Neville, Ferdinand and Scholes are rested and Saha is also on the list of absentees because he has a slight twinge. The Danes think it is because Ferguson has underestimated their team. 'Why didn't you play your stronger players?' the guy from *Ekstra Bladet*, Denmark's equivalent of the *Sun*, is asking, adopting a barrister's tone. 'Why did you leave out someone like Louis Saha when he has scored so many goals?'

'Saha's injured,' Ferguson snaps, 'and you should know your facts.'

He is grumpy because it is an unforgivably poor performance. Some of the players who have come in – Fletcher, O'Shea, Silvestre – have let him down badly, culminating in a scrappy goal from a Copenhagen corner seventeen minutes from the end. Copenhagen are not even a good side, but United struggle to play their passing game other than in occasional flashes. There was a Bruce Springsteen concert at the stadium four days ago and the grass has been badly trampled, with large areas worn down to the mud. It looks like someone's allotment, churned up and uneven. Ferguson, who believes a football pitch should be as smooth as a bowling green, is thinking about making an official complaint.

He takes these things extremely seriously. He is an expert when it comes to what goes to make an acceptable football pitch – how much water should be applied, how much sunshine is needed, the perfect length of grass. It is one of his specialist subjects and it drives him to distraction when United have to play on a rutted, pockmarked pitch where the ball will not run straight.

Sometimes, when we are finishing in the Old Trafford pressbox, an hour or so after a game, we will see him stride out on to the grass to run his eye over the playing surface, like a forensic scientist looking for clues at a murder scene. On one occasion we saw him haranguing the head groundsman, Tony Sinclair, on the day he received the club's Employee of the Year award. Sinclair looked distinctly uncomfortable as Ferguson fastidiously examined the goalmouth in front of the Stretford End, pulling up blades of grass and holding them to his face – even sniffing them.

TWENTY YEARS
6.11.06

Today is Ferguson's twentieth anniversary as manager and Tom Tyrrell of Piccadilly Radio presents him with a bottle of Bordeaux at the end of his press conference. Tyrrell, who has covered the club for forty years, bought this wine when Ferguson first came down from Aberdeen in 1986. 'I'll keep it for when you have done your first twenty years,' he told him at the time, and he has been true to his word. Ferguson is touched. He has signed one of Tyrrell's books: 'Thanks for having the faith in me to last so long. Alex.'

We have all been feeling pretty friendly towards the old man recently. Several sackloads of letters and anniversary cards have arrived at Old Trafford from supporters. The television schedules have been full of tribute programmes and the newspapers have been packed with eulogies. Words such as 'genius' and 'legend' have been used and a national debate has raged about where he stands in the managerial hierarchy. Is he better than Busby? Or Clough? Or Shankly? Or Paisley? Is he the greatest of all time?

He has had some terrific press, but when we see him at Carrington he looks uncomfortable with all the attention. He is distracted and uninterested, bordering on rude, obviously wanting to get it over as quickly as possible. Ken Lawrence, a freelance journalist, sidles over to say 'Congratulations', but Ferguson shifts uneasily in his seat, looking distant and withdrawn, like a pools winner who has forgotten to tick the 'no publicity' box.

He is not a showy man and he has asked for everything to be kept low key, with as little fuss as possible. He doesn't want any nostalgic one-off interviews, or special media events, or photo opportunities of him cutting an oversized anniversary cake. Barclays, sponsors of the Premier League, have arranged a commemorative 'Fergie and Friends' lunch at the

Manchester Hilton – but he plans to arrive through a back exit to avoid the cameramen.

'My anniversary is hard to escape but I must admit I am finding it hard to come to terms with,' he says. 'My first intention was not to pay any attention to it at all, lest it confuse and distract me. But it has become obvious that it is going to be thrust upon me, whether I want it or not.'

He doesn't want a 'carnival' or a 'circus' and he is noticeably weary, close to rolling his eyes, when the questions start. No, he doesn't have any anecdotes about his first memories of the club, or the struggles he had in his early years. He is asked if he remembers his first team talk, before a 2–0 defeat against Oxford United at the old Manor Ground, and he says he doesn't. Then the talk turns to the time he nearly lost his job because of poor league results in the 1989–90 season. Does he ever wonder how life might have been so different? 'No,' he replies again, looking into the middle distance, unwilling to elaborate.

We plug away for a few more minutes, groping for a way to make him open up, but his fingers might as well be in his ears. 'The future's more important to me,' he explains. 'You journalists are all going on about my twenty years here, what I've achieved and all the rest of it. But it really doesn't matter to me. I prefer to move on.'

Finally, he says something about his soup getting cold and wanders off.

'Cheerio ... and goodnight.'

It is when he has jumped in his Audi and driven the 100 yards from the youth academy back to the main Carrington building that his colleagues explain why he has been so grumpy. Oliver Holt, the *Daily*

Mirror's chief sports writer and Sports Journalist of the Year, has written that he cannot join in the 'orgy of back-slapping and misty-eyed remembrance'. Holt is one of Fleet Street's more courageous journalists, with enough awards to fill a removals van, and in his weekly column he argues that Ferguson should have retired when he said he was going to, at the end of the 2001–02 season:

> *The man is a living legend. He belongs in the pantheon with Paisley, Clough and Shankly. But strip it down and under his management Manchester United have won the European Cup once in twenty years. Celebrating his anniversary amounts to nothing more than a lazy and meaningless ballyhoo for a man who has stayed on too long. Whatever United go on to achieve this season, or in seasons to come, nothing changes the fact that Ferguson should have quit.*

The article was faxed to Ferguson when the team were in Copenhagen and it has been bugging him ever since. 'It's scandalous that some people think I should retire,' he says. 'There are people in the media saying I should hang my boots up. Well, I don't think anyone has got the right to say that. It's none of their bloody business. I've every right to work hard and still be here. Some people don't want to work, but I do. It disgusts me. I want to work and I will continue working.'

It is amazing that this seems to be the only article that has stuck in his mind when every other newspaper has carried page after page of flowery tributes. But there is history here too. Ferguson has never forgiven the *Mirror* for the way it treated him when Piers Morgan was the newspaper's editor and even now it probably ranks as his least favourite tabloid.

Morgan was an occasionally brilliant, yet ultimately flawed, editor, a great white in the world of tabloid sharks. He had an Arsenal season ticket and an Anyone But United mentality, and at times he seemed to goad Ferguson just for the sake of goading him. When United lost 5–0 at Newcastle in October 1996, Morgan was so delighted to see Ferguson on the wrong end of a thrashing that he decided it should be the newspaper's front-page splash. His colleagues thought he had taken leave of his senses but he did it anyway, under the headline '5–0'.

He also ran a very aggressive 'Save the FA Cup' campaign after United pulled out of the competition in 2000 to play in the World Club Championship in Brazil. All sorts of politicians, celebrities and football types backed the campaign and the *Mirror* splashed on it nearly every day for two weeks, regardless of what else was happening in the world. Ferguson was getting more and more wound up and snapped when the *Mirror* sent news reporters to 'doorstep' him at a champagne reception in Manchester. He allegedly yelled: 'Tell your editor to fuck off back to Highbury and stagnate …'

Morgan found this hugely amusing and took it as a victory for his campaign. Over time, it seemed to become his personal mission to get under Ferguson's skin. A few months later Ferguson appeared in court charged with speeding on the hard shoulder of the M602 in Eccles. He claimed he had been dashing to the loo because he had terrible diarrhoea and his lawyers managed to get him off on the basis that there were extraordinary circumstances. The next day, Morgan posted some Imodium to Ferguson with a note saying: 'Dear Alex, we Gooners have known you've been full of crap for years. Now we've got the proof. Love, Piers.'

It was strange for a man as intelligent as Morgan to be so empty-headed: going to war with United was a terrible blunder. Yet Morgan was relentless in his apparent desire to get at Ferguson, sniping about him in public, belittling him in print. He also played an enthusiastic part in accelerating Jaap Stam's departure from Old Trafford after Stam had brought out an autobiography which made personal attacks on Gary and Phil Neville and described David Beckham as 'no mastermind', and – the *pièce de résistance* for the *Mirror* – contained an admission that United should not have pulled out of the FA Cup. Nobody at United even knew Stam was writing a book. Morgan was particularly delighted because the Dutchman claimed Ferguson had made an illegal approach to sign him and was happy for his players to dive in European matches. The *Mirror* bought the serialisation rights for £15,000 – a snip, according to Morgan – and ran all the stuff relating to Ferguson on the first day.

The following morning, Morgan took a call from Stam's agent begging him to can the rest of the serialisation because Ferguson had hit the roof. 'Bollocks,' came the reply. 'I'm an Arsenal fan and Stam will be out of Old Trafford by the end of the week, which means we will win the league.'

Stam was sold within two weeks. 'I rang David Dein at Arsenal and we had a good laugh about it,' recalls Morgan. Except it didn't stop United winning the league, ten points clear of Arsenal, and the *Mirror* has suffered ever since. Morgan's vendetta drove away United-supporting readers, while Ferguson banned the newspaper for several months. Even though he has since let them back in, he hasn't forgotten how they behaved.

Morgan was sacked in 2004 and six months later the *Mirror*'s sports editor, Dean Morse, approached Ferguson, at a lunch to celebrate his 1,000th game as manager, and politely asked if there was anything he could do to improve the relationship between newspaper and club.

'Yes,' Ferguson replied, smiling. 'You can fuck off and die.'

KISS ME QUICK
7.11.06

Southend	1
Manchester United	0

Carling Cup fourth round

There is nothing quite so depressing as a seaside town in winter. Southend in November is the sort of place Morrissey was presumably singing about in 'Every Day is Like Sunday' – a seaside town they forgot to close down. Only the hardcore United fans have been tempted to Roots Hall, with its peeling paintwork and Lego-like stands. Few, if any, will take the slightest pleasure from a night that ends with a pitch invasion and some youths in Tommy Hilfiger doing the let's-all-have-a-disco dance as close as they dare to the away end.

Going out of the League Cup doesn't hurt United as much as it does other clubs but, as upsets go, losing to Southend is about as bad as it gets. It will not be talked about like the great FA Cup giant-killings: Hereford against Newcastle in 1972, Sutton versus Coventry in 1989, Wrexham against Arsenal in 1992.

And Ferguson is not as down as he was after the draw against Burton Albion. But it is still a bad night. A definite embarrassment.

To put it into context, Southend have not managed a league win in a dozen attempts and are rooted to the bottom of the Championship. In their last game, they were 3–0 down after twenty-two minutes to Wolves. This is the first time they have ever made it past the third round and they have absolutely no history of giant-killing. United are top of the Premiership, with twenty-eight points out of thirty-three. And this is the real deal too, a team packed with fêted names: Rooney, Ronaldo, Smith, Brown, Silvestre, Heinze. When the team-sheets are handed out in the pressbox half an hour before kick-off, the reporter from the *Southend Evening Echo* puts his head in his hands and says, 'Oh, Jesus, no … I was hoping they might play their kids.'

He doesn't seem very confident as he asks the club's press officer, 'Can you remember the year we lost 9–1 to Brighton for our record defeat? This could be a bad one.'

What happens next is Steptoe and Son meets Roy of the Rovers.

Playing in attack for Southend is Freddy Eastwood, a Romany gypsy who lives in a static caravan next to a dual carriageway in Basildon, with his wife, Debbie, his son, Freddy junior, and (post-*Footballers' Wives*) his daughter, Chardonnay. After half an hour, the referee blows for a free-kick. Eastwood measures out his run-up, twenty-five yards from goal, then hits his shot. Eleven thousand people are watching, hushed. Then they realise, a second after it has happened, that the ball is in the back of United's net.

There are two-thirds of the game for United to find an equaliser. They go straight down the other end and hit the post, but it is not until stoppage time that they get behind the Southend defence again, and Richardson can't make proper contact on his shot. The final whistle goes. Then comes the bizarre sight of the team bottom of their league, with one point in twenty-four, jogging round the pitch on a lap of honour while Eastwood, an unlikely hero, sprays champagne into the crowd.

Ferguson keeps his composure. He is a dignified loser and he shakes the hand of every member of Southend's coaching staff, and several of the players' hands too. He thanks the referee and the two linesmen. Then he does his bit for MUTV in a corridor that smells of stale sweat and liniment. 'This is a great reminder to everybody that football can smack you in the face,' he says. 'I may have been here twenty years but I'm not impervious to it. It can come up and smack you right in the face.'

He is philosophical. 'We don't like defeats at Manchester United but sometimes we have to accept them,' he says. 'There will be no suicides, no mass sackings, no need for counselling. We are disappointed because our club can't accept being beaten in any kind of competition, even a friendly. But we've lost only three times this season so there isn't much wrong with us. I know we'll be crucified by certain journalists but there's no need for a knee-jerk reaction. Our form in the league has been good and there's no need to go overboard.'

MORE IMPORTANT MATTERS
11.11.06

| Blackburn Rovers | 0 |
| Manchester United | 1 |

The *Southend Evening Echo* has dedicated twenty pages to what the *Independent* describes as 'the biggest night in Southend since the pier burnt down'. The club have rushed out a special-edition commemorative mug, for £5.99. T-shirts are available for a tenner, showing a picture of the scoreboard at the final whistle. Or for £25 you could buy a framed photograph of Freddy Eastwood's goal, signed by the man himself.

Eastwood isn't talking about it though. Richard Rae, one of the *Guardian*'s football writers, tracked him down in Essex but was turned away from his gypsy site by a woman who swore more than Billy Connolly. A couple of kids with BMXs and muddy knees confirmed he was at the right place, but it didn't seem worth hanging around. When the *Guardian* photographer turned up, a group of men piled into a flat-bed truck and chased their cars back on to the A127.

For a lot of United supporters it's history already. Southend was an embarrassment, there is no other way to describe it, but the Carling Cup is not a competition that captures their imagination. It is the Premiership, the FA Cup and the Champions League that matter this season and there is an impressive response from the players today.

Blackburn away, with a howling gale and aggressive opponents, is the kind of game where any team with realistic aspirations of being champions has to stand up, fight and dig out a result. There is a question mark hanging over United but they dominate the game from the first minute to the last. Saha scores the winner and Ferguson has taken off his unhappy head, Worzel Gummidge-style, and replaced it with the happy one.

GLASGOW
20.11.06

There is always a unique sense of occasion when an English team plays in Glasgow. United take on Celtic tomorrow, in a contest between Britain's two biggest clubs, and when we see Ferguson today there is a boyish excitement in him. We can see it in his face and hear it in his voice. His eyes sparkle, never seeming to fix on anyone or anything, and his accent progressively gets more and more Scottish.

When he comes into his press conference, at a hotel on the shores of Loch Lomond, he is smiling even before he lowers himself into his seat, scanning the room to pick out a few familiar faces and winking at a couple of his favourite reporters. He is looking forward to the game, United's first-ever competitive fixture at Parkhead, and enjoying being back in the city where he grew up. But the first piece of news, he says, is that he plans to drop Paul Scholes because he once scored the winner for England against Scotland. For that, he deserves to be punished. Scholes is sat beside Ferguson, smiling politely, as this little comedy routine unfolds around him. Ferguson is sorry, he says, but Scholes has dug his own grave. He looks at his player with an expression of *c'est la vie*. If Scholes is going to upset so many great people, he has nobody to blame but himself.

Ferguson is in full flow when, mid-sentence, someone's phone goes off. It is one of those bloody awful ring-tones – Gary Numan or something – and nine times out of ten an interruption like that would genuinely annoy him. Instead, he simply tuts with mock outrage, shaking his head in an exaggerated fashion, as if to say: 'Tch, kids today.' He sighs theatrically, playing up to the cameras, and then his shoulders are jigging up and down with laughter.

'You … un … professional … so … and … sos.'

Ferguson, it seems to us, is always on good form when there are Scottish reporters around, always that little bit happier in their company, as if it takes him on a nostalgic trip down memory lane.

Some of the Scots came down to Carrington for his last briefing and he made sure he put on a good performance. He talked about his days at Aberdeen, where he was the manager from 1978 to 1986, and the pride he had taken in breaking the Old Firm's hegemony, winning three league titles, three Scottish Cups and, in 1983, the European Cup Winners' Cup. He spoke about the atmosphere we should anticipate at Celtic Park and the passion of the Scottish supporters. He wondered whether it was something they put in the porridge.

Then his eyes lit up and he picked out someone in the front row. 'Christ almighty,' he spluttered, 'you're going grey!'

'Anyone would go bloody grey coming here to see you,' came the reply. Ferguson hooted with appreciative laughter.

The Scottish reporters tend to subscribe to the theory that he has mellowed with age, that his fuse was a lot shorter when he was managing north of the border.

At Aberdeen his closest friends included newspapermen such as Jim 'Scoop' Rodger of the Scottish *Mirror* and Glenn Gibbons of the *Scotsman*. But he also had a little black book in which he kept track of how often the Glasgow-based journalists failed to make the 300-mile round trip to his press conferences, making a note whenever they chose to go to Celtic or Rangers instead. He would turn on them if he hadn't seen them for three or four weeks and accuse them of snubbing his club and being biased towards the Old Firm. 'They don't want to come to Aberdeen,' he would tell his players. 'They think they're a superior people down in Glasgow.'

Back then, his nickname among his players was 'Furious Fergie', eventually shortened to just 'Furious'. And the stories of his temper are legend.

One favourite is of the time a player turned up for training with a perm. Ferguson, a short-back-and-sides man even in the era of Slade and Marc Bolan, made him wear a balaclava, telling him never to report to the club again in such a bloody awful state.

Gordon Strachan tells a story, from the 1986 World Cup finals, about not being able to sleep in the team's hotel in Mexico City. Not because of the humidity, or mosquitoes, but because he was in the next room to Ferguson – Scotland's interim manager after the death of Jock Stein – and was so in awe of him that he would lie awake at night listening to his nervous cough through the wall. Strachan, now manager of Celtic, has a long and occasionally acrimonious history with

Ferguson going back to the days when he played for him at Aberdeen. He remembers that Ferguson 'put the fear of death into players'. In one dressing-room rage he kicked the laundry basket with such force that a pair of pants catapulted through the air, landing on the head of one of Strachan's team-mates. Ferguson didn't even notice until he had stopped blowing his top. Then he looked up and exploded again. 'And you can take those fucking pants off your head. What the hell do you think you're playing at?'

DYING ON YOUR FEET
21.11.06

Celtic	1
Manchester United	0

Champions League, Group F

All the laughter stops tonight. The team lose, which is a minor miracle considering the way they dominate the match, and Ferguson is gruff and irritable in his press conference, in no mood for an inquisition. He cannot comprehend how his players could be so careless after having so much of the ball. United have given Celtic a lesson in everything apart from the art of putting the ball into the net. He is shaking his head, a fatigued expression on his face, trying to fathom out how they could possibly have lost.

He says United should have won comfortably, and it is difficult to disagree given the obvious imbalance of talent between the two teams. Yet United are not incisive enough inside the penalty area and for the first time, they conspicuously miss Van Nistelrooy. Celtic keep going, throwing themselves into every tackle. Ten minutes from the end, they are awarded a free-kick thirty-five yards from goal. Shunsuke Nakamura, their Japanese midfielder, wraps his left boot around the ball and suddenly it is spearing into the top left-hand corner of Van der Sar's goal. It is a once-in-a-lifetime goal, a swirling, dipping, piercing shot over the defensive wall and down and suddenly Ferguson is the one Glaswegian in Parkhead whose blood has not been converted into red wine.

Even then, United should salvage the draw that is needed to send them through. In stoppage time, the referee awards United a penalty and suddenly the Celtic Roar is replaced by a long howl of anguish. Saha picks up the ball but his eyes are glazed and his body language is all wrong. A few minutes earlier he had run clear on goal, only to imagine a non-existent offside flag. He paused, waiting for a whistle, when the first rule for a centre-forward is to score first and ask questions later. Now, with the chance to send United into the knockout rounds, he looks incapable of getting his butterflies to flutter in formation. Gary Neville watches him measure out his run-up and Neil Lennon, the Celtic captain, asks him what he thinks. Neville shakes his head – Lennon later claims – and says that Saha is going to screw it up because 'his head has gone'.

It is the first time all season that Saha has found Van Nistelrooy's shoes too big to fill. His nerve deserts him and when his shot – on target, to the goalkeeper's right, but not close enough to the corner and neither low nor high – is palmed away the Celtic fans reach a point of near-hysteria. Relief and joy and euphoric incredulity all come together to form an explosion of unremitting noise. A din that screeches through Ferguson's ears like fingers running down a blackboard.

He talks afterwards about how the team cannot get away with being so wasteful, how they will have to take a greater percentage of chances if they want to be successful in the Champions League. There is only one game left in their qualifying group, at home to Benfica, and he can scarcely believe that United's qualification is going to the wire after winning their opening three games.

He looks sick with misery, hating the feeling of defeat, hating that it has happened in Scotland, clearly angry with his players. Ferguson is not a man who is capable of hiding how he feels and, most of the time, he does not even try. We can sense everything from his abrupt, defensive tone and the way the skin is cinched around his eyes. The way he looks at us. The way he stares into our eyes, flashing us coded messages.

Peter Martin, the reporter for Radio Clyde, asks him: 'Are you angry with your players, Alex?'

Ferguson looks him in the eye. 'I don't think I'm angry with anyone,' he says, a flash of irritation sweeping across his face. 'Maybe with you for asking such stupid questions.'

He says it like a slap. Quick, like a cobra strike, and Martin's reflexes aren't ready. He gently tilts his head, as if to say: 'Did I hear that right?' Then he realises he did and for one awful moment he looks as if he might say something back. Or laugh. Or make some other dreadful mistake. He sneaks a look at the rest of us and we play dumb, offering him absolutely no support. We're bastards like that. If Ferguson is having a go at someone we will happily let him get on with it. Nobody will ever butt in and say: 'Hang on, Alex, that's a bit unfair.' We're far too gutless. And besides, it can be quite entertaining watching someone get it in the neck.

We have all been there at one time or another. The blood rushing to your head. The sudden sensation that your mouth has gone dry and sticky, as if you have swallowed a tablespoon of baking soda. Then afterwards, the sweeping sense of indignation and the horrible feeling that people are sniggering behind your back. Which they usually are.

THE SPECIAL ONE
26.11.06

| Manchester United | 1 |
| Chelsea | 1 |

The front cover of *Red Issue* carries a picture of Ferguson and Jose Mourinho deep in conversation. Ferguson is chuckling away, looking very pleased with himself, and Mourinho has a pained expression on his face.

Mourinho's voice bubble says: 'I never expected you to be clear at the top at this stage.'

Ferguson replies: 'Aye, me neither pal ...'

For forty-five minutes today United pass and move with wonderful precision. They knock the ball around.

There is pace and refinement and when Saha soothes his confidence with the opening goal, half an hour in, they have Chelsea on the rack. The crowd are on their feet, loud and excitable. The football is bold, incisive, beautifully choreographed. Everything is tipping in their favour.

But Chelsea are fortified against the possibility of losing football matches. Mourinho's team may not compare with United as crowd-pleasers. They may not ping the ball about in such a pretty fashion and work such elaborate, triangular patterns. But they are brilliantly efficient. The second half is theirs. They force their way back into the match, equalising with a deflected header. When the ball hits the net Mourinho is off, machine-gunning his fists, running down the touchline in his black overcoat and polished shoes. The Special One, the star in his own movie.

United stay top of the Premiership, three points clear, but there is an overwhelming feeling at the final whistle that it is an opportunity lost and, afterwards, Mourinho emphasises the point with a certain smugness. His is a world-class display in his press conference, talking up Chelsea's powers of recovery, gently questioning United's durability. He describes it as a psychological victory for his players and he guesses that Ferguson must be 'very disappointed'. Every sentence is laced with spin.

To watch Mourinho in these high-pressure situations is to witness a hypnotic presence. He isn't like a normal football manager. He is too chiselled, too debonair. Mourinho is Hollywood handsome, all Don Johnson and George Clooney. Prada scarf. Rolex watch. Expensive aftershave. He nods to the sound of his voice, as if he likes what he is hearing. He has an intense look on his face and when he has said what he wants to say – mostly, it is one long speech rather than the typical question-and-answer session – he nods curtly and slides out of his seat in one movement, his eyes darting around the room as he whacks open the door and floats away.

Ferguson seems almost doddering in comparison. For such a powerful man, his are surprisingly small steps. He wears a sensible coat, nothing too flash, and when it is cold, like today, his shoulders are hunched to his chin. He is not bothered about designer labels and he doesn't exude Mourinho's flamboyance or showmanship. At this point in Ferguson's life, he is not seduced by fame. He still gets his hair cut for eight quid at Trims in Cheadle Hulme and he owns one of the few cars at Carrington not to have blacked-out windows. He has sufficient power not to have to flaunt it.

Twenty-one years separate him from Mourinho and, in many respects, they are poles apart temperamentally. In one corner, the Glaswegian street-fighter; in the other, the Portuguese smooth-talker. Sir Chalk and Senhor Cheese – two men of vastly different backgrounds and lifestyles.

The paradox is that they share many of the same behavioural traits: the passion, the control freakery, the refusal to suffer fools, the desire for conflict, the humour, the attitude. Mourinho, like Ferguson, is capable of turning the toughest journalistic Rottweiler into a spaniel. Neither is a tall or imposing man, but their personalities are forceful enough to create the aura. They are hardnosed, driven, famously unapologetic, and they have the best CVs in the business. Maybe not the most controversial and outspoken men in football – but certainly on the group photo.

You wonder how long it will be before the friction starts to warp their relationship. Sooner or later one of them will say something the other doesn't like. There will be a reaction and suddenly they will be bustling past each other without even raising their eyes. For now, though, they genuinely seem to get on as well as can be reasonably expected for two men in such direct opposition.

'I like Jose,' Ferguson says. 'I see him as the young gunslinger who has come to town to challenge the old sheriff. He has a great sense of humour and there is a devilish wit about him. He's like me, he speaks his mind. I understand his passion for the club, so there's no problem. We were at a dinner in London the other week for a children's charity. There was good banter, honest conversation and I enjoy that. We get on well.'

At the final whistle they shake hands straight away. There is even a quick embrace and Ferguson invites Mourinho into his office for a glass of wine. Mourinho has come prepared, with a £200 bottle of Portuguese red, and for ten minutes they sit together and talk about football and life.

SUGAR LOUNGE
1.12.06

Ronnie Wallwork, a former United player, is in hospital after being stabbed at Sugar Lounge, a bar in Manchester where a lot of the footballers drink. The police are calling it attempted murder and Ferguson is asked for his reaction at today's press conference.

'I just hope the boy's going to be all right,' he says. 'I can't believe it. I'm shocked.'

He asks us if we have heard any updates and he shakes his head in disbelief. 'Jesus ... don't go to that Sugar Loaf!'

It is a serious subject but there is a squawk of laughter on the back row. Someone else joins in. Then, very soon, it is like that moment at school when the teacher is standing at the front of class and everyone has an uncontrollable fit of giggles.

Ferguson looks utterly bewildered, completely at a loss about what is so funny, until someone puts him out his misery.

'I think it's known as the Sugar Lounge, Alex.'

He lets the moment hang then he heaves with laughter. It is one of those rare moments when all the barriers come crashing down and everyone is on the same level.

'Ah well, Sugar Lounge then. Don't go there, whatever it's called ...'

He is still laughing when a reporter from *The Times* raises his arm. 'Don't your players drink in that bar as well?'

'No, no. Not at all. None of my boys ever go there.'

'They do, you know. They're quite often in there.'

'Listen, I'm telling you – they don't.'

'I'm sorry, Alex, but I've seen them there myself.'

His eyes squint at that revelation. Ferguson is not keen on his players being out at night, particularly if it means they have been drinking.

'Well,' he says, after a few long seconds, 'you shouldn't be in a place like that either ... it says more about you than me, son.'

BENFICA II
6.12.06

Manchester United	3
Benfica	1

Champions League, Group F

Mission accomplished. The team have had a scare but the important thing is that they have finally made it through to the knockout rounds, even if it is amazing that they make life so difficult for themselves.

Tonight is classic United: going behind, then springing into life and dragging themselves out of trouble. Never has a team won their opening three Champions League group games and failed to qualify, so Ferguson is probably a little embarrassed that his side nearly became the first. But the only thing that really matters is that they are in the draw for the last sixteen, courtesy of an impressive feat of escapology and goals from Vidic, Saha and Giggs. They have put Benfica in their place and Ferguson can joke about the 'torture' his team put him through: 'Why do my players take us right to the very edge so often? Why do they do it to me? It's as if the make-up of this club has a built-in requirement to take the difficult route.'

Hopefully they will learn from it. They may have to. All of Europe's top clubs – Barcelona, Madrid, Milan, Bayern Munich and so on – have made it to the knockout rounds. The serious business begins now and it does not reflect well on United's chances that they have hobbled over the line.

THE COMIC STRIP
8.12.06

The Sunday newspapers have linked United with a £10 million move for Charlton Athletic striker Darren Bent. Ferguson thinks it is hilarious.

'Jesus Christ, how do you lot come up with this stuff? It's Korky the Cat, Dennis the Menace stuff. Do you read Lord Snooty? Which comic is it you guys work for these days? Absolutely priceless.'

He is wheezing with laughter. 'I get the papers every morning and I have a good laugh about them. I get my cup of tea. I look at what you've written. I get an aspirin to make sure I get over it. And then I go about my day's work … still laughing.'

FERGIE AND HIS BUS PASS
29.12.06

It's Ferguson's sixty-fifth birthday on New Year's Eve and we have clubbed together to buy him a bottle of Pinot Noir, with a card that reads: 'Hope this is better than the paint-stripper Mourinho gives you. Many happy returns. The dailies.'

No official presentations though. We simply give it to Diana Law, asking her to hand it over after Ferguson has finished his press conference and driven back to the main building at Carrington. We are not sure if our relationship with Ferguson is ready for a public love-in yet and we are very aware that the Sundays would find it hilarious. We are not even sure whether buying him a present is a good idea, considering our grievances about access. It is the first time we have done anything like this and it needs a show of hands before we decide to go through with it.

Two abstain, one votes no 'unless it's Blue Nun'. Six of us chip in a fiver each, albeit with one complaining that it makes us look 'desperate'. Which, unfortunately, is true.

Still, you've got to make the effort, haven't you? We are going to need Ferguson if the team carry on doing well. He has generally been a lot better with us this season. And, besides, how can you fail to be impressed by someone who is on the verge of turning sixty-five yet still puts in enough hours to shame the average workaholic? Ferguson may have his faults but he is an example to us all in terms of his dedication and commitment. It has been an epic run. Nobody has beaten the system so emphatically. Nobody has done it for so long or with such tireless enthusiasm.

To most men, sixty-five is the time to slip into dotage as if it were a nice warm bath. Bus-pass time: pipe, slippers and port and lazy afternoons watching *Countdown*. Except that Ferguson was out of bed at half past five this morning and into Carrington with his hair still wet from his morning shower. 'Sometimes it is even earlier,' he tells us. 'I'll often get up at five. It's just the way I am, you know. Hard work and long hours do not scare me and I've always got up early. As a young boy, my dad used to get me up at six o'clock every day. So it's no different to when I was growing up. To me, it's just a normal way of life.'

Growing old, he says, does not scare him. 'The thing about turning sixty-five is that it is a milestone because it's the age when people normally collect their pensions. I'm waiting for the envelope to drop through the door. I'll get my bus pass and heating allowance and after the length of time I've worked I probably deserve them too. But the important thing is that I feel fine. I'm as fresh as can be.'

He doesn't look bad for it either. He jokes about being 'ravaged by time' but there isn't a hint of pot belly on his body. His hair, once chestnut, is greying and his face is full of worry lines and bags, like an officer from the Serious Crime Squad. Yet he still looks young for a man of his age, more like fifty-five than sixty-five.

Ferguson's enthusiasm for life is so intense that it is easy to forget he had to go into hospital in 2004 to have a pacemaker fitted after he was diagnosed with a heart condition known as supraventricular tachycardia, or SVT. Ferguson had wanted to keep it secret but someone sold the story to the *Sun*, making a tidy little profit in the process.

For most men, an experience like that could have been life-changing, the body's way of pointing out that it was time to take life at an easier pace. But Ferguson's a monster. He was back at work for half past six the next morning, talking about 'business as usual', and it doesn't seem to have altered his lifestyle one bit. Occasionally, he talks about trying to get more time off and scolds himself for not delegating more of his jobs. But he never goes through with it. He is still clocking up air miles, scouting foreign players and watching European games, still 'never out of bloody hotels'. He can still be found presenting prizes at some under-12s' competition in Collyhurst or on the edge of a muddy school field in Burnage, running his eye over some promising kid he has been told about. And he still gets by with an unfeasible lack of sleep: in bed by midnight, into Carrington before sunrise. Half an hour in the gym.

A bit of toast and cereal, a cup of tea, then into his paperwork.

You could make a comparison with Margaret Thatcher during her eleven years as Prime Minister – though not within Ferguson's earshot. One interviewer used that line before and Ferguson, staunch Labour, very quickly put him right. 'Please don't associate me with that woman!'

But there are similarities in terms of his ability to run his life with only four or five hours' sleep and the way he rarely suffers fatigue. 'It does become a little harder as you get older,' he says. 'Sometimes I will have a little catnap for ten or fifteen minutes at half four or five o'clock. But I don't see the big deal. There are plenty of people who are older than sixty-five but who still get up earlier than me to go to work. There are farmers and butchers and milkmen and bakers. These are the people I have to admire. Farmers, in particular, when you look at the elements they have to work in. I look at what they do and I think to myself: could I do that?'

We'd been apprehensive before we saw him. When he reached his twentieth anniversary his press conference was a tough and tetchy ten minutes. Today, though, we are reminded why there is so much more to admire about him than to dislike.

He speaks about how Rooney and Ronaldo are on course to be recognised as the most exciting players on the planet. He talks about his wish to reinvent the most exciting days of his life and his willingness to believe that the prizes can still be won in a certain, thrilling fashion. Then he tells us about his belief that there is more than a little good wine left in the glass. And why not? Bob Dylan qualified for his AARP (American Association of Retired People) discount card earlier this year but is still putting out chart-topping albums. Richard Steadman, the knee surgeon credited with saving Michael Owen's career, is sixty-nine. Others past the age of sixty-five are going strong: Bernie Ecclestone, Rupert Murdoch, David Attenborough, Ralph Lauren.

Someone asks, God knows why, if at his age he ever finds himself 'falling asleep on planes'. It is the kind of question that might have brought an explosion of right-eous indignation in the past. But he laughs it off and politely replies that, no, he doesn't fall asleep on planes – or not to the point where it concerns him anyway.

His sense of mischief kicks in and he tells us it is time we started working as hard as the people we write about. He teases the Sunday journalists about their 'five days off every week'. He talks about using his bus pass on 'the 4A to Govan Cross'. Then he raises himself off his seat and heads for the door with a big smile on his face.

'You haven't got rid of me yet,' he calls over his shoulder. 'No matter how many times you have tried. I'm still here. You lot will all be gone before I am. I'll see you all off.'

HAPPY DAYS
30.12.06

| Manchester United | 3 |
| Reading | 2 |

A text arrived today from Diana Law: 'The manager loved his wine. Thank you.'

We hope he enjoyed it. Football is a tough, unfor-giving business and there is something truly remarkable about the way Ferguson seems to have come through all the turmoil of last season. Rumours of his demise were clearly exaggerated. He is fit and healthy and he says today that he plans to carry on working until 2009 at the earliest.

'I have a few more years left in me as manager. Yes, it is one of the most significant mileposts in life's journey but I cannot say I feel on the verge of becoming an old man. Quite the reverse, in fact. Many people work well into their eighties these days and I shall take umbrage if my friends in the media try to typecast me as a pensioner.'

His team, he says, are keeping him young. Winning games and scoring goals. They are six points clear of Chelsea after this victory and sixteen from Liverpool in third place. They have played twenty-one league games and won seventeen, scoring forty-seven goals and conceding only thirteen. It is championship form and Ferguson cannot resist pointing out that the journalists and supporters who 'suggested not so long ago I was past my sell-by date and presiding over a crumbling empire' have been noticeably quiet recently.

He seems tickled by the memory – 'I think we've put that one to bed' – and he is entitled to be a little smug. When we saw Mourinho at Old Trafford three weeks ago he looked like a man who could not see how his team could possibly fail. But since then Chelsea have dropped points against one mid-table side, Reading, and one in the bottom six, Fulham, and there have been stories about several fallouts behind the scenes at Stamford Bridge. Key players have been injured or lost form. Words such as 'flop' and 'misfit' have been used to describe Michael

Ballack and Andriy Shevchenko and, suddenly, Mourinho seems to have stopped taking the handsome pills. He has started to look tired and stressed and he gives the impression of being emotionally exhausted. 'Maybe I am not such a good manager,' he says today. 'Maybe my players are not such good players.'

It is an astonishing statement for a man of Mourinho's vanity and self-adoration, and the glint in Ferguson's eye is almost satanic. He has waited a long time for the opportunity to have some fun at Chelsea's expense and he has become increasingly emboldened of late.

At one press conference he forgot to switch off his mobile and it started ringing as he was taking the first question.

His face was a picture. 'It's Jose,' he said, scrabbling about in his coat pocket and grinning mischievously. 'He's panicking already.'

CHELSEA'S BLIP
20.1.07

Something strange is going on at Chelsea. They lose 2-0 at Liverpool today and Abramovich's seat in the directors' box is empty. The pundits on *Match of the Day* reckon it is Chelsea's worst performance since Mourinho took over and, when the cameras zoom in, his body language is startling, to say the least. He has an impassive face and there are dark rings beneath his eyes. His hands are jammed into his pockets and his hair looks wild and greasy for a man who is usually so impeccably groomed. Every time we see

Mourinho these days he looks a little bit worse than the last time.

A few months ago Mourinho was untouchable. Now, the rest of the country is peering into Stamford Bridge like rubberneckers at a motorway pile-up. The sports pages are full of stories about political infighting and backstabbing, and Mourinho looks like a man leaving a casino at four in the morning. The entire club has gone into temporary meltdown. And it has all happened so amazingly fast.

> *Mourinho future hangs in balance*
> *Chelsea at war*
> *Abramovich won't back down in Jose feud*
> *Roman's cold war with Jose*

Chelsea is such a nest of vipers it is difficult to know how much is fact and how much is rumour spun into something it is not. Yet Stamford Bridge is a breeding ground for Fleet Street informants and there is clearly something seriously wrong. There have been strategic leaks from the boardroom and the dressing room, and the consensus is that Mourinho and Abramovich are barely on speaking terms. Abramovich is said to want more style and panache from his team, and when he has pumped so much money into the club – around £500 million at the last count – it cannot be easy for an employee, even one as arrogantly self-assured as Mourinho, to find out what the Russian is for 'kindly butt out'.

Never before has Mourinho had to deal with a sequence of five league results that has gone: draw, draw, draw, win, defeat. It is commonly known as 'the blip'. Except, for Chelsea the blip never used to be anything more than a blink of the eye, a momentary lapse or, at the very worst, a bad forty-five minutes. Until recently they seemed immune to a sustained collapse and it was impossible to think of Mourinho and his players without taking it for granted they would invariably find a way to win. Now, they look virtually unrecognisable from the robotic, methodical team that has dominated the Premiership for the last two seasons. And this is Ferguson's opportunity, maybe the only opportunity he will get.

At every press conference now there are half-a-dozen questions about the soap opera at Stamford Bridge and the implications for the top of the league. Ferguson doesn't usually like to discuss other clubs' business but he takes a keen interest when it comes to Chelsea, and his information is that 'Shevchenko seems to be at the core of it'. It is obvious, he says, there is something in the air but, intriguingly, he insists he doesn't want Mourinho to leave because he would miss the sense of competition and the challenge of beating him.

It is a diplomatic response but we wouldn't be surprised if his fingers are crossed behind his back. Ferguson has suffered badly at the hands of Mourinho and, at the very least, he must take great satisfaction from the fact Chelsea have spent £30 million on one striker while United have sold Van Nistelrooy for £10 million and still been far more prolific. So far this season United have scored fifty-two goals in twenty-three games, thirteen more than Chelsea and ten more than this time last season.

Ferguson's theory is that the team are more fluent and cohesive with Saha rather than Van Nistelrooy in attack and that they were previously too reliant on one player to score all the goals. Saha may never accumulate scoring records like Van Nistelrooy but he is sleek and athletic and more of a team player. He roams right and left, creating space, running into it. One moment he is in front of you, the next he is on the wing and suddenly Rooney or Ronaldo will be coming through the middle. Always, there seems to be an attacker in space. Always, Scholes or Carrick seem to pick them out. Scholes's passes are forward both in geography and thinking. Carrick is more of an acquired taste but he has an appreciation of space and is starting to show he is a United player in the truest sense.

Ferguson has also brought in Henrik Larsson, a former Sweden international striker, on a nine-week loan from Helsingborgs. Larsson is a former European Golden Boot winner, with three World Cup campaigns on his CV and a Champions League medal with Barcelona. He is thirty-five now but he looks lithe and sharp and eager to impress, and it is an outstanding piece of business on Ferguson's part.

As for Van Nistelrooy, he is having a successful first season at Real Madrid, on course to be the leading scorer in *la Liga*, but there have been times when he has seemed slightly obsessed, and maybe a little aghast, by the success his former employers have had without him. He was always a restrained public speaker in Manchester but his choice of language has become noticeably more colourful since he moved to Spain. He has admitted 'exploding' with anger in front of Ferguson at the end of the Carling Cup final, describing it as 'the end of everything'. He has talked of Ferguson 'kicking my soul' and complained about being 'stabbed in the back'. Which is not strictly accurate. Ferguson has been accused of many knifings throughout his managerial career but on each occasion the blade is always plunged through the victim's chest.

Not that this really matters any longer. The fans have stopped singing Van Nistelrooy's name and it is noticeable how Ferguson seldom, if ever, refers to him in public. The most prolific striker at Old Trafford for thirty years has become a fading memory, consigned to the gulag of indifference just like Alan Green, Brian Barwick and so many others.

ARSENAL AWAY
21.1.07

Arsenal	2
Manchester United	1

We arrive at the Emirates stadium today wondering whether this is going to be the day United in effect finish off Chelsea in the title race. The newspapers are packed with new revelations about divisions and rifts at Chelsea. The Stamford Bridge family tree is depicted as a network of cliques and there are reports that Mourinho will be sacked at the end of the season, that the arguments with Abramovich have led to an irreparable rift, and that he is already looking for a new club.

Judging purely by results, sacking Mourinho would be an act of madness. Yet Chelsea operate by their own rules and Mourinho has not only apparently fallen out with Abramovich, his relationship with Peter Kenyon and the director of youth development, Frank Arnesen, has reputedly been strained. There is a clash of egos.

Several clashes, in fact. Behind the scenes at Stamford Bridge they used to look on proudly at Mourinho's sophisticated mind games and the way he sought to undermine anyone he perceived as an obstacle to his ambitions. Now, it seems, his charm has worn thin and this is the time when United have to capitalise. Chelsea are too strong, too belligerent, too damn good, to allow the blip to extend into anything more prolonged, but substantial damage has already been done and when Ferguson takes his seat in the dugout he knows a win will take United nine points clear with fourteen games to go – i.e. the sort of gap that can feel like a chasm for the side in second place.

The misery of what comes next is made all the worse because, at first, everything goes to plan. For the opening hour United are the better team, brisk and business-like, probing for Arsenal's weaknesses. Evra surges up the left and whips in a perfectly measured cross. Rooney is free at the far post and flings himself at the ball. It thuds against his forehead and the squash of United fans behind the goal is suddenly a writhing mass of euphoria.

Mentally, this is the point when United are cracking open the champagne, eye to eye with the title. Arsenal look beaten. United have their foot on Chelsea's throat. The clock is ticking down and Ferguson is on the touchline, checking his watch and barking out instructions.

Football clubs can be extraordinarily inventive when it comes to finding ways to inflict misery on their supporters. The United fans are going through their victory songs when a ball comes across the penalty area and Neville, a man you would normally bet your mortgage on, doesn't react quickly enough.

There are only seven minutes to go. Robin van Persie slashes in the equaliser and Ferguson's shoulders slump.

The momentum is with Arsenal and the killer blow is landed in stoppage time. Emmanuel Eboue gets a yard past Evra. His cross is fast and whipped, and Thierry Henry has peeled away from Vidic. His header is immaculate and then he is off, on his victory run, pursued by his team-mates.

Two-one.

Daylight robbery.

ARSENE WENGER
26.1.07

Ferguson is still upset about the way his players threw the game away. He hasn't slept. He has been up to three, four, five in the morning, trying to get his head around what went wrong. He is tired and grouchy and he has taken umbrage about some of Arsène Wenger's remarks after the match.

Wenger had rubbed salt into United's wounds by saying the title would have been 'over' if United had held on. Critically, he also said he had been analysing United's statistics and had noted a trend of the team conceding goals in the final twenty minutes of matches, indicating there might be an underlying problem with stamina. After seventy minutes, he said, they were 'not the same side'.

The irritation in Ferguson pours out in a stream of expertly delivered barbs.

He calls Wenger 'petty' and accuses him of talking 'a load of nonsense'. He accuses the Arsenal manager of trying to score cheap points and he says there is no evidence to back up the claims. 'I can't think why he has said it,' he tells us, and then he leans forward and smirks wickedly, 'but I think it's about making him look great again.'

Then he puts on his most sarcastic voice.

'I'm … the … great … Arsène … Wenger.'

It is a world-class putdown, great newspaper copy, and Ferguson looks as pleased as punch. What he says will dominate tomorrow's sports pages and we get the impression he is looking forward to reading the headlines already. Wenger will be 'blasted' and 'slammed' and Ferguson is grinning mischievously. He seems to like the idea of his old rival spraying a mouthful of coffee over his breakfast table.

Wenger's press conference is a couple of hours later at Arsenal's training ground in Hertfordshire, and the London hacks try to get him to bite back, but with no success. He claims it is a misunderstanding and says he doesn't want to get involved in spats, bust-ups, feuds and wars-of-words. Which surprises everyone because, usually, Wenger is more than happy to have the final say when it comes to verbal sparring with Ferguson.

At the height of their feuding, long before Mourinho pitched up on the scene, the rivalry between Ferguson and Wenger became so bitter and twisted there were complaints from the Metropolitan Police and government ministers. The FA wrote to both clubs demanding an official ceasefire and the League Managers' Association offered to mediate. There was even talk of arranging a peace summit on neutral territory before everyone accepted what was blindingly obvious: that *entente cordiale* was not a possibility.

Manchester's football writers interviewed Wenger after a game at Bolton Wanderers and he was trembling with anger.

'What I don't understand,' he told us, 'is that he, Ferguson, does whatever he wants and *you* are all at his feet.'

Wenger is well over six feet and surprisingly scary when he wants to be. He has a pale, lined face with hooded eyes and he was pointing an accusatory finger every bit as long and bony as ET's. 'In England you have a good phrase,' he said. 'It is "to bring the game into disrepute". The managers have a responsibility. Yet Ferguson does what he wants. He lays explosives. He should go abroad and see how it is over there.'

When we asked him to explain he stopped us in our tracks.

'One thing is simple. I will never answer any more questions about this man. I am not going to answer any provocation from him any more. It is simple, I will not respond to anything.'

James Lawton, the *Independent*'s chief sports writer, had one final question.

'Is that the end of diplomatic relations for good?'

Wenger looked down, blinking very quickly, and hissed: 'I have no diplomatic relations with that man.'

He stayed true to his word for about three weeks before slipping back into the old routine. The London journalists are always amazed they can ask Wenger whatever they like about Ferguson, or Mourinho, and nine times out of ten he will have something to say. It would be easier sometimes for him to brush it off with something like: 'I would rather you asked me about my own club.' But it rarely happens.

As for Ferguson, his sights are firmly fixed on Mourinho these days and the feuding with Wenger has been downscaled to a part-time hobby. Nowadays, it is nothing more malicious than two old neighbours bickering over the garden fence about who has the better lawn. Yet it is Wenger, not Mourinho, whom Ferguson dislikes. He has criticised him over the years for lacking grace in defeat. He has argued with him on the touchline. Arsenal are renowned for playing beautifully elaborate football and Ferguson, like every lover of the game, admires the way they treasure the ball. But he has also suggested they like to kick their way to victory compared to his own halo-wearers at the top of the Fair Play League.

Wenger speaks five different languages and is one of the few football managers to have a master's degree, earned from Strasbourg University in economics and sociology. Yet Ferguson has never seemed impressed. 'Intelligence! They say he's an intelligent man, right? Speaks five languages! I've got a fifteen-year-old boy from the Ivory Coast who speaks five languages ...'

That is not to say there is not a mutual sense of respect. Both men appreciate what the other has brought to their sport, and there are sides to Wenger that, if pushed, Ferguson would admit he admires – but he would have to be pushed hard.

Ferguson has his love of films and music and horses and wine, whereas Wenger can come across as being as grey as John Major's *Spitting Image* puppet. Wenger admits spending his free evenings watching tapes of old German football matches and he once confessed he had no knowledge of central London at all, despite living in the capital since 1996. He said his wife wanted to take him out for dinner to celebrate his birthday but that he had insisted on certain conditions: the restaurant had to be close to his north London home and it had to be an early booking so he could watch *Match of the Day* at 10.30 p.m.

Ferguson is wary about what goes on behind that inscrutable face. For years, he would invite Wenger into his office for a drink after Arsenal had played at Old Trafford and, every time, Wenger politely turned it down. Ferguson always took that as a snub. Then Arsenal won the league at Old Trafford in 2002 and suddenly Wenger decided that he would like a glass of Manchester United's wine. Ferguson doesn't forget things like that.

Nor has he forgotten that Wenger refused to shake his hand after United beat Arsenal in an epic FA Cup semi-final at Villa Park en route to the 1999 treble. Giggs won the match with a sixty-yard slalom through Arsenal's defence but Wenger was still ruminating about Peter Schmeichel saving Dennis Bergkamp's penalty in the final minute of normal time and marched briskly down the tunnel. When the two managers shake hands these days there is only the briefest contact of flesh.

BACK ON TRACK
31.1.07

Manchester United	4
Watford	0

A freewheeling win. Watford are certainties for relegation and they are obliging opponents for a club that is fully committed to swift, first-time passing and imaginative, penetrative running. Ferguson is wreathed in smiles and he seems to have got the Arsenal game out of his system. 'People can curl up and die in the face of disappointment,' he says, 'but men of purpose and ambition do something about it.'

Arsenal, he says, should be regarded as nothing more than a blip. 'It was gut wrenching. I certainly didn't sleep a wink, repeatedly going over the match in my mind, doodling on bits of paper, watching the video, asking myself over and over again how we could let the points slip through our fingers. But as far as I'm concerned it's the challenge presented by a big setback that drives me on and if I've got my players figured out correctly, and I know I have, they will be feeling the same way.'

He is very positive, very pumped-up, but he must be worried Chelsea have been let off the hook. The crowd seem to recognise it too. The atmosphere is good tonight, but there has been a palpable change at Old Trafford since those days, pre-Abramovich, when the fans were so spoilt with success they would frequently sing: 'It's all so fucking easy'. With Chelsea on the scene, nothing can be taken for granted any more. It is dangerous to assume anything.

Ferguson, however, is making all the right noises, convinced that his players can hang on. 'We're still in an excellent position,' he says. 'Winning the Premier League this season lies in our hands.'

And here's the thing: Chelsea have become so hated, so terminally unpopular, he has noted a trend, for the first time in his twenty years at the club, of other clubs' supporters taking United's side. Strangers, non-United supporters, have been stopping him in the street to offer words of encouragement. Taxi drivers have been telling him how they cannot bear the thought of Chelsea making it a hat-trick of titles. Letters containing good-luck messages have arrived from all around the country. 'Even Liverpool fans,' Ferguson says.

This is a completely new phenomenon and he seems bemused by it, as if it might be some kind of elaborate prank. But it is very real. Even when Chelsea are at their best they do not, and cannot, tug at the heartstrings in the way United do. There is a lot to admire, and it is only envy that stops some people from recognising the quality of their football, but Mourinho is essentially a pragmatist, and his team, to the average punter, have become as romantic as a cold sore. They are not a spectators' team, a side that grabs your imagination and makes you quicken your step on the way to see them, whereas there is something captivating about the way Ferguson has taken United to the top of the league and the way they are trying to take on Chelsea by playing football the way it is meant to be played. Adventurously and with flair.

The turnaround is nothing short of incredible because, once, it felt as if the whole country was desperate for United, and Ferguson, to fail – and, ideally, in the most excruciating way possible. No other club has inspired a book title such as *Manchester United Ruined My Life*. Or a television show such as *The Greatest 100 Goals Scored Against Manchester United*. Or had England fans singing derogatory songs about them at Wembley. Even when they won the European Cup in 1999, Ferguson was very conscious there were millions of Englishmen cheering on Bayern Munich in the final. Afterwards, he guessed there would be 'more than one person throwing themselves off London Bridge'.

For that hostility to have transferred to Chelsea is one hell of an achievement, especially given that there was a time under Mourinho's predecessor, the endearingly eccentric Claudio Ranieri, when they were many people's 'other' team, and most neutral supporters were happy for them to bloody United's nose.

Mourinho took over in 2004 and, at first, he bewitched everyone. He was the coming man, infuriatingly handsome with his well-cut dark suit and excitingly modern take on the role of football manager. There was a period indeed when he was the most admired personality in the game. He didn't look, or sound, like the average football manager. He was too chiselled, too debonair. Chelsea won trophies and set records, and the critics, if not the purists, were won over. He was made for television, our first celebrity manager since Brian Clough, and he did something that nobody thought possible – transforming Abramovich's Chelsea empire into something weirdly cool.

What he is discovering now is that it is no longer enough to win but to win with style and, most importantly, with grace. The novelty factor has worn off, replaced by resentment and, in some cases, open hostility about Abramovich's riches and Mourinho's feistiness. Peter Kenyon, who brags Chelsea will be 'the biggest club in the world by 2016', does not help either. In football grounds across the country, every Saturday afternoon, there is a hush of expectation when the scores are read out and an anguished sigh when the news comes through of another Chelsea victory, or a loud cheer of undisguised joy on the rare occasions when they fail. Drinkers congregate around the television screens in pubs, watching the scores flash up on Sky Sports and willing Jeff Stelling to announce in giddy tones that Petr Cech has just picked the ball out of his net.

Not all the antipathy is warranted. Yet Chelsea, in their current format, are not an enjoyable team to watch. The manager pouts and gesticulates and preens for the camera but the players, despite their cosmopolitan extraction, play remorseless old English football. The template is built on an immaculate defence and muscular, athletic midfielders rather than nimble ball-players such as Scholes and Giggs, and the common result is a 1-0 victory, often with a late goal as opponents tire. They grind out wins, playing an aggressive, pressing, zonal game, whereas the philosophy at Old Trafford is attack, attack, attack. 'We have to put on a show,' says Ferguson. For a short time – but only a very short time – this was not the case when he experimented with 4-5-1. United believe the best form of defence is to keep the ball at the other end of the pitch and the beauty of this is that every game is memorable for its 'wow' factor. The emphasis is to entertain – to win, but also to be the Harlem Globetrotters of the Premiership. Rarely do they attract the same newspaper critiques that attach themselves to Chelsea. For United, it is not enough to be 'methodical' and 'efficient' and 'functional'. They want to be 'dazzling' and 'bewitching' and 'exhilarating'. And that is Ferguson's doing. It is not enough to win – he wants to win playing spellbinding football. Style matters.

Mourinho gives the impression he couldn't care less if Chelsea have overtaken Don Revie's Leeds on the hate scale. He is in the business of winning football matches, he says, rather than winning friends. And it is true, as he says, that there are no trophies handed out at the end of the season for being popular. Even so, it is amazing how a man once described as a 'breath of fresh air' for the English game has metamorphosed into a cartoon villain and how the initial fascination with Chelsea's wealth has led to so many misgivings about the Russian oligarch sitting in the executive boxes. An ABC mentality – Anybody but Chelsea – has taken root and the more they bicker and brag and snipe the more they become a permanent reminder, to the man on the street, why the cricket commentator John Arlott once said of football that 'the bad guys outnumber the good ones by about 200 to one'.

If that sounds terribly harsh, you can guarantee worse is being said in pubs, offices and factory floors the length and breadth of the country. To love Chelsea it is necessary to embrace Mourinho and, really, that should be a lot easier than it actually is. We should be able to forgive him his bad points because of his mix of talent, drive and showmanship. But the point is this: you can have all the money in the world but it cannot buy history and tradition. Nor can it buy class, and there are times when the modern Chelsea team have the soul of a pickpocket. Mourinho complains about referees. He belittles smaller clubs. He has put together arguably the most functional team ever witnessed in top-flight football and he is blessed with a fiendishly brilliant tactical brain. But he is dedicated to the idea of being permanently extraordinary. He has an abrasive, unforgiving edge and his policy is that you are either with him or against him. Mostly, he thinks people are against him.

He also has a brutal tongue. Towards the end of last season Ferguson said in one press conference that he would not give up on the league until it was mathematically impossible and that he was still living in hope that Chelsea might be susceptible to a 'Devon Loch moment'. Mourinho's response was cutting, to say the least. He said he wasn't aware of the story of the 1956 Grand National loser but he knew of a Portuguese proverb that stood as a warning to Ferguson and it was known as *morrernapraia* – or, translated, dying on the beach.

He compared them to two swimmers at sea, himself being the 'good swimmer' and Ferguson 'the fellow who wants to chase me' and he demonstrated his full range of swimming strokes as he explained to the press what happened next. 'He shouldn't chase me,' he said. 'He should say to the boat: "Please take me a little bit closer." He's so enthusiastic chasing me – gasp, gasp, gasp – but he has a heart attack. When he reaches the beach, he dies. That, my friends, is our Devon Loch.'

Mourinho had already said he was more concerned about bird flu than the chances of United catching and overhauling his team. His one-liners can be cruel in their impact. Even when Chelsea won his first championship, eighteen points clear of United, his attention was diverted by Ferguson taking his team on a lap of honour at Old Trafford. It didn't matter to Mourinho that it was just Ferguson's way of thanking the crowd for their support. 'If they had done that in Portugal,' he remarked, 'they would have had bottles thrown at them.'

Football would be a dull place, of course, if everyone behaved impeccably, and Chelsea's fans are entitled to point out that, from time to time, Ferguson has been known to pick the occasional fight. Yet Mourinho wouldn't walk if his wickets were scattered all over the square. He deserves better than to be labelled, in the words of one UEFA official, an 'enemy of football', and it is easy sometimes to find yourself warming to the man. But there are no guarantees that if United win the league he will be at all gracious. He might congratulate Ferguson and come out with some standard platitudes but, deep down, it will be that Chelsea lost the league, not that United won it.

BIGGLES
2.2.07

Ferguson is over his spat with Wenger and his press conference today is a friendly little session. He is in his tracksuit top when he comes up the stairs, whistling a happy tune, and his eyes light up when he sees that James Mossop, an old friend from the *Sunday Telegraph*, has put in a rare appearance. 'James, how nice to see you,' he cries out. 'What are you doing slumming it in these parts?'

He is in sparkling form, astonishingly relaxed considering the pressure he must be under. He talks about how much he is enjoying watching his team play. He feels in great shape, the players are in great shape. Everything, in fact, is in great shape. He talks in a you-guys-aren't-so-bad kind of way and when he realises he is actually enjoying himself he doesn't stop. Even when he takes issue with one reporter for allegedly misquoting him it is done light-heartedly, with him declaring in a loud voice that 'people have been hanged for these kind of things, you know'.

A soft-focus Ferguson has come into view, his observations marinated in humour. There are still moments of seriousness. He is very aware Mourinho may be watching on television and his strategy is clever: to look and sound as assured as he can.

The only thing that has been rankling with him recently is the incessant reports in the Spanish newspapers that Real Madrid plan to sign Ronaldo. This has been going on for several weeks and Ferguson's message is clear. 'We only sell players that we want to sell,' he says. 'There is no way that Ronaldo is leaving this club.'

The word from Old Trafford is that Ronaldo has been offered a new contract but Ferguson denies it. 'His current deal runs to 2010,' he says, and then he is laughing again. 'I'll be in my wheelchair by then. You'll be pushing me up the hill so I can have a game of darts at the British Legion.'

'We know that, Alex,' says Stuart Mathieson of the *Evening News*. 'But you'll still be the manager here ...'

Ferguson is still laughing when we ask him about the silliest story of the season so far. At the start of the week, person or persons unknown made four 'spy flights' in a Cessna over Carrington, with someone on board apparently filming the training sessions. The *Mirror* ran the story over three pages, claiming that another Premiership club was behind it – but Ferguson isn't so sure.

United suspect the *Mirror* is trying to pull a fast one and Ferguson is beside himself with joy when David McDonnell brings it up.

'Amazing!' he exclaims. 'It's amazing that the *Daily Mirror* correspondent asks about this one, isn't it?'

'Just doing my job, Alex,' McDonnell smiles.

Ferguson loves that. 'Just doing your job … but I saw you flying the plane (impersonating looking through binoculars). I could see you up there in your Biggles hat and your Biggles goggles …'

He is roaring with laughter now. 'Biggles McDonnell! Biggles of the *Mirror*!'

ENGLAND DUTY
6.2.07

International week: a chance for Ferguson to catch up on some paperwork. He still doesn't allow himself any time off but most of his players are away and it gives him an opportunity to go through the mountain of letters on his desk. Or run the kind of errands that he never gets the chance to do in a normal week. Ferguson's job is so time-consuming he once confessed to David Meek that he had forgotten to get Cathy a Christmas present. He remembered on Christmas Eve but the shops were shut. So he slipped a cheque into her Christmas card. 'A bummer idea,' he recalled, 'she tore it in two and dropped it in the bin.'

England have a friendly against Spain at Old Trafford and the FA is using Carrington as its training base. Which gives us, the media, a rare opportunity to see a little more of the practice ground than just the pressroom. The FA does not operate by United's restrictions and there is a training session every morning of which we are allowed to watch the opening fifteen minutes. The FA has a small army of press officers and after these sessions there can be as many as a dozen players put up for interview. The players have it drummed into them that it is part of their duties to speak to the newspapers, and everything is divided between the different broadcast and written journalists to suit everyone's requirements. There are no set-in-stone time constraints and when it comes to Steve McClaren's briefings there is nothing like the intensity of when Ferguson is in the seat.

The McClaren press conference is a strange experience, particularly for those of us who are used to dealing with Ferguson. Here is an England manager who is so desperate to be liked it would be of little surprise to find him standing at the doorway handing out Liquorice Allsorts. Someone will ask a routine question about injuries or formations and he will enthusiastically nod his head: 'That's a very good question. I'm glad you've asked that question. I'm *really* glad you've asked that question.' Or someone will make a light-hearted remark and he will tip his head back and roar with a kind of laughter that sounds forced.

For someone who spent two and a half years at Old Trafford as Ferguson's assistant, McClaren doesn't seem to have cottoned on that football managers get good press by inspiring confidence and winning matches rather than buttering up reporters. It is not just a question of being a good guy or a bad guy, of being liked or disliked, approachable or aloof. All these things are secondary to the quality that is essential for a top manager: the capacity to dominate and take control.

When Ferguson walks into a room there is immediately a hush of anticipation. If someone is slouched in a seat, that person will instinctively sit to attention, bolt upright. We ask the questions. But he is generally in control.

McClaren has a very different approach. He has learned the name of everybody who matters in Fleet Street. He has had television coaching. He has employed the celebrity publicist Max Clifford to get him 'in' with the tabloid editors. Off-duty, McClaren is a likeable man. Yet put him in an FA blazer and place him in a room of journalists and he takes on the role of a new stepfather: matey and jocular, obviously doing his best, but largely viewed with suspicion, however hard he tries.

He is relatively new in the job but some of the newspapers already have their knives out and McClaren is plainly conscious of his shortage of admirers. He sent a carefully selected list of the 'Number Ones' a text message on Christmas Day along the lines of: 'Dear (insert name), have a fantastic Christmas, best wishes, Steve.' There is nothing wrong with being friendly, of course, but there is a difference between friendliness and strategic sweet-talk, and the journalists were generally stunned by this message given that their newspapers had enthusiastically put into place the beginnings of a 'McClaren Out' campaign. Then just before midnight on New Year's Eve, the same journalists' phones bleeped again. 'Dear (insert name), have a happy and prosperous new year, looking forward to seeing you in 2007, Steve.'

The average England press conference now is an ego-destroying interrogation, far worse than anything to which Eriksson was subjected. Eriksson was an owlish little man, with his rimless glasses and stacked shoes, and he could be fist-eatingly boring. Yet he didn't really give a fig what was in the newspapers and in an odd way that earned him kudos. He was always unflappable, whereas McClaren looks like he needs a Bloody Mary as soon as the questions get tough. He is not an easy man to quote. There is never a single moment when you find yourself listening to him, thinking 'this is great stuff' while hoping that the batteries in your tape recorder don't conk out.

The top managers are confident enough to march to a different drumbeat from the rest. They don't need the gimmickry of PR or clever little 'buzz phrases' when they are possessed with judgment and nerve. Ferguson comes into this category, as do Mourinho, Wenger, Benitez and, overseas, the likes of Luis Felipe Scolari and Marcello Lippi. But there are times with McClaren when his lips don't seem to move and you find yourself thinking: 'who the hell is operating this guy?' He straight-bats questions with formulaic, carefully structured sound bites and when someone chucks in a googly he cannot think on his feet. He freezes in his seat and clams up, like a panicking supply teacher. It is what a comedian would know as 'dying'.

BOMBAY MONEYLENDERS
9.2.07

An email has gone out from Old Trafford telling us off for being too scruffy. Some of the directors have complained about our appearance and we have been asked to wear suits if we want to fly with the team in future. United have drawn Lille in the next round of the Champions League and it is made clear that we will not be welcome on the plane if we flout the rules by wearing denim.

The order has come from the board but Ferguson, as always, is aware of everything that happens at Old Trafford and he is braying with laughter when he comes into the pressroom.

'I want to see this new dress code then,' he announces, checking us out from head to toe, and it is one of those moments when you desperately hope your shoes are polished and your flies are done up.

He is tut-tutting, shaking his head with faux disgust, racking his brains for the killer line. Then his eyes sparkle as it comes to him.

'You look like a bunch of Bombay moneylenders,' he says. 'Your mothers wouldn't be proud of you.'

Then he claps his hands together and says he wants to get down to business because there is a new signing to tell us about.

Our mouths fall open.

'What new signing?' we ask simultaneously and he wheezes with more laughter, chuffed to bits with the combination of his wit and our gullibility.

To see Ferguson right now is to observe a man who is utterly in love with his work. Last weekend, United went to Tottenham and thrashed them 4-0 with goals from Ronaldo, Vidic, Scholes and Giggs. It was their biggest ever win at White Hart Lane and when the cameras panned on Ferguson he was laughing and joking in the dugout, totally relaxed – until one moment, deep into stoppage time, when we were treated to a wonderful insight into what makes him tick. Ferdinand made a mistake and Ferguson was out of his seat, throwing his arms in the air and furiously swearing, while Rooney and Giggs were collapsing in giggles in the next row. There are not many managers who could blow a gasket when their team is winning by four goals at White Hart Lane but this, perhaps, is what makes Ferguson different from the rest. The man, at his very best, is a perfectionist.

The only time his stare becomes disquieting today is when he is asked about the 'kicking' that Steve McClaren has had in the newspapers.

England lost 1-0 against Spain. It was a dishevelled performance, full of misplaced passes and dreary, sideways football, and there were 58,000 people inside Old Trafford letting McClaren know exactly what they thought of it. His smile was the thinnest of slits in his post-match conference and there was nothing subtle about the next day's headlines.

The country is going through its first cold snap of the winter and the *Sun* mocked up McClaren as a snowman, with a carrot nose, under the words 'England in Snowman's Land'. McClaren has talked about wanting to find the 'real bull' but some of the reporters misheard him and thought he said 'rainbow', and the *Mirror* superimposed a picture of him between Bungle, Zippy and George from the children's television show.

Ferguson is keen to stick up for his former colleague. 'One of the big problems of the England job these days is you press,' he tells us. 'The players are fearful of putting in a bad performance because of the reaction there will be in the press. You lads will not agree with that. You think it's your duty to do what you're doing but I don't see how you're going to get a positive response when you treat England the way you do.'

Fair enough. Some of the criticism has been over the top, maybe personal, and there are some journalists who clearly take a sense of pleasure out of the national team doing badly. The England manager's job is close to becoming a poisoned chalice and it doesn't reflect well on our industry that what Ferguson says, interesting as it is, won't appear in many of the newspapers simply because it contains an anti-media vibe.

A FRENCH FARCE
20.2.07

Lille	0
Manchester United	1

Champions League, first knockout game

Claude Puel, the Lille manager, is a friend of Arsène Wenger's and used to play for him at Monaco. That doesn't automatically make him an enemy of Ferguson's but it is useful information when analysing their relationship. Ferguson, to Puel, is someone to view with extreme caution. Puel, to Ferguson, is not a man he wants to befriend.

The tone was set when Lille drew 0-0 at Old Trafford last season and Ferguson complained, long and hard, about the French tactics, accusing Puel of sending out a team that had tried to kick their way to success. Giggs left the pitch with a fractured cheekbone and Ferguson talked about 'punches in the back, elbows in the face and kicks'. In Ferguson's world, there is no more devastating snub than to refuse to shake hands with an opposition manager and he studiously ignored Puel when the sides met again at the Stade de France.

We asked Ferguson about it at his pre-match press conference yesterday and he laughed it off, claiming it was simply because Puel had disappeared in the Lille celebrations. It was a diplomatic answer but we weren't sure whether to believe him. Ferguson versus Puel is not a rift to compare with Clough and Revie or, indeed, Ferguson and Wenger, but it is a rift, none-theless, and worse is to follow tonight.

For eighty-three minutes it is a grey game, on a grey night, in a grey stadium. Then United win a free-kick, twenty-five yards from goal, and Giggs clips it into the goal while Tony Sylva, the Lille goalkeeper, is lining up his wall. Sylva barely moves. His wall is only in the construction stage but the referee has given Giggs permission to take it early.

Bedlam is the best description of the scenes. Lille's players crowd round the referee, screaming in his face. He is flashing yellow cards for dissent, ordering them to back off but they are bug-eyed with anger, refusing to accept what has happened. It takes at least three minutes before the game finally restarts and, straight from the kick-off, something extraordinary happens. The Lille players down tools. Gregory Tafforeau, the captain, hoofs the ball into touch and then starts to follow it. A white-haired guy – later identified as the team's goalkeeping coach Jean-Noel Duse – appears in the technical area and, at first, it looks like he is just unloading a stream of invective at the referee. Then it becomes apparent he has more sinister motives. Tafforeau is walking off the pitch and Duse is signalling for the other players to follow, waving them in like a lifeguard at high tide.

All hell breaks loose. It dawns on Ferguson what is happening and he is out of his dugout. Some of the

United players run over and Ferguson is incandescent. He gives Neville a sharp push in the back and orders him to get on with the game. Neville takes exception to being singled out and gives him a mouthful.

The atmosphere is poisonous when the game restarts. Bottles and flagpoles are thrown from the crowd towards anyone in a United shirt. It is a night that has 'UEFA investigation' stamped all over it.

The press conference is a must-see event and Ferguson doesn't disappoint. 'I've never seen anything like it,' he says, and his anger grips the room. 'It is an absolute disgrace what has happened tonight. I've seen a lot of bad things in football over the years but nothing like that. It is totally wrong.'

The goal, he re-iterates, was perfectly legitimate and Lille should just have accepted it. 'They were trying to intimidate the referee, incite the fans and create a hostile atmosphere. Gary Neville was struck to the side of his head and there were other objects thrown at our dugout. It shouldn't be allowed.'

He is angry with his own players too. 'We should have taken a quick throw-in,' he says. 'We should have gone down the other end of the pitch and scored a second. That's what I was telling Gary. I told him he should have stayed on the pitch. It was our job to get on with the game and if we had taken the throw-in quickly it may have defused the whole thing. Gary was trying to be the peacemaker but there was no need because the problem wasn't with us.'

Puel is next in and his argument is very, very flaky. He denies that his players were trying to abandon the match and he says they were simply trying to lodge a protest with the fourth official. Paddy Crerand, the former United player, can be seen in the second row, in

his role as MUTV analyst, shaking his head incredulously and struggling to stop himself from laughing
out loud. We all feel like that, to be honest. But Puel carries on. His club will appeal against the result to UEFA,
he says. He wants the game to be replayed and he says
he isn't bothered by anything Ferguson has to say.

'I don't understand why Alex Ferguson has said
anything on the matter. He shouldn't have said anything but we have had these problems with Ferguson
before, haven't we? He likes to influence referees and
he enjoys trying to create polemic situations. That is his
style. But I don't want to be bogged down with him.'

It is interesting what happens here – all the French
journalists take Puel's side and all the English journalists back Ferguson. The French seem to think
their entire values as a sporting nation are being
challenged and they concentrate their questions for
Puel on the perceived injustice of Giggs's goal. They
flash us dark looks and scowl exasperatedly when
we demand an explanation for the walk-off, and at
one point Puel rolls his eyes for their benefit, as if to
say: 'Who the hell are these guys?' Then at the end of
the conference the reporters from *L'Equipe*, *Le Monde*
and the other French newspapers start to remon-
strate with us because of the tone of our questions.
They say we have it wrong and that it is 'tradition'
in France to walk off the pitch to complain to the
fourth official.

We have no time for an argument. It is essential we
speak to Neville to see how he is, so we make our way
to UEFA's 'mixed-zone' interview area: a long, snak-
ing walkway in which we wait behind barriers and
try to bribe, beg and bully the players into talking to
us as they leave the stadium.

All the players have to come through and Neville, as captain, is usually happy to stop for a very brief interview. Others will march straight past as if they would rather nail their toes to the floor than talk to us. On England duty some players even avoid talking to us by pretending they are on their mobiles, a ruse that was exposed when a player's phone started ringing in the middle of one 'conversation'. But Neville doesn't go in for those tricks. He either says yes or no, and it is usually yes.

Van der Sar is first through and he stops for half a dozen questions with MUTV. Saha is next and he knows some of the French journalists, so he stops too. The other players head straight for the bus. Then Neville appears and he has a lump the size of an egg above his right eye.

'Any chance of two minutes please, Gary?'

'No,' he clips, not even breaking stride.

We wait for him to snake back round and a journalist from one of the Sunday newspapers leans forward.

'Gary? Just one question?'

'I said no, didn't I? Are you deaf?'

LUNCH WITH FERGIE
1.3.07

Ferguson comes to the Football Writers' Association's managers' lunch at Haydock Park today. It is a great do and he is in cracking form, holding court, telling stories and wheezing with loud laughter as he recites, from one to eleven, the line-ups of his favourite Scottish teams from the 1970s, even breaking into song over dessert.

The picture is of a man without a care in the world. United are at Liverpool this weekend, one of the last major obstacles if they are to win the league, and yet he doesn't seem the slightest bit agitated.

Everything is going swimmingly until we get to the point when the managers traditionally begin to drift round the tables for individual interviews.

David Moyes, of Everton, comes over first, followed by Wigan Athletic's Paul Jewell. Sam Allardyce, the Bolton manager, heads over to speak to the Sunday newspaper reporters and everyone seems happy to talk. Except Ferguson won't budge.

An *Evening News* reporter drifts over apprehensively and asks if he can have a couple of minutes.

Ferguson laughs teasingly. 'The Evening Blues? The Manchester Evening Blues? No thanks. Go and interview FC United of Manchester ...'

Our interviews with Jewell and Moyes wind up and we look plaintively in Ferguson's direction. He is still laughing, enjoying watching us squirm.

'Come on Alex, you know you'll enjoy it.'

'Boys, you've got more chance of getting an interview with the Pope.'

THE MOMENT
3.3.07

Liverpool	0
Manchester United	1

There is always one moment in every season when everything falls into place and the team that are top of the Premiership know they are going to finish as champions. One moment when the worrying stops and everyone at that club knows it is going to be a season to cherish. A goal, or a miss, or a referee's decision. A defining moment when everything turns and all the hard work comes together.

Go through Ferguson's twenty years at Old Trafford and his career is littered with such moments – Steve Bruce's header against Sheffield Wednesday in 1993, Eric Cantona's volley at Newcastle in 1996, Andy Cole's lob against Tottenham in 1999 and today, at Anfield, it is another of those seminal days when it is impossible to leave the stadium without feeling that we have surely witnessed the defining moment of the 2006-07 season.

Liverpool have been the better team. Rooney has come off injured and Scholes has been sent off for swinging a punch at Xabi Alonso. Ninety-two minutes have been played when Ronaldo shapes up to take a free-kick, over by the left touchline. It is the last chance to win the game and the Kop is whistling for full time.

Everyone expects Ronaldo to cross but he hits it, hard and true, and Liverpool's goalkeeper Pepe Reina is partially unsighted. He dives to his right and the ball bounces off his shin. It is football's version of the yorker. The rebound falls, fortuitously, to John O'Shea and, suddenly, in the very last minute, at the home of United's most despised rivals, he has the chance to win it.

Everything seems to go into slow motion. Ferguson is crouched in his seat, the upper half of his body leaning towards the pitch, his mouth forming a little 'o'. O'Shea brings back his right boot. It's in. And Ferguson is out of the dugout, dancing a grandfather's jig of delight on the touchline, and it is the celebration he reserves only for special occasions: a running skip, a clap of the hands and a jerky sequence of peculiar little hops and twirls.

A true test of any championship team is to go to a fortress such as Anfield and win. United are now twelve points clear, albeit having played two more games than Chelsea, and their goal difference is so superior it is worth a bonus point. They are, in effect, thirteen points ahead and the United fans are, for want of a better description, going loopy.

The celebrations at the final whistle are long and impassioned. No one even tries to pretend it is just another three points. Ronaldo rips off his shirt and throws it into the away end. Evra is next. Then Giggs. Soon, half the team is bare-chested. Neville, whose dislike of Liverpool is legendary, does his version of the Mancunian Haka. Rooney, who has come off with blood streaming down his leg, limps out barefooted. The away end is a scene of delirious jubilation and Ferguson is soaking it all in, flushed with pride, arms aloft. He has a rubicund glow and he is still beaming thirty minutes later when he does his television interviews. 'It's a massive result for us,' he says, and we know we are listening to someone savouring that rare experience of complete accomplishment. 'You cannot minimise the importance of this victory. It is a championship win, there is no question about it.'

CRISTIANO RONALDO AND PLASTIC SURGERY 17.3.07

| Manchester United | 4 |
| Bolton | 1 |

The mood at Old Trafford now is that of champions-in-waiting. There are long, enthusiastic chants of 'we want our trophy back' and 'we shall not be moved' and a touching moment when Ferguson is invited on to the pitch before kick-off to collect February's Manager of the Month award. There is a huge, vibrating roar of approval and a standing ovation. Ferguson walks on to the pitch, waving to the crowd and the fans rise to salute him. It is a spine-tingling mix of affection and gratitude and, above all, sheer admiration. He raises a triumphant arm and the volume goes up again.

What a difference a year makes. This time last season it was impossible to start a conversation about United in any Manchester pub without someone saying it was time for him to go. The phone-ins crackled with animosity and a browse through the fans' websites would habitually uncover page after page of vitriolic essays demanding his removal from office. Many of the dissenters were anti-Ferguson because of his support for the Glazers – in other words, there were as many political reasons as football ones for the disillusionment – but it feels hugely paradoxical now that he was demonised in such a way. Or that three weeks into the season five season-ticket holders with a pot of paint and a spare bedsheet took it upon themselves to make a 'Fergie Out' banner and stand outside the gates at Carrington for two hours, chanting for him to go.

What is clear is that there are a lot of people, from a lot of different walks of life, with a lot of egg on their faces. At one point last season the newspapers were so convinced Ferguson would be frogmarched kicking and screaming into retirement the debate ceased being about when he would go, or even if, but of who would replace him. Guus Hiddink and Paul Le Guen were both prominently mentioned which, in hindsight, is laughable in itself – Hiddink has just been convicted of tax evasion and given a six-month suspended prison sentence and Le Guen went to Glasgow Rangers and was sacked after six months in which he seemed to take his inspiration from the theory of chaos.

All that feels like a distant memory now because Ferguson has had some wonderful press this season, with more than one correspondent ungrudgingly acknowledging they were too hasty to write him off. Richard Williams, the *Guardian*'s chief sports writer, has written that it is time to 'shut up and join in the applause', although he points out he was 'not the only person who got it utterly, absolutely, laughably wrong'. Matt Dickinson, *The Times*'s chief football correspondent, has predicted Ferguson could be dishing up the 'world's largest humble pie' at the end of the season, and that he might be 'surprised how many willing eaters he would find in Fleet Street'.

The win is United's sixth in succession in the Premiership and it is another performance that has Ferguson applauding warmly from the sidelines. Bolton are a strong team, competing with Arsenal for the fourth Champions League spot, but United have rattled eight past them this season and when you see the way Ronaldo runs the show it feels like we must have dreamt what happened in the World Cup.

We didn't, of course, and this is where Ferguson comes into his own because what we have here is a classic example of his man-management at its very best. Ferguson has never spoken about it publicly, but after the World Cup he flew to Portugal to take Ronaldo out to dinner and convince him that, if he placed his trust in the Manchester United family, he could beat the hate mobs at opposition grounds. Ferguson told Ronaldo he wanted to build the team around him and that there would be only place to go if he left Old Trafford: down.

These little touches of genius – for that is what they are – have been an essential part of Ferguson's success and that heart-to-heart in Lisbon is up there with his very best work because Ronaldo's form this season has put him on the way to achieving what was once thought impossible at Old Trafford, eclipsing the players who wore the club's number seven shirt before him: David Beckham and Eric Cantona.

To see him right now is to witness a player whose speed across the ground, with the ball under total control, can make traffic bollards of the most accomplished defenders. Ferguson has always encouraged his wide players to play with freedom and not be frightened about running at full-backs but he has never had a wide player who has taken the art of wing play to such dimensions. Ronaldo may not have invented dribbling but he has elevated it to its highest tier. Nobody – not even George Best – has tormented opponents so mercilessly.

He flicks the ball with the outside of his left boot while leaning back, looking at the clouds. He conjures up shots that dip at the last moment, like a beach ball on a windy day. He looks one way and caresses a pass in the opposite direction. He has strapping shoulders and the torso of an Olympic swimmer, nothing like the classic rake-thin winger of old. But when he moves with the ball he looks like he wouldn't make footprints in snow. It is a blur of white boots and gelled hair and improvisational brilliance.

Defenders try to kick him. They yank his shirt, stand on his feet, scratch his neck, prod, poke, pull and pinch and, in the worst cases, try to point him in the direction of the local hospital. And none of it works. Ronaldo, like Best, knows how to ride a challenge. Unlike Best, there is never a flicker of retaliation. Everything with Ronaldo is so beautifully packaged and polished he would rather hurt his opponent with the ball.

When he first arrived in Manchester, at the start of the 2003–04 season, he wore braces on his teeth, his forehead was pockmarked with adolescent pimples and after a dazzling start his obsession with stepovers and showy pyrotechnics marked him down as a playground show-off who had stayed young too long. There were times when he would get into a good position and try another piece of extravagant, showboating skill rather than a simple pass, and team-mates, most often Neville and Van Nistelrooy, would drag their hands down their faces and spread their fingers into the air as if they would cheerfully throttle him.

Ferguson, in time, has turned him into a far more accomplished package. His work now is informed by an adult intelligence of when to pass, when to keep it and when to try his tricks. The ball is welded to his right toe and even when Bolton surround him with three, four, sometimes five defenders they are powerless to do anything about it.

Henrik Pedersen, the right-back, is so befuddled Sam Allardyce substitutes him only twenty-eight minutes into the first half. It is the ultimate indignity but Pedersen is traumatised. And in the press conference afterwards a reporter from the *Bolton Evening*

News asks Allardyce whether Ronaldo's performance could leave his defenders with psychological scars. 'Scars?' Allardyce replies. 'We're going to need a fucking plastic surgeon after that.'

FERGUSON AND GEOFF SHREEVES
19.3.07

Manchester United	1
Middlesbrough	0

FA Cup sixth round replay

This has been such an aggro-free season it is easy to be lulled into a false sense of security. The more we have seen of Ferguson, the more we have become convinced that he has taken a strategic decision that falling out with journalists is not worth the hassle and that it would be better for everyone to work in peace. A large part of this is because of the ubiquitous television cameras. But he has also mellowed in line with the turnaround of his team and the admiring headlines they have received. Even when something is written that offends him the rebuke comes via the press office these days rather than the public ordeal of being bawled out. Ferguson has been serene and good-humoured and his temper has been kept on a leash – which is just the way we like it.

Tonight, though, it breaks loose and when we hear what has happened in the tunnel it is clear that The Hairdryer has been only in hibernation and that Ferguson is still as accomplished as anyone in sport when it comes to terrorising men with microphones.

The man whose eyebrows are scorched is Geoff

Shreeves, Sky's pitch-side reporter.

Ronaldo has won another man-of-the-match award and at the end of the game that means collecting a bottle of champagne and answering half a dozen or so questions from Shreeves in the tunnel. It is one of his first interviews without using an interpreter and Ferguson is watching the television in the dressing room. Ronaldo has been the outstanding player, scoring the decisive penalty after having his heels clipped by Jonathan Woodgate. But he has a habit of going down under minimal contact and Shreeves begins by asking whether he could have stayed on his feet, even though the television replays show he was caught. Then Shreeves wants to know why Ronaldo always seems to be embroiled in controversy when he plays Middlesbrough. Ronaldo is bemused but smiles politely and comes out with a line that is pure Ali. 'I don't know,' he replies, 'maybe it is because I am too good.'

He handles it superbly. But Ferguson is protective of Ronaldo to the point of being a surrogate father and he is furious that one of his players has gone to collect a bottle of bubbly and found himself being interrogated about being a serial diver. He thinks the line of questioning is pointed, to say the least, and he is off his seat, out of the dressing room and marching through the labyrinthine corridors to find Shreeves.

Gareth Southgate, the Middlesbrough manager, is in the interview area, taking questions from *Match of the Day*'s Ivan Gaskell, when Ferguson suddenly appears. He is shouting, calling Shreeves a 'fucking bastard'.

This is the point when the subjects of his wrath

usually freeze to the spot and either blurt out something completely wet or lose the power of speech entirely. Except Shreeves refuses to accept what is happening. He looks Ferguson in the eye and tells him in a firm voice to stop shouting because he is out of order. It is very apparent that he is not going to accept being sworn and shouted at. 'Do not talk to me like that,' he says.

Ferguson is not used to being rebuked in the middle of a full-blown rant. He splutters back: 'Fuck off to you.'

Shreeves tell him again: 'Don't talk to me like that. Don't even think of it.'

'Don't you think about it,' Ferguson yells back. 'Fuck off, right?'

Shreeves refuses to back down. He doesn't think he has done anything wrong. At least half the country thinks Ronaldo goes down too easily, or has done in the past. Earlier this season Southgate was all over the sports pages calling Ronaldo a 'diver'. Ferguson, in turn, described Southgate, the Premiership's newest manager, as 'very naïve'. Resentment has been festering and when Ronaldo scores tonight he runs past the Middlesbrough bench and dedicates the goal to Southgate. There are shouts of 'cheat' and Queiroz has to be pulled away from confronting Southgate's backroom staff. The game ends with the Middlesbrough players trying harder to kick Ronaldo than to get an equaliser, and one of their substitutes, James Morrison, gets a red card for chopping him down by the corner flag.

'Listen,' says a red-faced Shreeves, 'are you going to do an interview in a professional manner or not? Do you want to do it or not?'

But Ferguson isn't interested. 'You fucking be professional,' he says. 'You be professional. You're the one.'

Shreeves tries to defend himself some more, but it is useless and he begins to stutter.

'I'm entitled to ask … Cristiano gave the right answer …'

Ferguson is turning to go.

'Fucking hell with your answers,' he says, and then it is Shreeves's turn to lose his rag.

'Don't talk to me like that. Go away. If you want to behave civilly, fine. But don't talk to me like that.'

'Fuck off!'

Ferguson has said enough and disappears. There is a short silence, maybe ten or fifteen seconds, and then Gaskell apologises to Southgate.

'I'm sorry Gareth, but I'm going to have to ask that question again.'

The news has seeped through to the pressroom by the time Ferguson does his MUTV interview and when we see his face it is obvious he is still angry. 'I watched the interview with Sky and it was a poor interview, a disgraceful interview,' he says. 'He was stretching it out, hoping Cristiano would trip himself up, but he doesn't know how intelligent the boy is. It was a poor interview and I'm disgusted. Sky should have a good look at themselves.'

ROME
3.4.07

Geoff Shreeves has emailed Ferguson with a request that they put the slanging match behind them and don't let it affect their working relationship. Sky pump an awful lot of money into the Premiership and normally get privileged access at Old Trafford, second only to MUTV. But Shreeves's bosses are acutely aware of what Ferguson has done to the BBC and that there have been at least three occasions when he has threatened to boycott Sky in the past, even when his son Jason worked there as a producer. The first was in 1993 after the cameras zoomed in on a touchline row with Gerry Francis, then the QPR manager. The following year Sky upset him again when they set a series of Eric Cantona's illegal tackles to music, and he was livid again in 2003 when a television crew made the mistake of interrupting him and Cathy on holiday in France to ask about David Beckham's impending move to Real Madrid.

Jason, incidentally, became Sky's senior football director before changing careers to become an agent in 1999. On one occasion, seeing his father's pained stare during a particularly tense match, he was famously heard to yell in the production room: 'Get the cameras on Fergie, he's looking angry!' Ferguson found that story rather amusing when it got back to Old Trafford, chuckling with journalists one day that 'even my family are playing up the Fergie-fury angle'.

The issue with Shreeves is whether or not it was fair to ask Ronaldo in effect: 'why is it always you?' Ferguson is angry because he thinks Shreeves was trying to lead Ronaldo into saying something he might later regret. Shreeves's argument is that he would have been accused of ducking the issue had he merely patted the player on the back and complimented him on his performance. The truth is probably somewhere in between, but the important thing is that it doesn't seem to have caused any lasting damage. One thing about Ferguson is that he has more respect for victims of The Hairdryer if they are willing to stand up to him. Shreeves, by all accounts, refused to budge an inch as they went toe to toe in the tunnel and Ferguson might even be secretly impressed because when we check in at Manchester airport today – the team play AS Roma in the first leg of the Champions League quarter-finals tomorrow – there is confirmation that he is willing to speak to Sky, and Shreeves, after the game.

Ferguson is in a good mood on the plane and the only spark of anger comes when we are interviewing him at Ciampino airport and a Scandinavian tourist starts to click away with a camera phone without asking permission. This is one of Ferguson's pet hates. 'Have you finished?' he thunders and even when the tourist scuttles off Ferguson is so annoyed he can barely concentrate for the next couple of questions. 'It's unbelievable,' he says, 'that someone can just come up to you and stick a camera in your bloody face.'

His tactics are always interesting before these big games because he will invariably plan in advance what he wants to say to the media and how to exploit the headlines for his own benefit. Today, for example, he is no admirer of the referee Herbert Fandel, and his carefully delivered message is that he wants the officials to be 'strong'. It is a classic Ferguson ploy. Before home games he will often appeal for the fans to get behind the team and intimidate the opposition. Or there have been times when he deliberately seems to want to disrupt United's opponents by getting under their skin.

Before the quarter-final against Inter Milan in 1999 UEFA fined him £2,000 after he voiced his distrust of Italians. 'When an Italian says it is pasta,' he said, 'I check under the sauce to make sure.' He went on to predict Inter's tactics would include 'scheming, diving, referee-baiting, the full works' and he was at his most provocative again before the quarter-final against Real Madrid in 2003, claiming that the Spaniards would try to 'get' the referee and that the draw had been fixed because 'they don't want us in the final'. *Marca*, the Madrid newspaper, responded with a front-page headline of 'Hooligan Ferguson', and the Real coach Vicente del Bosque said Ferguson was being 'ridiculous'. UEFA agreed, describing the comments as 'unfortunate and silly' and fining him £4,600.

Today, though, Ferguson is on his best behaviour. He talks at length about his admiration for the Italian game and he is full of praise for the Roma coach Luciano Spalletti, describing him as a brave and inno-vative tactician. He congratulates Roma for knocking out Lyon in the last round and he makes it clear that he thinks United are facing one of the strongest teams left in the competition.

He could hardly be more complimentary, but there is muttering and headshaking in the seats where the Italian journalists are congregated. At one point, a reporter from *La Gazzetta Dello Sport* asks him in a slightly accusatory tone why he does not seem more concerned about Totti. There is none of the reverence that is usually afforded to Ferguson in other coun-tries, where he is sometimes applauded in and out of press conferences. The whiff of controversy is in the air and another Italian wants to know why United have written letters to their 4,500 travelling fans warning them there is a 'real danger' of being attacked by Roma's hooligans, the Ultras.

The answer should be obvious given that three Middlesbrough supporters were stabbed in the Campo de Fiori before a UEFA Cup tie last season. Liverpool's supporters have also encountered problems in Rome dating back to the 1984 European Cup final, when there were numerous stabbings, and United have advised their fans to avoid several areas of the city.

The letter has been published on the club's website and the Italian press have picked it up. Italian journalists have always been a rather bloodthirsty lot and United have been accused of staining the reputation of the Eternal City with 'racism' and a 'weather forecast of violence'. Spalletti has been quoted as saying he is 'extremely annoyed by this slur against our city', and everyone – from the city's leading political party, the Democrats of the Left, to the chief of police and the head of internal security – has had their say. The mayor, Walter Veltroni, is on the main television news tonight and he says he is so angry he has complained to the British Embassy.

'We always do this,' Ferguson tries to explain. 'We write to our supporters with advice before every European trip.' He says the Rome authorities have been 'very co-operative' and he predicts it will be a trouble-free evening, but you can tell from the Italians' faces that they are unimpressed. Veltroni has held his own press briefing: 'Rome is a city that welcomes everyone in a hospitable manner. This letter is unfortunate and unpleasant and I regard it as dangerous because it creates a negative climate. I would like to assure

Manchester United fans that they are welcome in our city and that the true image of Rome is very different to how it has been portrayed by their club.'

POLICEMEN IN BLACK
4.4.07

AS Roma   2
Manchester United   1
Champions League quarter-final, first leg

As Walter Veltroni points out, Rome is a city of culture and elegance, from the pavement cafes and upmarket boutiques on Via Veneto to the serenity of the Vatican and the sense of architectural awe inspired by the Colosseum. But it is also a city in which large groups of young Italians carry knives and operate by their own rules, and there are eighteen United fans in hospital tonight, ten with stab wounds. Another fifty have to be bandaged up inside the Stadio Olimpico after some unforgivable scenes involving the Italian police. In the relative sanctuary of the pressbox some of our number could be forgiven if they were struggling to concentrate on the football. Jonathan Northcroft of the *Sunday Times* and James Fletcher of the *News of the World* were trapped on the Ponte Nenni, one of the 'no-go areas,' when thirty Italian youths carrying flares and broken bottles advanced on three Irish lads before the game. Northcroft managed to break free but Fletcher tried to run away; thirty yards later, sprinting at full pelt, he was intercepted by a fist. Jim Clarke, a photographer for the *Sun*, was kicked to the ground close by and £4,000-

worth of camera equipment was whipped from his neck.

The trouble is so extreme it dominates the news agenda. United's fans have been attacked with knives, bricks, bottles, coshes, catapults, an axe and even a stepladder. Yet the Ultras, it seems to us, have rivals to the title of the most formidable firm in Rome. The police (*carabinieri*) may not have such an extensive weapon collection but they also have their own set of rules and, of course, they have the law on their side. At the end of the first half Roma take the lead and their supporters rush towards the divide segregating the away end. A small group of United fans react and the *carabinieri* charge, lashing out indiscriminately with their batons, hitting anything that moves, battering limbs and heads. Anyone within range is struck. Some fans try to make gestures of peace and are beaten to the ground. A few are trapped and go down under a flurry of baton strikes. Others turn to flee and the police swarm after them.

The reaction is so savagely over the top the television cameras and photographic lenses are trained on what is happening in the stands rather than on the pitch. Supporters with nowhere to escape can be seen in a state of blind panic. One guy, in his fifties, is curled up in the foetal position, trying to cover his head and pleading for mercy as the blows rain down. His watch is smashed, hanging limply off his wrist, and he is shaking with fear. The television pictures zoom in on a middle-aged man, with a camera round his neck, and there is blood gushing from his forehead. A younger adult, possibly his son, is trying to pull him away and one of the riot cops, decked out in black Robocop gear, is swinging at them with his baton. A woman in her twenties is filming what is happening and one of the police officers snatches the camera from her hand. She goes after him to protest and his colleagues wade in, hitting out violently with their fists and their truncheons.

Many of us have friends and relatives in the away end and it is unnerving watching it all unfold, feeling utterly helpless from a comfortable seat 100 yards away. What begins five minutes before half-time lasts until the opening exchanges of the second half and it feels like the *carabinieri* are enjoying themselves so much they don't want the fun to stop. After the game we are waiting on a media coach to take us to the airport and they are having an informal debrief in the same part of the bus park. We can see them embracing each other, clasping hands and kissing each other on the cheeks – celebrating, it seems. One guy, sweaty and breathless and with his helmet tucked under his arm, is swishing his baton through the air to re-enact his best shots. His mates are laughing and clapping.

On occasions like this we have to file stories for the news sections as well as our usual match reports, and the word from United is that they want a full UEFA investigation. There are conflicting reports of how many people have been hospitalised and the extent of their injuries, and that makes it a long night because as well as the mayhem in the stands it is also a difficult match to assess for the sports pages.

On the face of it, there is more reason for consternation than confidence. Scholes is sent off for two first-half bookings and will miss the return leg. Ferguson is already without Neville, Vidic and Evra through injury – i.e. three first-choice defenders – and Roma look like an accomplished, adventurous team.

Yet Rooney scores a fine breakaway goal in the second half and Ferguson looks happy enough in his interviews. 'The away goal is always invaluable in these two-legged fixtures,' he says. 'This is a good result for us.'

It is midnight before we leave the stadium and when we arrive at the airport there are dozens of supporters with bandages over their heads and blood on their clothes. Some ask us what Ferguson has said about the trouble and they are distinctly unimpressed to learn that he refused to talk about it. We are horribly late getting on the plane, maybe as late as we have ever been, and as we shuffle past the directors we apologise for keeping them on the runway for so long. The atmosphere feels very flat – a combination of losing, fatigue and the shock of seeing so many heads being cracked – and we are glad to be leaving Rome behind, to be honest. The flight home is in near-silence.

LA DOLCE VITA
10.4.07

Manchester United	7
AS Roma	1

Champions League quarter-final, second leg
Manchester United win 8-3 on aggregate

Tonight is one of those occasions when it is easy to understand why, in 1958, a twenty-one-year-old Bobby Charlton told Arthur Hopcraft, one of the doyens of sportswriting, that playing football at Old Trafford was like walking into a 'theatre of dreams'. It

is a night when Manchester United's play is so thrill-
ingly packed with one-touch, fluent, penetrative
football it could be set to cha-cha music. A night when
words feel slightly superfluous and the aggregate
score belongs to a sepia-tinted past. Nobody wins 8-3
in the modern game, we all thought, and certainly not
against the Italians. It is an evening so crazy that it
defies logic and explanation. An epic, lyrical performance, full of everything that is good about the club
and the team.

Ferguson says it is his 'greatest European night at
Old Trafford' and it is a legitimate statement because
when the team-sheets were distributed before kick-
off there were audible groans from the crowd. Saha
had joined the list of injured and Ferguson not only
had to scratch together a team missing three-quarters
of his first-choice defence but Smith was starting in
attack for only the fourth time since recovering from
his broken leg. Fletcher was in 'the Keane role' and
O'Shea was deputising for Neville.

The list of absentees makes it unrealistic to expect
anything but an evening gripped by tension. Yet the
tone is set in the eleventh minute when United surge
forward and Carrick expertly lifts the ball over Doni,
Roma's goalkeeper. When Smith makes it 2-0 six minutes later it is a story of great personal triumph but
there is hardly time to pause. Within two minutes
Rooney has made it three and suddenly the Roma
defenders are wearing the pained expressions of
climbers stranded on a rock-face.

To see a team famed for its smothering negativity
being torn apart with such contemptuous ease feels
almost surreal. Roma had conceded only four goals in
their previous eight Champions League fixtures but

tonight the reputation of Serie A is obliterated in front of a worldwide audience and, in the pressbox, the Italians are banging their laptops shut, flapping their arms wildly and in one or two cases abandoning any pretence of impartiality to rise to their feet and scream loud, impassioned disapproval. Italians, as Ferguson pointed out before the first leg, pride themselves on parsimonious defending and have won four World Cups because of their thou-shall-not-pass mentality. It is the nation that gave us *catenaccio* – the defensive system patented by Inter Milan in the 1960s and translated as 'door-bolt' – and legendary defenders such as Franco Baresi, Claudio Gentile and Paolo Maldini. And yet here is Roma, the second-placed side in Serie A, being taken to the cleaners, with thirty-eight countries tuning in live.

When Ronaldo makes it 4-0 just before half-time it is too much for one of the Italian football correspondents, and he flounces out of the pressbox with tears of rage stinging his eyes, not to be seen again. There is a further peacock-like spreading of United's feathers after the break and the sense of awe increases with each goal. Ronaldo gets the fifth, Carrick the sixth and soon afterwards the 'oles' start, followed by giddy chants of 'we want ten'. Daniele De Rossi, the Italian World Cup winner, salvages a modicum of pride with a consolation goal but this is the final twitch before rigor mortis sets in and by the time Evra makes it 7-1 Ferguson is signing autographs for the fans behind the dugout.

The final whistle has the effect of smelling salts for the Roma defenders. Ferguson uses the word 'uncanny' and he questions whether there has ever been a better performance in the club's fifty years of

European football. Yet there is no hint of smugness. Ferguson never gloats in the face of an overwhelming victory. Or seeks to deflect the glory on to himself. If anything, he seems strangely restrained. A couple of people even remark that he seems slightly subdued, although that is not to say he is anything but proud and triumphant. 'To score seven times in a Champions League tie you think is an impossibility,' he says, sat back in his chair with an expression of rare and complete satisfaction. 'The quality of our game was so high that once we scored the second and third goals I was thinking: "this could be something really big here." But even so, I wasn't expecting that.'

United, he does not need reminding, managed only three goals in their six Champions League games last season. Tonight they have equalled that total inside the opening nineteen minutes. 'Hopefully what we have seen is not a one-off,' Ferguson continues, 'but the quality was so high it is difficult to think we could ever get that again. It was a fantastic performance: the speed of our play, the penetration, the confidence, the clinical nature of our finishing. Everything. It was just perfect.'

THE MORNING AFTER THE NIGHT BEFORE
11.4.07

The problem about scoring seven goals against an Italian side with the best defensive record in the Champions League is that it raises the question: have United peaked too soon? A number of other questions also have to be asked. Is this really the same team that were held to a scoreless draw against Burton Albion last season? Can they ever play like that again? And how is it possible to improve so drastically by selling the club's top scorer? The whole thing is, quite frankly, bizarre.

The rout is described in the *Independent* as 'one of the most exhilarating, affirmative and historic performances the European Cup has ever seen'. Oliver Kay hails a performance in *The Times* that 'will be replayed all over the world as confirmation the Manchester United phenomenon has been reborn'. Henry Winter, the jewel in the *Daily Telegraph*'s crown, says the life was drained from Roma like 'the Trevi fountain in a drought' and the *Daily Mail*'s Paul Hayward points out 'there have been international rugby matches that have ended less than 8-3'.

Ferguson often tells a little white lie about never reading the newspapers but they are lined up on his table today.

Seventh heaven in Theatre of Dreams
Fantasy Football
Rampant United lead the charge
Rout of Roma
Seven wonders of sublime United

After the game, in the 'mixed zone' interview area, it was one of those rare occasions when all the United players were happy to talk. The Italians were stunned. Some, like Totti, barged past without saying a word, their eyes smouldering with anger. Others looked dazed, shaking their heads with exaggerated slowness when we asked for interviews. Christian Panucci, a defender with forty-eight international caps, was one of the few to stop and we asked him what it was like to face Ronaldo. 'If he starts off with the ball at his feet, you can't catch him,' he explained, shaking his head mournfully. 'It's like he's Valentino Rossi. Or Juan Manuel Fangio. If you give me an engine, maybe I could keep up with him. Otherwise it's helpless, just helpless.'

Italian football has not been humiliated like this since Juventus lost 7-0 to Wiener SK of Austria in the 1958 European Cup, and their newspapers reflect a sense of national shock. 'I do not recall such an apocalyptic quarter-final or such a devastating first half in the history of the game,' Roberto Beccantini writes in *La Stampa*, describing Roma as 'stunned, then swept away, then destroyed, then humiliated'. *La Repubblica* singles out Ronaldo and says the defenders who were assigned to stop him 'looked like car-sick kids who vomit their elevenses at the first sharp curve'. Totti, the golden boy of Italian football, is 'Captain Disaster' in *La Gazzetta Dello Sport*.

WEMBLEY BOOKED
14.4.07

Manchester United	4
Watford	1

FA Cup semi-final

It is always easy to tell how Manchester United are doing by the number of autograph hunters waiting outside Carrington. This time last year we would roll up and there would be only a sprinkling of supporters by the gates. The numbers have risen all season and when we turn up for Ferguson's briefings now there are large throngs loitering with intent in strategic positions along the kerbside. Some are in place from sunrise. Every car is a legitimate target and, for us journalists, it can be jaw-achingly embarrassing as they swarm around at each set of barriers, peering through the windows to see who is inside and holding out their autograph books in anticipation. The disappointment when they realise it is a non-footballer is immense and barely disguised.

The supporters have plenty to be excited about right now and Watford were never going to stop United booking a place in the first FA Cup final at the new Wembley. To their credit, the Premiership's bottom club provide stiffer opposition than AS Roma, but class comes out in the end. Rooney scores twice, Ronaldo and Richardson get the others, and Watford's manager Adrian Boothroyd is philosophical. 'I was at Old Trafford for the game against Roma,' he says. 'I stopped taking notes at one point and started clapping.'

It has been an outstanding week for United, with eleven goals in two games, and the other good news is that Ronaldo has agreed to sign a new contract. Madrid's newspapers, particularly *Marca*, have been reporting an end-of-season transfer for Ronaldo as being a done deal and this is Ferguson's chance to put them in their place.

Madrid, he says, have no regard for anyone but themselves. 'There was never any reason for Cristiano to think about leaving other than that thing about people perceiving Real Madrid as *galacticos*. Or whatever the hell it is they call themselves. They have a pre-conceived notion of themselves at Madrid, don't they? But you couldn't say they are ahead of Manchester United.'

Ferguson is amazingly proud of United's status as the biggest club in the world and he hates the idea that Madrid, or anywhere else, should think they are a more attractive proposition.

Someone asked him once whether Arsenal could ever rival United in terms of size after their move to the 60,000-capacity Emirates stadium and he nearly fell off his chair. 'Rival United? Arsenal? Never! They will need three stadiums and thirty-three teams to rival us as a club. Nobody is as big as Manchester United. Nobody ever will be either.'

THE GLOVES ARE OFF
17.4.07

Manchester United	2
Sheffield United	0

There have been times this season when United have blown away their opponents with the quality of their football and times when the Premiership is so imbalanced they have won comfortably without hitting top form. The supporters inside Old Trafford might be disappointed this is not one of the more illuminating nights but it is unrealistic to expect them to scintillate every week, and Ferguson's face is still suffused with a broad smile at the final whistle. They may not have come close to their thrilling best but it is another match ticked off, courtesy of goals from Carrick and Rooney, and it keeps them coasting along at the top of the league.

The win is vital because there have been the makings of a Chelsea comeback recently. Chelsea's season may have been pockmarked with internal disputes and byzantine politics but nobody could question the durability of Mourinho's team, and since their mid-season blip they have won eight consecutive league games without conceding a goal. They have beaten Arsenal in the Carling Cup final to lift the season's first silverware and they have defeated Blackburn Rovers to make sure the FA Cup final is a contest between the two leviathans of English football. How Mourinho has managed it in a period of unremitting off-field crisis is anybody's guess but it is potentially among his finest achievements. He has had to contend with a devastating injury list, with Petr Cech, John Terry and Joe Cole among the long-term absentees. His five major summer signings – Shevchenko, Ballack, Ashley Cole, John Obi Mikel and Khalid Boulahrouz – have all had sub-standard seasons. Then there has been all the infighting with Kenyon and Arnesen and the daily ritual of his future being debated all over the sports pages. The backdrop has been so poisonous it would have rocked any other club to the foundations. And yet here are Chelsea, still fighting, still plugging away.

The gap has come down to six points and, as predicted, the bickering has started. April is always the month when the insults start to fly and Mourinho has already described United as 'lucky' to be top. Ferguson has taken exception to that and, like a schoolmaster admonishing a naughty third-former, suggested that Mourinho should 'button his lip for the rest of the season'. But Mourinho has never been a man to take advice on professional courtesies. He has questioned Ronaldo's habit for winning dubious penalties and he has complained so many times about referees favouring United that Ferguson has threatened to bring out a dossier on Chelsea's many different controversies with match officials. Mourinho, he says, is 'the last person who should ever talk about referees'.

Ferguson has also accused the Premier League of showing favouritism to Chelsea because of the way they have structured the fixture list. The response was classic Mourinho: 'Alex is an intelligent man but his problem is he thinks other people are stupid. They are not and can only laugh.'

It is a soap opera of the cheapest kind: two men at the very top of their profession bickering and backbiting. Yet let's not be too pious because, let's face it, it is also hugely entertaining and if this is the way it is going to be for the rest of the season – tit-for-tat sniping, dirty tricks and wars of words – we journalists love it as much as anyone. Her Majesty's Press enjoys nothing more than a good old-fashioned feud, and Ferguson v Mourinho is promising to become every bit as rancorous as Ferguson v Wenger or indeed Mourinho v Wenger. If is there is one thing for certain, it is that this is going to run and run.

A FULL HOUSE
23.4.07

A big press conference today. Milan, the famous *rossoneri*, are at Old Trafford tomorrow for the first leg of the Champions League semi-finals and it is standing-room only in the Europa suite. At Carrington there are only a dozen of us at some briefings, but today, in a room decorated with photographs of the club's most celebrated European nights, there are roughly 150 newspaper journalists, thirty radio reporters and another twenty television crews. Lorries with satellite dishes are parked on the concourse. Press-packs in different languages are handed out and Ferguson is flanked by an interpreter as he takes his seat behind a cluster of brightly coloured microphones. Everything has to be translated and there is a distinct feel of the 1970s sitcom *Mind Your Language*. The Italians are on one side, looking tanned and aloof in their dark shades and sharp suits. A group of Portuguese journalists is on Ronaldo-watch. The back row is filled by Japanese reporters. There are South Koreans, Americans and Scandinavians dotted round the edges. All of Europe's influential football newspapers – *L'Equipe*, *Marca*, *Bild* and so on – are represented, and the English dailies have sent their best teams of reporters.

Ferguson is wearing a summer suit, his hair is neatly brushed and he spends most of the conference in international ambassador-of-the-club mode. A Dutch journalist wants to know whether he thinks Van der Sar is the Premiership's outstanding goalkeeper. A Norwegian radio reporter asks for a comment on Solskjaer. A Portuguese reporter wants a reaction to Eusebio being in hospital. Another asks whether Ronaldo is the most exciting player in the world and Ferguson nods sagely. 'To my mind, he's the best,' he says, 'and you can't say that lightly given the fantastic footballers around.'

Strictly speaking, it is not a great press conference. Most of the foreign journalists just want a quick sound bite about the players from their countries and it is difficult to get any real flow or momentum. But at this stage of the competition it is always about more than the match anyway. These events are an opportunity for Ferguson to show the club in the best possible light and he does it with understated brilliance. Every question is answered thoughtfully, he is sparing with his time and when the Italians start to grill him about Milan he eloquently eulogises about what he regards as one of the great names in football.

Milan, he points out, have won the European Cup six times, compared to United's two. It is the fourth time in five seasons they have reached the semi-finals – their eleventh in total – and their squad reads like a Who's Who of the Champions League's elite. They have eight players with at least one winner's medal and, in the case of Paolo Maldini, four. They have a sweetly gifted midfielder-cum-striker, Kaka, who is fast replacing Ronaldinho as the star of Brazilian football, and they have three of the more influential players from Italy's victorious World Cup: Andrea Pirlo, Gennaro Gattuso and Alessandro Nesta. Ferguson has tried more than once to sign Gattuso. Maldini, the club's symbol of class and continuity, is his 'favourite player in Europe over the last fifteen years'.

The irony is that Milan's involvement in the competition is questionable, to say the least. At the start of the season, they were found guilty in a referee-rigging scandal, banned from the Champions League and deducted fifteen points in Serie A. Milan appealed and UEFA's emergency panel re-admitted them with extreme reluctance because there was 'no choice' legally. Now, eight months on, Milan are threatening to embarrass UEFA by reaching the final. They have all their best players available and will walk out at

Old Trafford as favourites, if only because of the injury problems that are handicapping United.

Before European games we are allowed, under UEFA regulations, to watch the players train for fifteen minutes at Carrington and when we roll up to the practice pitches this morning there are only ten senior outfield players going through the usual drills.

Ferguson says it is an 'injury crisis of major proportions' and describes the squad as 'down to the bare bones'. The first question from Sky sums it up – 'Have you got enough players to make a squad?' – and he reluctantly has to accept it will be difficult to put together 'an adequate bench'.

He has no time, however, for feeling sorry for himself. 'I don't have any fears,' he says, and he is as upbeat as could be expected for someone who might have to field a completely new defence. 'The injuries have come at a bad time for us. But I see the mood in the camp and it pleases me. It's difficult to think we can get to the standard we got against Roma, because that was a once-in-a-lifetime result, but we should still expect a very good performance. The quality of our opponents and the importance of the occasion demands the very best from us.'

The press conference has been a success and there is a classic Ferguson moment at the end, as everyone is rising to their feet, when an Italian journalist tries to get his attention.

'Mr Ferguson, what do you think of the Italian match-fixing scandal?'

But Ferguson is preparing to leave, only half paying attention.

'Scandal?' he asks.

'Yes,' the Italian calls out, 'the scandal ...'

'Scandalous,' Ferguson replies deadpan. And then he's out of the door.

LIVING ON YOUR NERVES
24.4.07

Manchester United	3
Milan	2

Champions League semi-final, first leg

There are times with Manchester United when it feels like there must be something in their DNA that stipulates they can never do things the easy way. When you think you have worked them out, they come up with something new to scrape your nerve-ends. Even when everything seems lost, it is never over until the Fat Lady has a heart attack. 'Nobody scores more late goals than us,' Ferguson says proudly, and it is a quality that adds to the romance surrounding the club.

On evening games, each newspaper is waiting for the journalist's match report before it can go to press and there isn't time to write it at the final whistle. Instead, we submit a series of staggered extracts known as a 'runner', the first of which is filed at half-time, the second after about seventy minutes and the 'top and tails', meaning the introductory paragraph and the closing line, five minutes before the final whistle. In theory, it is the only way to get the copy over in time for the early print run. In practice, it has a nasty habit of biting us on the backside.

After the European Cup final in 1999 Ferguson told us he had deliberately requested some of the early editions so he could read our reports of a match that Bayern Munich were winning 1-0 until stoppage time. We weren't sure whether he was just teasing but if he did ever get his hands on those newspapers he would find large swathes of text, all written and sent after eighty-five minutes, dedicated to United's tactical failings and paying tribute to their opponents. Before the game turned upside down thousands of words had been submitted telling the gloomily depressing story of German efficiency steering United towards defeat. Long passages were dedicated to the obduracy of the Bayern defence and the inability of United's strikers to have any impact. Journalists buying the European editions of their newspapers on the streets of Barcelona the next morning turned to the sports pages with a mixture of dread and embarrassment.

Tonight is another occasion when the shout of 'rewrite' reverberates through the pressbox and the blood pressure hits the roof. At half-time United are 2-1 down and it looks hopeless. Kaka has scored two sumptuous goals, dancing through the redesigned United defence, and it is easy to see how Milan put out Bayern in the quarter-finals. Old Trafford is watching in leaden dismay and Milan are letting their minds drift to a straightforward-looking return leg at the San Siro.

But United just never give up. The first half has been a story of Italian control and sophistication. The second is of United's speed, agility and sheer bloody-mindedness. On the hour, Scholes clips a wonderful pass and Rooney controls the ball on his chest and beats the goalkeeper Dida. Kaka has had the game in the palm of his hand but then he puts one wide, another high, and it is here that the night no longer belongs to him and falls into Rooney's possession. Giggs picks up the ball and breaks forward with pace and purpose. As he crosses the halfway line the clock ticks past ninety minutes. United are the early-leavers' nightmare. Giggs slips a diagonal pass into Rooney and he takes his shot early, thumping it with his right foot, hard and low. And then he is lying on the turf, with his knees tucked up to his chin and he is screaming into his clenched fists. It is 3-2 and United stand on the verge of the final.

It scarcely seems credible that an Italian team could be so careless. But this is what United do: they make life difficult for themselves, offer their rivals hope then react like no other team. They take us to the brink, leave us with our fingernails bitten to the quick then invariably find a way to win. It is a team built on skill and flair but most of all a love of drama. The most devastating second-half team on the planet – despite what Wenger says.

Ferguson's press conference is relatively low-key bearing in mind the importance of the match. 'We were the better team,' he says but he is unhappy about the defending, accusing them of conceding 'two terrible goals', and when you hear the irritation in his voice it is fair to assume he has made the point forcibly in the dressing room. He cannot stay angry for long, however. There is too much to cherish. In the first light of morning, this result will be put in perspective and Kaka's goals will feel a lot more devastating when taking into account the away-goal rule. But tonight it is all about the drama. There is no more exciting sight anywhere in football than United chasing a game and for the first time Ferguson says they have shown they can win the competition. 'We are in a fantastic position,' he says. 'I think we will

score again over there. It won't be easy going to Milan
– but it won't be easy for them either.'

PORTUGUESE MAN OF WAR
27.4.07

The relationship between Mourinho and Ferguson is
officially declared bankrupt today. Mourinho has
been chipping away and Ferguson comes prepared to
his press conference. He knows what he wants to say,
exactly how it should be and by the time it is finished
the myth that is their 'friendship' is shattered.
Mourinho, he says, has 'no respect for anyone but
himself'.

Ferguson has been building up to this moment for
some time and the only real surprise is that it has
taken so long. Mourinho has already suggested that
referees are in favour of United and that Chelsea are
being assailed from every side by all manner of devi-
ous plots. His complaints have become increasingly
hysterical as the season has gone on and the allega-
tions have been upgraded to a firmly declared
conspiracy theory about the reasons for United's position at the top of the table. 'The problem for Chelsea,'
he says, 'is that we not only have to face difficult
opponents but also new football rules. One is that
you're not allowed penalties against Manchester
United. Another is that you're not allowed to give
penalties in favour of Chelsea. If I am wrong, I will
have to visit the optician. But it seems to me United
are forbidden to lose.'

Even by Mourinho's standards it has been an extraordinarily tempestuous week. While United have been

grappling with Milan, Chelsea have been contesting the other Champions League semi-final with Liverpool. He has questioned whether Liverpool would resort to dirty tricks to nobble Didier Drogba. He has mocked their form in the league and he has judged Rafael Benitez's record by speculating that the same results at Stamford Bridge would have got him the sack.

Benitez's theory is that Mourinho is friends only with managers of teams that are no threat to Chelsea and if that is true it seems to extend to the players too. Ronaldo has been on Portuguese television to argue that referees are equally fair to everyone and that 'the whole world knows how Mourinho is'. Mourinho has responded by calling him, among other things, a 'liar'.

The anger in Ferguson spills out in a long, impassioned diatribe. 'Just because Cristiano has an opinion does not mean he is a liar,' he says. 'Jose seems to be on some sort of a personal crusade about regulations and his suspicions in the game. He has accused referees. He has insulted Liverpool, a club with great history. He suggested their players were going to hunt down Drogba. Jesus Christ, it goes on and on and on. It's a rant, all the time, and it's really disappointing.'

His face shows that he means business. 'It's all calculated,' he says. 'He's a very clever man and by saying that no one is allowed to get penalties at Old Trafford it puts terrible pressure on the referees in our future games. He is trying to get a penalty kick awarded against us and that is wrong. That, without doubt, is calculated and, if we do get a penalty kick against us, he wins. There's no doubt about that: a penalty against us and Mourinho wins the war.'

There are times with Ferguson when you just place the tape recorder in front of him and let him speak. Questions are superfluous. And he hasn't finished yet. 'In some people's eyes he's a hero, you know,' he says disbelievingly. 'I don't know who's a villain or who's a hero here?' He accuses Mourinho of 'thumbing his nose' at the football authorities and he questions why the FA have not taken disciplinary action. 'I am surprised, absolutely, because it just goes on and on and on.'

He carries on for a few more minutes and, finally, when he has got everything off his chest he lets us know by outstretching his arms and giving us a little nod. 'Anyway,' he says, looking out of the window to the fields around Carrington and smiling broadly, 'it's a lovely day, isn't it? The birds are whistling here … and the sparrows are waking up at Stamford Bridge coughing.'

The laughter takes the sting out of the air and the rest of the press conference is a light-hearted affair. But this is a huge story for the newspapers – the first time Mourinho has properly felt the lash of Ferguson's tongue in his three seasons in England – and there is more to come when Ferguson sits down in front of the MUTV cameras.

'I don't know what the matter is with the lad,' he says, and his use of the word 'lad' is a brilliantly subtle put-down. 'He just seems to be having a go at everybody. He has questioned the regulations. He has questioned the referees' integrity. He has questioned Liverpool's integrity. And when you think about the history that Liverpool Football Club have got, Chelsea don't even compare.

'You just can't go around saying these things all the time. But it tells you he has no respect for UEFA or anyone else but himself. To suggest we are changing the regulations is bringing a suspicion into the game that we are corrupt. Which is one hell of a statement to make. You bring that kind of suspicion into our game, which is the most honest in the world, and we're finished, all the principles are gone.'

AHCUMFIGOVIN
1.5.07

The more we see of Mourinho the more it seems he is auditioning for Monty Python's Silly Party. His response to Ferguson's onslaught is that he doesn't want to fall out with someone he admires, but he is still irritated by Ronaldo and describes him as having had a 'difficult childhood' and 'no education'. It is an astonishing thing to say and Mourinho is on very thin ice. He has been getting increasingly personal and it is obvious a mindset exists at Stamford Bridge, perhaps because of their wealth, where they believe they should be able to say what they want, when they want, and get away with it. It is a dangerous way to live because, in football, you can light only so many fires before you torch yourself.

Mourinho has been talking about winning a Quadruple, but at the weekend Chelsea's hopes of catching United all but evaporated with a 2-2 draw at home to Bolton Wanderers. It was a critical slip-up. They are five points behind with three games to play and their misery is exacerbated tonight in the second leg of their Champions League semi-final against Liverpool. The tie finishes 1-1 on aggregate and after extra-time it comes down to penalties. Liverpool go through and Mourinho looks as down at the final whistle as at any time since he came to Stamford Bridge. If he were Basil Fawlty – and sometimes it's a close-run thing – this is the point where he would be reaching for the shrapnel wound in his knee.

United's return leg against Milan is in the San Siro tomorrow night and when we asked Ferguson which team out of Liverpool or Chelsea he would like to face in the final he wouldn't be drawn. He didn't want to offend anyone or look overly presumptuous about reaching the final. 'I'll take anybody,' he said. 'I'll play the Glenbuck Cherrypickers if I have to.'

We looked collectively blank and his eyes lit up.

'Oh, come on, who are the Glenbuck Cherrypickers?'

Tim Rich of the *Daily Telegraph* was the only reporter who had heard of them.

'They were Bill Shankly's old village team.'

'Correct,' Ferguson yelped. 'And what was a cherrypicker?'

'Was it a hoist?'

'A hoist?' he exclaimed, shaking his head. 'No, son, a cherrypicker used to stand at the top of the mine-shaft and take the stones out of the coal.'

He looked thoroughly pleased with himself. 'Education,' he said delightedly, 'it's quite cheap, you know.'

He was in a genial mood when we arrived at Malpensa airport. While Chelsea were drawing with Bolton at the weekend, United came back from 2-0 down at fifth-placed Everton to score four goals in the last half an hour. It was another comeback of stagger-ing proportions and at the final whistle we were treated to the sight of Ferguson cavorting on the pitch, jumping into Ronaldo's arms and doing a theatrical 'cut' sign with his arms, as if to signify that it was all over. He promised the Bolton manager Sam Allardyce 'two kisses and a cuddle', which was a rather scary thought, but he still had Mourinho in his sights and turned on him again.

'What he has said about Cristiano is below the belt,' he said. 'To bring class into it is totally wrong. Maybe his tactic is to try to unsettle the boy but he is barking up the wrong tree. It is below the belt. Very below the belt.'

His words are almost spat out. 'Coming from a poor background does not mean you are uneducated and it does not mean you have no principles,' he continued. Ferguson is so proud of his working-class roots in Glasgow he has a sign on his office wall reading 'AHCUMFIGOVIN' – i.e. 'I come from Govan'. If there is one thing guaranteed to rile him it is snobbery, particularly when the offender comes from within his own sport. 'The difference,' he says, summoning one of his more devastating put-downs, 'is that there are people from very poor backgrounds who have principles, whereas there are people who are educated but who have no principles at all – and that, without question, is the case here.'

REALITY CHECK
2.5.07

Milan	3
Manchester United	0

Champions League semi-final, second leg
Milan win 5-3 on aggregate

The music stops tonight. Ever since the demolition of AS Roma Ferguson has allowed himself to believe it was possible to win another Treble, and the disappointment is brutal, to say the least. The Champions League has conjured up some of his finer memories from his twenty years at the club but it has also left many scars and there can be few more chastening experiences than this master-class in the art of retaining possession. Milan's is a symphony of brilliant forward play and suddenly, horribly, United revert to looking more than one level shy of greatness. They have come a long way in the seventeen months since they were knocked out against Benfica last season, but not quite far enough, and an audience with Ferguson is a melancholic experience. 'I expected better,' he says. 'I really expected better.'

His words are delivered with unmistakable sadness. The Premiership might be the priority this season but Ferguson's life in management has been dedicated to chasing the European Cup and here he is, eight years since the Treble, the most prolific British manager in history but still nowhere closer to winning the competition for a second time to secure his place in European terms alongside Clough, and put him only one behind Paisley.

The disappointment has to be put in context, and the United fans in the top tier of the San Siro can remind themselves that their team could be champions of England after the next round of Premiership fixtures. Nonetheless, everything has been going so well recently that tonight feels like a jolt to the system. Ferguson could be toasting his ninth title if United beat Manchester City in their next game and Chelsea fail to win at Arsenal but here, in torrential rain, soaked to the skin and with his hair flattened to his forehead, there is only the deepest form of despair.

Ferguson, it should never be forgotten, has accumulated more trophies than any other British football manager, past and present. Yet under his management the biggest club on the planet have reached only one European Cup final in twenty years. And tonight, as Kaka, Gattuso and Clarence Seedorf produce a level of football beyond the scope of Rooney, Carrick and Scholes, it is tempting to wonder whether the European dynasty Ferguson was so desperate to forge will ever materialise. Or whether we are kidding ourselves when we keep saying 'next year'.

Maybe in the warm afterglow of a ninth championship it will not matter so much but Ferguson's pathological desire is to win and it will not have escaped his attention that when United last played at Anfield the Liverpool supporters in the Kop stretched out a banner, over thirty feet long, mocking his record in Europe compared to Paisley's.

Paisley 3 Ferguson 1

Nottingham Forest's supporters also derive a wicked sense of pleasure from the fact Ferguson has never been able to emulate Clough's achievements in the European Cup. Clough won it twice, in 1979 and 1980, and in his inimitable way he was never slow to let the football world know of the disparity. 'For all his horses, knighthoods and championships,' he once said, 'Alex hasn't got two of what I've got ... and I don't mean balls.'

Ferguson never thought that worthy of a response – his relationship with Clough was never better than lukewarm – but there is one of Clough's maxims with which he will empathise. 'You win something once and people can say it's all down to luck,' Clough

used to say. 'You win it twice and it shuts the bug-
gers up.'

Winning the league will be much more than a consolation prize but Ferguson sets his own standards
and he has never hidden the fact it would be a permanent regret if the Nou Camp were to be a one-hit
wonder. The European Cup, he says, is the pinnacle
of his ambitions and no season passes by without him
expressing sorrow that he has delivered it to Old
Trafford only once before. 'We should have done
better,' he will say. 'We have consistently qualified for
the quarters and the semis but we haven't won enough
trophies in Europe. Real Madrid have won it nine
times, Milan have won it six times and then there are
clubs like Bayern Munich, Liverpool and Ajax who
have all won it four or five times. For a club like ours,
we should definitely have won it more than we
have.'

There is nothing much more he can add tonight but
the words that do come are nearly all gracious. He
talks of his side running out of legs. He pays tribute to
Milan and he accepts they were the fresher, slicker,
more enterprising team. What he might also say, however, is that in the single most important match of
United's season his most lauded players, the A-listers,
went missing. All season we have speculated about
this side being on the cusp of greatness but when we
see the way Milan pass the ball maybe we should re-
assess what the term 'greatness' means.

At his press conference yesterday he seemed to be
jotting something down and when we looked afterwards there was a piece of paper on his table with the
words: 'Milan 1 Man Utd 2'. We couldn't be sure he
had written it himself – it does not feel very Ferguson-

like – but tonight, amid a backdrop of theatrical thunderclaps, it quickly becomes clear that whoever did was guilty of gross over-confidence. The first goal comes after eleven minutes, the second after half an hour and Ferguson has made a calamitous blunder by recalling Vidic to defence. Vidic, a broken-nosed type of centre-half, has been marvellous all season, the steel to Ferdinand's silk. 'He comes from Serbia,' the song goes, 'he'll fucking murder ya' and in the context of trench warfare he would always be on the frontline while others are licking stamps back at HQ. But it is only four weeks since he broke his collarbone and the initial estimate was that he would be out until the FA Cup final in three weeks' time. His reactions are ponderous, to say the least, as Kaka drills in the first and it is his mistake that leads to Seedorf doubling the lead.

At 2-0, the mind goes back to United's semi-final against Juventus at the Stade delle Alpi in 1999. Then, like now, United were rocked by two early goals, only for Keane – having picked up a yellow card that would rule him out of the final – to inspire a three-goal comeback with a performance Ferguson later described as 'the most emphatic display of selflessness I have ever seen on a football field'. Now, eight years on, United need another Keane, someone to inspire and cajole and take the game to the Italians. But no one steps forward. Carrick and Scholes allow the game to pass them by. Rooney and Giggs stay on the edges. Ronaldo, the best player in the Premiership, disappears. Milan are more confident on the ball: Kaka, Gattuso, Pirlo and Seedorf bossing midfield, pounding every blade of grass. Gattuso goes in so hard on Fletcher he loses a shin-pad although, tellingly, not the ball. Later on, he tackles Ronaldo, wins possession again and triumphantly punches the air. Alberto Gilardino scores the third with twelve minutes to go and when we check our notes at the final whistle we cannot find one occasion when United have forced Dida into a truly testing save. It is a drubbing.

When Ferguson walks into the pressroom the television is showing Liverpool's goals from the 2005 final. He resists the temptation to put his foot through the screen and he faces the truth with dignity. His team simply could not cope, he says. His demeanour is as bleak as we have seen all season and he accepts what everybody already knows: they have been outclassed. 'We're obviously disappointed,' he says. 'Having done so well to get here, I have to say we never came out of the blocks. We lost two goals very cheaply and at this level you just can't do that. You have to defend much better.'

For Ferguson, that fierce protector of his own, this is unusually forthright criticism. 'We needed to see through the opening twenty-five minutes without cutting our own throats but both goals were very cheap,' he continues. 'We shouldn't be losing goals like that. In credit to Milan, they were very well prepared for the game. They were much sharper to the ball, pressing us very well. But I still expected more from my team. The name of the game in Europe is don't give the ball away. Unfortunately we did give the ball away. Milan kept the ball far better than us.'

He is gracious and dignified, but mostly he is just despondent, and there is a sympathetic tone to our questions. The Italians, however, are not so sensitive and there is a brief interrogation in which they want to know whether a) the Champions League is 'too big' for Rooney and Ronaldo and b) why the team is so perennially 'unsuccessful' in Europe. 'What do Manchester United lack in the Champions League?' one reporter asks. 'You always arrive at the semi-final or the quarter-final, but what do you lack? What do you need to become a team as great as Milan?'

Ferguson doesn't properly address the second part of the question but when he dissects the performances of Rooney and Ronaldo it is unusual to hear him accepting criticism of his players. 'They have had a disappointing night,' he agrees. 'Wayne did okay but Cristiano had a disappointing night, and he knows it. They're still young, still improving, and when you see the professionalism and experience in the Milan side it's a good indicator of where we want to be. But that doesn't apply just to Rooney and Ronaldo. It applies to all the players.'

There is, he points out, still a league title to be won but when we next see him, in the departure lounge at the airport, he is sat in silence with his hands in his pockets, clearly suffering.

CHAMPIONS OF ENGLAND
7.5.07

United beat City 1-0. Chelsea drew 1-1 at Arsenal and, finger by finger, Jose Mourinho's grasp has been prised off the Premiership trophy. It has been an epic battle but Chelsea have finally waved the white flag and Ferguson sheepishly admits he has a 'fuzzy' head when we see him today. He spent last night celebrating with family and friends in Wilmslow and, live on

Sky Sports, he managed to spill champagne down his trousers in his excitement. He was meant to be popping it open in the style of a Grand Prix champion but drenched himself instead. True to form, he found it hilarious.

There are television cameramen waiting for him in the car park at Carrington. He has agreed to a one-off press conference and they follow him through the double doors and up the winding stairs, and when he gets to the top something happens that has never happened here before.

It is applause – a standing ovation, no less – and it is long and respectful and thoroughly deserved. When the clapping dies down Ferguson puts his hands out and does the old Tommy Cooper joke: 'Who told you to stop?' So the clapping starts again. And when Diana Law comes up the stairs he starts another round of applause just for her. Clapping with the rest of us and jigging with laughter.

His cheeks are glowing as he goes around the room, shaking hands, patting a couple of his favourites on the back, and then something else happens that has never happened here. He orders us champagne. 'There's a big bottle of bubbly in my office,' he calls over to one of the press officers. 'Send someone over. There are some plastic glasses here (pointing at the coffee machine) so let's get a drink for these boys.' And in the rows of seats, we are looking at ourselves, thinking: 'Bloody hell!'

The next hour is slightly surreal: sipping champagne from supermarket cups, reminiscing over the last couple of years and sharing a little piece of the glory with a man who, this time eighteen months ago, was unanimously rejected as a dead man walking.

One thing is for certain: never again will anyone in this room doubt Ferguson's capacity for battle nor suggest that age has warped his talents. Never again will we leave ourselves in a position where, genuinely, it would not be inappropriate for one of us to tug on his arm and say: 'Jesus, Alex, we got it wrong, didn't we?'

He seems to sense our embarrassment. 'You lot are so bad,' he says. 'You really aren't the best judges, are you?'

He starts to laugh as he chides us for having ever dared to question him. 'Don't worry, I know you were forced into it by your idiots of editors. And I know you won't report that! Because if you do, they might just ask if you agree …'

We cannot help but feel slightly sheepish as we ask whether he was badly affected by the criticism. 'Listen,' he replies, 'I'm experienced enough to know it is the name of the game. If you are not doing well at this club, you are going to get criticism. But there's no point taking it personally.'

It feels a little incongruous to point out he has, in fact, spent the last twenty years taking criticism personally. What we are witnessing here is Ferguson at his very best, holding court, making a mockery of all those claims that he had passed his best-before date. 'Even when we got knocked out against Benfica I felt that if we stuck together we would develop into a really good team,' he says. 'We made our decisions. Then it was just a case of sticking together. We looked at the squad, we knew there was enough youth and certainly enough ability. What we tried to instil in the players' minds was that we had to get a good start. For the previous two seasons nobody went with

Chelsea early on and they had a clear run. We felt we could be there with them. But we did better than that. We managed to stay in front of them. Which was not easy because Chelsea were chasing all the time.'

When he talks of making 'decisions' it is a rare reference to the break with Keane and Van Nistelrooy and we ask him whether they were the most difficult choices he has had to make. 'Well, Roy was, certainly, because he was such an influence at the club … (he pauses) but I'm not sure about Van Nistelrooy being a big decision at all.' Interesting.

The follow-up question is whether the squad is more harmonious a year on, and he nods in agreement. 'You need a good team spirit and this season, from day one, we have just gelled. I've kept referring to that all season. The spirit has been brilliant in the dressing room.'

'So was Van Nistelrooy's departure important to the spirit?'

Another pause. 'I'm not getting into that.'

It is the only time in an hour of his company that he clams up and, even then, it is accompanied with a knowing smile rather than the conquering stare. He ranks his ninth Premiership title as his 'greatest achievement' and when you consider where it has come from, and the depths to which United plumbed last season, none of us thinks of this as a knee-jerk reaction.

Typically, he is already thinking to the next title and another go at the European Cup. 'Why should I give up?' he says. 'It's easy to retire. I decided to retire a few years ago and I regretted it within days. I feel invigorated by our young players. Last season I was tired. I wanted to get on my holiday, get started for the new season. But this season I just feel invigorated.'

He still feels young and energetic, he says, and he still has his health. 'Age creeps up on you very quickly. I still think I am fifty-eight, you know. Then I see in the papers I am actually sixty-five and I think: "I can't be sixty-five, can I?" I do wonder sometimes where the years have gone. Then I wonder how I compare with five or six years ago. I don't notice any dramatic changes in myself. But there must be some because age does that to you.'

One reporter asks if he will emulate Sir Bobby Robson by managing at the age of seventy. But he draws a firm line.

'No, no.'

'Sixty-nine then,' someone quips, and he smiles appreciatively.

Deep down, he would rather have won the league at Old Trafford and it is a mild disappointment that only one of his nine titles has been confirmed on United's own ground. But winning it at City is not a bad alternative. To put it into context, the souvenir stalls outside the City of Manchester stadium were selling Milan scarves and flags. City's dislike of United borders on obsessive. The enmity is so extreme that City's employees are forbidden from having red company cars and – seriously – diners in the executive lounges get blue ketchup to splash over their chips.

Ronaldo scored the winner from the penalty spot, his twenty-third goal of a season that has seen him win the Professional Footballers' Association's Player of the Year and Young Player of the Year awards, as well as a landslide victory in the Football Writers' Association's vote. Van der Sar kept out a late penalty and, after that, Chelsea had to win at Arsenal. Ferguson turned off his mobile and defiantly didn't switch on his television until the game was seventy-five minutes old. 'I went to see my grandson play in the morning because he had a cup final of his own. Then I went home and watched the racing on telly and when that was finished I had nothing to do but twiddle my thumbs. So I watched the last fifteen minutes.' Chelsea had a goal disallowed and spent the final moments camped in Arsenal territory. 'I was in agony,' says Ferguson. 'I was sure Arsenal were trying to throw it away.'

United have won twenty-eight of their thirty-six Premiership games, compared to Chelsea's twenty-four. They have scored eighty-three goals to Chelsea's sixty-three. They are seven points better off, with two games to go. Their goal difference is a Premiership-record – plus-fifty-seven, seventeen better than Chelsea – and they have eight players (Van der Sar, Neville, Ferdinand, Vidic, Evra, Scholes, Giggs and Ronaldo) in the PFA's Team of the Year. Ronaldo is the first player in history to win all three Player of the Year awards, and a Portuguese reporter has travelled to Carrington to ask Ferguson to assess the winger's contribution.

'He has won all the awards and it just shows you that even the journalists in England can get it right every now and then,' Ferguson tells him. 'Did you know that in 1999 they picked David Ginola for the football writers' award? We won the Treble that year. In fact, the only thing we didn't win was the Boat Race – and they still gave it to Ginola! Can you believe that?'

As for Premiership Manager of the Year, who else but Ferguson? He will be presented with the award before the final game of the season and it is telling that even Arsène Wenger has already stated that nobody deserves it more than his old *bête noire*.

'You might have lost one friend and made another,' Ian Ladyman, the *Daily Mail's* Manchester man, says to Ferguson.

Ferguson grins back. 'I might even buy him a drink,' he says.

Not that Ferguson seems willing to prolong the argument with Mourinho. He will be taking a 'nice bottle' to Stamford Bridge for United's next game and, suddenly, he has nothing but good things to say about Mourinho again. Mourinho has been on television to congratulate United as 'deserved champions'. He has also rung Ronaldo to apologise and Ferguson is happy to declare a ceasefire – at least until the FA Cup final.

'Jose has been very complimentary and I expected that,' he says. 'I'm sure he understands that, winning and losing, you have to deal with it in the right way. If you win you don't need to gloat and if you lose you don't need to go bananas about it. You have to accept defeat and he has done that.'

The champagne runs out soon afterwards and Ferguson has to go through the seventy-five text messages on his mobile. 'Okay, boys?' he asks, and then he is heading to his car and the 100-yard journey back to his office. 'Astalavista!' he calls over his shoulder.

SCHADENFREUDE
9.5.07

Chelsea	0
Manchester United	0

There cannot be many better sights for a Manchester United fan than watching Chelsea's players standing in line to applaud the newly crowned champions out of the Stamford Bridge tunnel. Two years ago, when Mourinho won his first Premiership title and Chelsea came to Old Trafford in their final away game, the guard of honour was United's responsibility and Gary Neville could barely make eye contact with the victorious players. Now it is Chelsea's turn to suffer. John Terry, for one, looks like he is clapping burglars into his house.

The guard of honour is a relatively new tradition in football. For the winners, it is the point of maximum smugness. For the losers, it is the equivalent of being placed in stocks and pelted with rotten tomatoes. There is something noble, almost Corinthian, about the way a team as supremely competitive as Chelsea will grit their teeth and put on a respectful front for the side that has toppled them as champions. But it is an exercise in forced humiliation. The television cameras tend to focus on the losers rather than the winners. Everyone puts on a brave face, straight-backed and dignified, and tries to hide what they are really feeling. But it is impossible.

The rumour beforehand is that Chelsea's supporters plan to turn their backs to the pitch in a synchronised snub. Instead, they mostly stand, arms folded, watching in silent indignation. Some applaud. Others whistle and respond with a defiant chant of 'Chelsea'. But this isn't an easy night for anyone connected with Chelsea – the supporters, the players, the accountants, the Russians and, most of all, Mourinho – and Ferguson has chosen a team that seems strategically designed to exacerbate their torment.

This is Manchester United-Lite: a team of reserves and maybes with only eighty-one Premiership appearances between them all season.

Kuszczak. Lee. Brown. O'Shea. Heinze (capt). Eagles. Fletcher. Smith. Richardson. Solskjaer. Dong.

The look on Terry's face is a picture. Here is the England captain, as proud and competitive as anyone in professional football, corralling his team-mates into two neat lines and making sure they are all respectfully in position, and then out comes Ferguson's second string, including three players making their first Premiership starts. Chelsea are not even clapping out the real champions. They are clapping out the understudies and there is utter disdain on Terry's face.

This is only the start of the indignation. 'You're not special any more,' United fans sing at Mourinho. 'That's why you're runners-up,' they gloat after a promising Chelsea attack peters out. Then 'sacked in the morning', as Mourinho comes to the touchline. In Germany, it is called *schadenfreude*. In Stretford and Collyhurst and Gorton and Chorlton-cum-Hardy it is known as 'taking the piss' and there are few fans with more biting wit than United's. After Chelsea's game at Arsenal, Mourinho had marched over to his club's supporters and made an unusual gesture for everyone to keep their chins up. Now, three days on, there are thousands of United fans doing the same, gleefully cackling 'keep that chin up'.

The match is a dead rubber. A few weeks ago this fixture was hyped as a title decider and tickets were selling on eBay for the price of a Mediterranean holiday. Yet Ferguson is resting his first-team for the FA

Cup final. Mourinho has left out some of his big-hitters too and the game starts slowly, deteriorates from there and ultimately means nothing apart from gloating rights.

The outstanding performers are United's supporters and at one point Mourinho turns to them with a half-smile. Later, however, his cover is blown and he loses his cool when a free-kick is awarded against his team. He is out of the dugout, wagging his finger at the referee and when he is ordered back to his seat he misunderstands and thinks he has been sent to the stand. No sooner has he climbed into the seats behind the dugout than he is informed of his mistake and sheepishly has to make his way back. It is an embarrassing faux pas greeted with another crowing chorus of 'you're not special any more'.

This, unmistakeably, is Mourinho's maximum point of vulnerability. When he was at his peak he strutted about Stamford Bridge as if he owned London. He was 'new-school', with an excitingly vigorous approach to management and a wardrobe to die for. Tonight, he is wearing a dowdy grey Chelsea tracksuit. His eyes are circled with dark smudges. His thick plume of once-silky hair is a greying bouffant. His glare is wild.

In the opposite dugout, Ferguson looks splendid in his long black overcoat, smartly creased trousers and polished shoes. He is unhappy about some of the Chelsea tackling but, generally, he sits back and enjoys the moment. And when your eyes flash across to Mourinho sniping at the referee, jabbing out a finger and flapping his arms in disgust, it is impossible not to think how the roles have reversed.

COLLECTING THE TROPHY
13.5.07

Manchester United	0
West Ham United	1

The rain falls hard on a humdrum town. It is a typical Mancunian day: the final home game of the season is to be played out in a late-spring downpour. But the weather scarcely matters when the Premiership trophy is waiting to be presented. There are no early-leavers today. It has been 1,093 days since this shiny, metallic piece of job satisfaction belonged at Old Trafford and, for the most part, the crowd are willing the game to end so the business of receiving the trophy can get underway.

West Ham do their best to spoil the party – winning saves them from relegation and their celebrations at the final whistle are long and raucous – but the game is merely a sideshow to the main event: the fireworks, the tickertape and the sight of the trophy adorned in red, black and white ribbons. This is the moment Ferguson has been waiting for. Lifting the trophy.

It is fifteen minutes before the small army of Premiership roadies have erected the winners' podium and when the trophy finally appears it somehow looks larger in real life than in photographs. A white-haired chap, stiff-kneed and grandfatherly, wearing a black overcoat and a proud smile, carries it out of the tunnel and he is identified as Jack Crompton, the goalkeeper from the championship-winning side of 1952. Behind him follow five of the Busby Babes: Bill Foulkes, John Doherty, Jeff Whitefoot, Wilf McGuinness and Albert

Scanlon. Six happy old men, aged from sixty-nine to eighty-five, old enough to remember playing in this stadium when it was being rebuilt after two direct hits from German planes in the Second World War.

They form a guard of honour on the pitch and the volume cranks up as Ferguson's backroom staff, led by Carlos Queiroz, appear from the tunnel. There are loud, appreciative cheers. The crowd are on their feet and Queiroz waves appreciatively to the fans behind the goal. In many ways, it has been as remarkable a journey for Queiroz as it has for Ferguson. He, too, has been labelled a has-been and had his work dissected in the media. He, like Ferguson, has come out the other side. He is a good guy and it is a nice moment.

Ferguson is next. His arms are raised and *This is the One* by the Stone Roses starts to play. John Squires on the guitar, Reni's drums, Mani on bass and Ian Brown's sweet vocals. It is an unusual choice as United's club anthem but it works brilliantly as Ferguson turns to salute the Stretford End and then the corner of the South Stand where, on a September day in 2005, V-signs were flashed at him. He walks on a few yards, soaking up the applause, and when he sees the club's mascot Fred the Red there is the surreal sight of the oldest manager in the Premiership leaping into the arms of a fancy-dress red devil with a forked tail and little black horns.

He is wearing a black waterproof coat and a cap that seems a size or two too large and bears the words '2007 champions'. The entire squad follow behind, all in fresh kits, and Rooney is the first to reach the podium and collect his medal. Neville and Giggs are the last and, between them, it is their privilege to lift the trophy.

The noise is incredible but the crowd fall obediently silent as Ferguson takes the microphone: 'All I want to say is that it's been a fantastic season for our club,' he begins, and there is an affectionate cheer and instinctive applause. 'Every one of us – you supporters, the staff and (pointing at the players) these lot here – have been absolutely fantastic. I can't speak highly enough of them. It's been a wonderful year. Thanks for your support and let's hope we can do it again next season.'

The party starts in earnest after that and a clan of mini-Fergie grandchildren join him on the pitch. The players' wives and girlfriends appear and a stampede of little boys and girls is let loose. Liberty Giggs gets her first appearance on national television. Noah Solskjaer waves to the North Stand. There is Luka Vidic and Aaron Scholes and many, many others. Ronaldo starts the lap of honour with a Portuguese flag tied round his neck, and his mother, Dolores, holding his hand. Rooney is wearing a jester's hat.

At one point Ferguson breaks off and waves triumphantly to the directors' box. David Gill can be seen belting out 'Glory Glory Man United' with the rest of the crowd. The Glazer brothers, perhaps the palest people in the whole of Florida, have put in a rare appearance but clearly don't know the words. Sir Bobby Charlton, straight-backed and dewy-eyed, looks emotional and at one stage he turns to his right and gives a thumbs-up to someone in the pressbox. Charlton comes from an era when reporters were not viewed with suspicion and he remains on first-name terms with many of the football writers. When he was younger he used to turn out in some of the press matches and, to our eternal shame, there is a famous story about him misplacing a pass in one game and a journalist on the same team throwing out his arms, in genuine disgust, and raucously screaming at the legendary, World Cup-winning hero of millions: 'For Christ's sake Bobby! To feet, man! TO FEET!'

The lap of honour is possibly the slowest in history. The players are determined to milk every moment. This is Giggs's ninth championship, a new record. It is United's sixteenth in total, only two behind Liverpool now, and the first under Neville's captaincy. Neville is still not fit and won't make it back for the FA Cup final but he is in his kit and kissing his badge. 'It has been three years of suffering,' he says. 'There were times when I'm sure every player, plus the manager and the fans, were all doubting whether we were going to get there again. One year becomes two, then three and you start to think: "is it going to be ten or twenty?" You have to give great credit to the manager for sticking to his guns, never panicking. The whole empire was said to be crumbling but he's been proved right yet again.'

The turning point, he says, came towards the end of last season. 'There was a period of six months when it became a little too easy. We were becoming a club it was easy to knock. We went out of Europe early, we went out of the FA Cup at Anfield, we lost two or three league games. We just had enough. The club had had enough. We were getting battered for every single defeat or draw and after two years you think: "right, that's it, stop this now." Ronaldo, Saha and Rooney started playing together and all of a sudden the speed in our play – what I call the

Manchester United way – returned. Quick, counter-attacking football. Defending one minute, the ball in the back of the opposition net ten seconds later. We had lost that for some reason for the previous couple of years.'

Neville remembers 'not many people giving us a chance' at the start of the season and it is difficult to disagree. The fanzines are out tonight and they put it in perspective. 'The men in white jackets would have been around with their straitjackets if you'd suggested we would win the league with two games to spare and still be in with a shout of the Double, as well as reaching the semi-finals in Europe,' according to one *Red Issue* writer. 'It has been a truly remarkable year that has exceeded all our expectations. Gone are those sterile 4-5-1 formations and instead we've seen thirteen away wins, eighty-three goals and eight occasions when we've scored four or more.'

United We Stand is equally effusive. 'The reason Ferguson's ninth title win is so satisfying is because it was so unexpected. The consensus was that Ferguson's logic seemed flawed. The *Manchester Evening News* told us that United would be going for Kaka, Gattuso and Patrick Vieira. Instead, we sold Van Nistelrooy, bought Michael Carrick and a new reserve keeper. Ronaldo's Old Trafford future was questioned and Ferguson's assertion that United could win the league seemed delusional. What happened next was staggering.'

The front cover has the simple headline: 'Champions'. On *Red Issue* there is a photograph of Ferguson holding the Premiership trophy. 'I've got my hands full here, Jose,' says the speech bubble. 'Can you grab the polish?'

ONE GAME TOO FAR
19.5.07

| Chelsea | 1 |
| Manchester United | 0 |

(after extra time)
FA Cup final

The first FA Cup final at the new Wembley. The stadium looks fantastic, its arch forming a giant Alice band on the London skyline, but United came here to win a trophy rather than admire the view and it is a dreadfully flat way to end the season. Wembley might be pleasing on the eye but there is one rule that has always applied to this stadium: it is impossible to enjoy unless you win.

For the Chelsea supporters the memories will be cherished, from Drogba's Cossack dancing in the post-match celebrations to Mourinho sticking up his fingers at Abramovich and the rest of the football world. Not two, but six – for each trophy he has won in his three seasons at Stamford Bridge. For the neutral it is a complete stinker of a match: 120 minutes of dreary, risk-free football. And for Ferguson it is his idea of hell: watching John Terry collect the trophy from Prince William, gritting his teeth as Mourinho goes on one of those fist-pumping touchline dashes, looking away as Lampard throws his shin-pads into the crowd and, all the time, knowing he has been tactically out-manoeuvred. It is a mixture of anti-climax, profound sadness and, above all, helplessness, and at the final whistle he doesn't seem to know what to do with himself. Mostly, he wanders between his players, his hands in his pockets, saying very little.

The Premiership matters much more than the FA Cup, of course, and when he and Cathy reach the French Riviera he should not torture himself too much with what might have been. Nonetheless, it is a gruelling experience, full of regret and what-ifs. The players look tired. It has been an arduous season. The pitch is spongy, speed-destroying and energy-sapping, and when the game kicks off United spend the first few minutes warily passing the ball around inside their own half, simply trying to get the measure of the surface. When Chelsea get possession they do exactly the same and the pattern is set. Slow starts are as traditional at cup finals as the crowd singing *Abide With Me* and booing the FA's dignitaries but today, in this pristine stadium, it lasts for the opening forty-minutes. The first half has all the drama of someone blowing out a candle at bedtime.

The standard improves as the game goes on but the surface is dead and Mourinho's tactics are gratuitously designed to suffocate United. Outplaying United on the day football returned to Wembley would have created a legacy of young supporters around the world. But they don't even try. 'On our first day this week,' he later reveals, 'I asked the players: "do you want to enjoy the game, or do you want to enjoy after the game?" They said they wanted to enjoy after the game.' In other words, do you want to contribute to a pretty game or do you want to win ugly? Mourinho ordered his players to double up on Ronaldo and keep a 'minimum of six players' behind the ball at all times. 'People say United are a very dominant team but I don't agree,' he explains. 'They are a team that kills opponents on the counter-attack so, first of all, don't let them counter-attack.' And there lies the Mourinho philosophy: controlled power, tight discipline and won matches.

It is not entertaining but it is staggeringly effective. Football, to Mourinho, is an art – though not in the sense that a high-minded aesthetician such as Ferguson could ever comprehend – and his instructions pay off four minutes from the end of extra-time. An exchange of passes between Lampard and Drogba to create space, poor anticipation from Ferdinand and a split-second delay as Van der Sar leaves his line. The pause is long enough for Drogba to reach the ball first and clip his shot into the bottom corner. It is the goal that rescues Chelsea's season and ensures Mourinho is in effect unsackable for another year. Ferguson has already brought on Solskjaer, anticipating a penalty shoot-out. There is no time to do anything and they fail to create a single half-chance before the final whistle goes. It is a dreadful way to lose.

There are cinemas in Manchester that are smaller than Wembley's 'media theatre' and when Ferguson arrives the red rose on his suit has already been discarded. His disappointment is measured in calm tones. Two or three players under-performed, he says. Rooney and Scholes have run themselves into the ground but he is disappointed with Ronaldo and a few others. He thinks the team look fatigued and he isn't surprised it has been such a poor spectacle. 'I had the feeling that would be the case,' he says. 'Chelsea are not the type to go gung-ho against anyone. They make sure they don't lose first of all.'

There is a subtle dig in there somewhere. Ferguson and Mourinho have been careful not to say anything derogatory about one another in the build-up to this game. But Mourinho doesn't shake Ferguson's hand at the final whistle. Ferguson will not have liked that and he also thinks Mourinho's complaints about United's penalty count have worked to Chelsea's advantage. He is convinced United should have had a penalty – in the first period of extra time Michael Essien clipped Giggs's heels as he shaped to shoot – and he believes the referee Steve Bennett was intimidated into not giving it.

'It's the same theme with Mourinho all the time,' he says. 'He puts the referees under pressure before every big game. There are twenty-two great players out there but all he ever talks about is the referee. That's the way he is. Maybe it has worked for him today because I was disappointed with the referee, I must say. For an FA Cup final I expected better.'

Bennett is not the kind of referee who thinks match officials should have to explain themselves to journalists. We knocked on his changing-room door after he had made a series of contentious decisions in a Manchester City match a few years ago. Bizarrely, he would not open the door by more than a couple of inches and insisted we wrote our questions on a piece of paper and put it beneath the door. Once we had done that, there was a five-minute wait before it was pushed back bearing single-word answers.

It is at this point of the conference, anyway, that someone notices that the rose on Ferguson's suit has disappeared and asks him where it has gone. 'It's lying in the dressing-room,' he replies.

Then he smiles for the first and only time. 'Do you want it?'

He is squinting to see who has asked the question. 'We've lost and someone is talking about roses?' he says. 'Can I escape please?' And on that note he rises to his feet and heads for the door. His hands are in his pockets – his hands always seem to be in his pockets when he is unhappy – but at least he is smiling.

TAKING ON THE WORLD (PART II)

In the *Daily Telegraph*, Tony Francis has called him The Man Who Can't Retire. Gary Neville reckons it might be another ten years before Ferguson steps down. Ferguson is not saying and maybe doesn't even know himself. The rest of us just have to guess. And hope that when the day finally arrives he is not denied a happy ending.

The conventional path, at the age of sixty-five, would have been to walk away at the coronation of his ninth title, to bow out at the top and collect his gold clock for twenty years' service. Except anyone who suggests that is showing a complete lack of understanding of what makes Ferguson tick. Football is the thing that makes sense of his life. It is an addiction. He has tried to fight it, but resistance is futile. Without football, the future looks blank and scary.

He has tried the conventional route before and he hated it. He had planned to step down at the end of the 2001–02 season, at the age of sixty. But life without football would feel like a prison sentence. 'It was a mistake,' he says. 'As soon as I announced that decision I knew I was going to regret it. Spur of the moment, you see. You should never do things spur of the moment. A man of my age should have known better.'

The story goes that Cathy kicked his feet as he was having a birthday nap and informed him she had been speaking to their three sons. 'We've reached a decision,' she told him. 'I've had a chat with the boys and they think you're off your head. Even if United have got a new manager you have to go elsewhere.'

It is scarcely imaginable what could have come of United if Lady Ferguson hadn't been so pro-active. 'I needed someone to kick me,' her husband admits. 'I wouldn't have done it myself.' He was worried about having to 'kowtow and say I'm sorry' and United had already lined up Sven-Göran Eriksson to replace him. Ferguson's first call was to the club's legal director Maurice Watkins. 'I told him I'd changed my mind and he went: "I knew it, I knew it. I told you that you were off your head. Now you have dropped me right in it."'

Five years on, he has added two league titles, an FA Cup and a League Cup to his collection. As he looks to the future, the thought of retirement seems to alarm him more than the prospect of Abramovich bringing in another batch of the world's most ostentatiously extravagant players. Ferguson has given his life, and measured it out, in terms of football. How else would he get his kicks? What else is there? Playing the piano? Reading books on wine?

The answer is nothing, but he is going to have to cut himself free one day. Retirement isn't something he can file away in a drawer. And here is the million-dollar question. How will he make his retreat? The sporting world is full of heroic figures who have badly blundered when it comes to deciding how, and when, to make the break. The stories are legion of managers finding that without the exoskeleton of football their lives become shapeless and empty. Ferguson must never allow his name to be added to the list.

Most managers live on borrowed time, knowing they will eventually be moved on. But in Ferguson's case he has won so much and done so much he is in the rare position where he can choose his own day of departure. And that, perhaps, is the hardest bit.

It is certainly not something he likes to talk about. Ask Ferguson about his plans for retirement and he will usually fudge the question, change the subject or make a joke of it.

'I don't want to go anywhere,' he told us on one of the last occasions. 'I'm enjoying the company of you gentlemen too much.'

Then he turned to Diana Law and gulped with laughter. 'Di,' he said, 'mark me down as the liar of the year.'

Pressed further, all he will say is that he wants to carry on for as long as he is a) happy and b) healthy. He is energised and enthusiastic. He is still as sharp as a pin and losing the FA Cup final will only harden his resolve. Between them, Abramovich and Mourinho have provided a unique challenge but it has slowly brought the best out of Ferguson. 'Why should I retire?' he argues. 'That's the easy option. I don't know how long exactly I'm going to last but I'm enjoying it and I'm going to carry on doing this job until I stop enjoying it.'

The only time he has allegedly considered quitting in recent years came after everything had blown up with Keane. Sir Bobby Robson tells the story of visiting Ferguson at home in Wilmslow in late-November 2005, with United ten points behind Chelsea and the newspapers full of crisis headlines, and being dismayed to find his friend at such a low ebb. Ferguson, he says, was in a bad way, thinking about the future, and confided that he was considering 'packing it in'.

'I was almost angry with him,' Robson recalls. 'First, I demanded to know what the heck he was going to do instead. Secondly, I asked him, having worked so hard to build a great club and a great young team, why would he want to hand it over to someone else and risk it being spoiled?'

Robson managed to talk him round but Ferguson is clearly not as immune to the pressure as we all assume. It may have been only a passing phase, a bad day or a spur-of-the-moment thought, but maybe the tumultuous start to that season, Keane's expulsion, Chelsea's dominance and the added pressure of the Glazer takeover affected him more than we will ever know. Everyone has their bad days and their low moments.

The pressure in football is so suffocatingly draining there is a trend in the modern game for managers to take gap years. Gordon Strachan and Alan Curbishley have both stepped away from the dugout for a breather and when Paul Jewell left Wigan Athletic he was so emotionally wrecked his chairman Dave Whelan spoke of fearing for 'his health and mind'. But here is Ferguson, a generation older than Jewell and still going strong. Shankly left Anfield at the age of sixty. Clough, his face ravaged by the excesses of drink, bid farewell to management at fifty-eight. Paisley lasted until he was sixty-four and Busby closed his reign at Old Trafford when he was sixty-two. When the arguments start about who is the greatest manager of all, nobody should forget how Ferguson has beaten the system.

When the act of retirement finally comes the lesson of history is that he must make a clean break. The old-timers at Old Trafford still remember the problems when Busby stepped down in 1969 but stayed on as general manager and then director. They talk about how quickly the team deteriorated and how his replacement, Wilf McGuinness, found it too tough an act to follow, lasting only eight months before being sacked. 'I thought I would be given the time to do a good job,' McGuinness recalls. 'But at Manchester United you live in a fairytale world. Everything is beautiful until it isn't.'

Busby returned as manager for another six months before handing over to Frank O'Farrell, who was never accepted by the senior players. Probably because he wasn't Busby. O'Farrell says the jury had been sent out before he had sufficient time to present his case, and the verdict was 'guilty of not producing a miracle in eighteen months'. United did not win the league again until Ferguson's first title in 1993.

For us – the football writers – there will be a strange sense of loss when Ferguson does finally pack it in. Life will be a lot duller without him. He is not a hero of ours, exactly, but we all admire him in different ways and he will probably be fully appreciated only when he is no longer around. Of course he can be infuriating but he would say the same about us as well and, having put the 2005–06 season behind us, he has almost become cuddly at times in his ninth championship-winning year.

An educated guess is that Ferguson has two more seasons left in him. But it would be no surprise if he were still in the dugout at the age of seventy. Or maybe Neville's correct and Ferguson will still be haranguing journalists, referees and opposition managers as a white-haired geriatric in 2017. Life at Old Trafford might be an emotional rollercoaster but Ferguson will forever be the boy in the front seat, his arms in the sky and a huge grin on his face, asking to go around one more time.

Index